Between the salt and the ash

Manchester University Press

For Kate, Gruffydd and Elma Dilys

Between the salt and the ash

A journey into the soul of Northumbria

Jake Morris-Campbell

MANCHESTER UNIVERSITY PRESS

Copyright © Jake Morris-Campbell 2025

The right of Jake Morris-Campbell to be identified as the author of this work has been asserted in accordance with the Copyright, Designs and Patents Act 1988.

Published by Manchester University Press
Oxford Road, Manchester, M13 9PL

www.manchesteruniversitypress.co.uk

British Library Cataloguing-in-Publication Data
A catalogue record for this book is available from the British Library

Portrait of author, p. 207 © Andy Martin (martintype.co.uk)

ISBN 978 1 5261 7537 3 hardback

First published 2025

The publisher has no responsibility for the persistence or accuracy of URLs for any external or third-party internet websites referred to in this book, and does not guarantee that any content on such websites is, or will remain, accurate or appropriate.

EU authorised representative for GPSR:
Easy Access System Europe, Mustamäe tee 50, 10621 Tallinn, Estonia
gpsr.requests@easproject.com

FSC
www.fsc.org
MIX
Paper | Supporting responsible forestry
FSC® C013056

Typeset in Kuenstler by R. J. Footring Ltd, Derby, UK
Printed and bound in Great Britain by
TJ Books Limited, Padstow, Cornwall

Contents

Prologue: First foot	3
Introduction: Lights of the North	13

Part I. The sea on sanded feet

1	The compass takes its weigh	31
2	Coastline of castles	51
3	Salt pans and sand dunes	71
4	The Spine Road	97
5	Harvest from the deep	121

Tirtha: Tyne	141

Part II. Stringing Bedes

6	Following the Don	147
7	The Ash Path	169
8	Ghosts of the East End	189
9	What kingdom without common feasting?	209
10	Light moved on	231
11	The big meeting	247

Tirtha: Wear	264
Davy	266
Coda	269

Contents

Glossary of Northumbrian dialect terms	274
Acknowledgements	276
Notes	278
Index	286

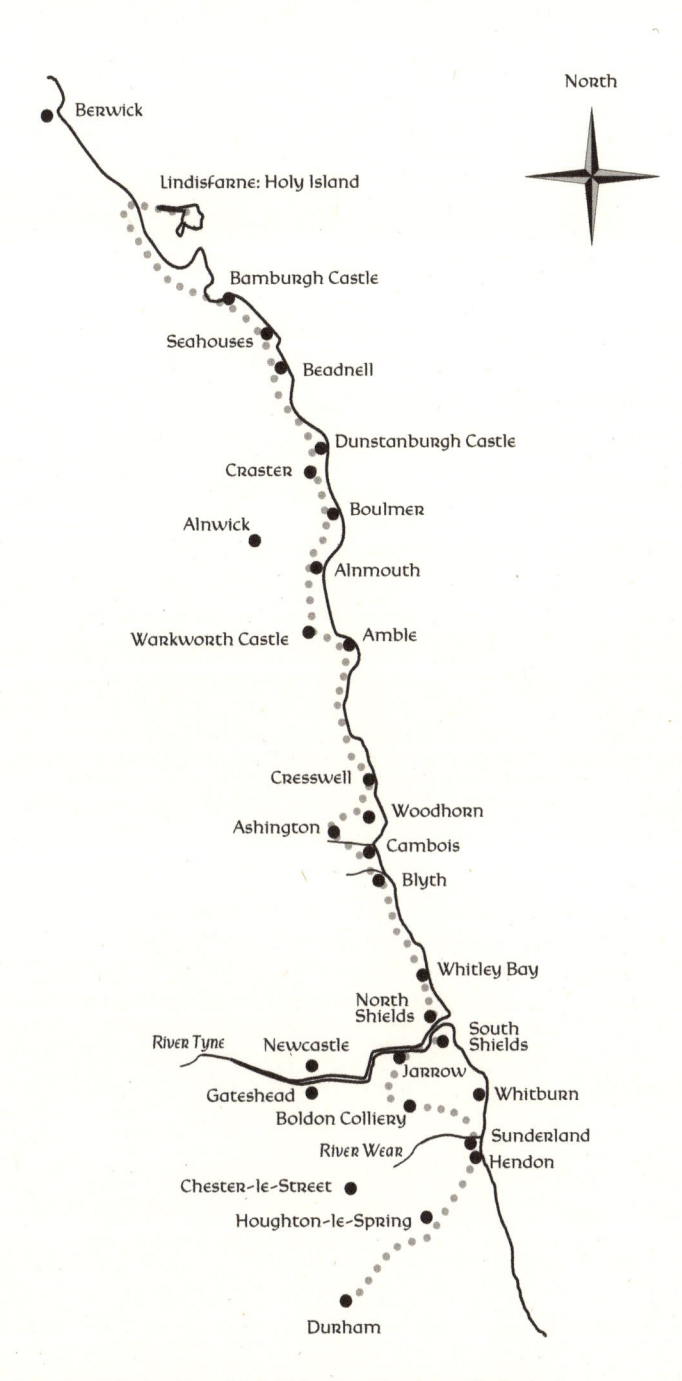

A North East English Camino: Holy Island to Durham Cathedral

I bent to the lamp. I cupped
My hand to the glass chimney.
Yet it was a stranger's breath
From out of my mouth that
Shed the light. I turned out
Into the salt dark
And turned my collar up.

    W. S. Graham, *The Nightfishing*[1]

As aw was gannin' t' Durham
Aw met wi' three jolly brisk women
Aw asked – what news at Durham?
They said – Joyful days are cumin

    William Martin, 'Marratide'[2]

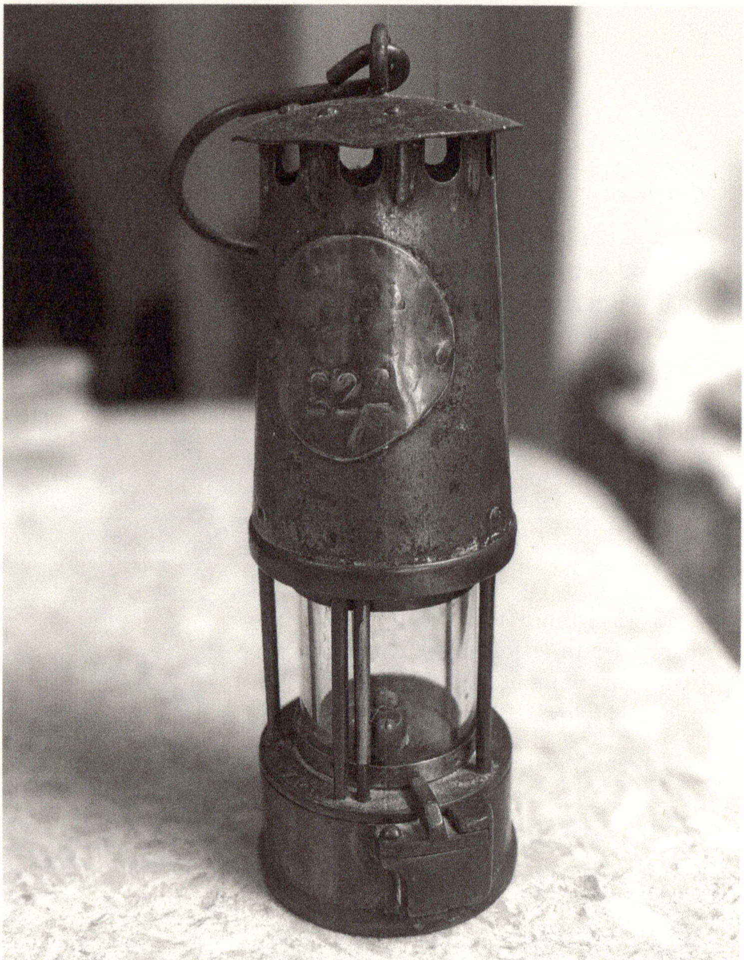

Prologue: First foot

My daughter is snoozing on me. Elma Dilys is a few days old; her feathery breathing matches the rhythm of my chest. Slow fall, slow rise. I trace her crown and fontanelle with a little finger, half asleep myself. It's the tab-end of 2021. I've had enough of bad news, so the telly's off. I try to relax into this moment, which I know won't last. Beyond the blinds the streetlights blink on. Winter is here.

My son Gruffydd is being read to in his bedroom by his mam. Suddenly, the knocker goes and I can hear my wife Kate carrying our eager toddler downstairs. I rise to my feet with Elma asleep over my shoulder, the four of us meeting in the hall. I open the front door. On the step, huddled in down jackets, are my grandparents. My nana holds forward a bag: *here, this is for you*. Inside the Lidl carrier, safely bubble-wrapped, is her father's davy lamp. *I want you to ha'd on to it.*

In the middle of the twentieth century, when Nicholas Moore was working for the Harton Coal Company in a shaft below Boldon and then later at Westoe, where he'd be sent three miles beneath the North Sea, this little steel and brass-plated cylinder was his only source of light. As Nick craned his shoulders and neck to chisel fossilised plant matter from the bowels of Britain, its tiny flame would have barely lit his sweaty, smudged brow.

I see Nick dreaming of his daughters back home, my nana Lana still a bairn-in-arms. I peel away the wrap and hold the lamp up from its scythe-like handle. Time collapses, distance unfurling. With a *poof* the wick flares. In the reflection of the little glass casing, I see Nick's eyes. In the wink of his smile, I turn to see my own children, to whom one day this heirloom will be passed down. My grandparents beam. Turning, saying they need to be off, they kiss both of their great-grand-kids. *They're an absolute joy, Jake.* And they're right. I set Nick's black torch down and hold fast to the future. Joyful days are coming.

It's two minutes to midnight. Now I'm standing outside their front door in Harton, South Shields. It's the late 1990s. An icy wind is rattling up off the Tyne, carrying with it the boom of ships' horns. Fireworks start flying, liquorice allsorts in the sky. In my fist I clasp a triangular hunk of coal. It has been varnished smooth and shiny. Through the door I can hear screeches of drunken chatter, the bass of the radio – Five and B*Witched, Boyzone and Jamiroquai – then the opening bars of Auld Lang Syne. It's starting: ten, nine, eight....

More fireworks, car horns, clouds whose underbellies are lit amber by sodium streetlights' glare. Suburbia pushes the last year out to the blackness of the sea, where the pepper-pot lighthouse rings its halo round the town, and the new one comes whooshing in.

My granddad opens the door: *Happy New Year, son*! He's beaming, red-faced and merry, wishing me *many happy returns*. I know my job. I step over the threshold, the coal held out like I'm one of the three wise men carrying myrrh, frankincense, gold. I present it to my nana, who's puckering up, offering me a bottle of Stella. *Don't tell your Mam!* Adults are leaning into each other as felled trees, smooching,

Prologue: First foot

sloshing drinks. On the news: Big Ben and the Thames; a huge fireworks display in Sydney; the Eiffel Tower. Here, the closing notes of Burns' lines ring out as the coal goes back on the mantlepiece, beside a brass ornament of a miner shovelling, his back bent double as he digs a hole he'll never get to the bottom of.

Twenty-five years later, I am carrying on tradition. On New Year's Day, early in the morning, I place the coal in my three-year-old son's hands. Gruffydd is the first foot through the house this year: the one who will bring blessings and warmth to our abode for the year ahead. In the Scottish version of the ritual practised at Hogmanay, the first foot, who is supposed to be tall, dark and handsome, carries with them salt, bread, coins, coal and whisky: those staples of good cheer and sustenance.

 I have held dear to that piece of coal for years, kept it close by on a bookshelf where I work. It has crossed the threshold of many houses, including my parents-in-law's in Shropshire, where I inducted them into the custom on a glistening night at the end of 2016, a year that, by the time it ended, we were all glad to see the back of. This little piece of coal, smaller than a shuttlecock, is one of my most treasured items. Even though it was mined to be burned, if my house caught fire, it would be one of the few things I'd rescue.

 I wrote a poem about my great-granddad Nick and the legacy of his work in my first collection of poetry. It was a little contrived imagining the full toil of his graft, but what's utterly heartfelt to me is the ringing echo of his voice. When I pick up his lamp, I hear him calling across the decades. I know, it's absurd. This person I never met, who died long before I was born, but still I hear him. Maybe it's because he was born on the same day as me, only seventy-eight years earlier. He tells me that he's glad I didn't have to endure his grind, that he's proud of my education, the things I've learned. He tells me that he looks down still on Lana, and that he's happy that those who came after him are getting on, not just getting by.

Of course, these are the things I have projected into his voice by dint of the upbringing I've had in the times I've lived through. This lamp which bears such scars, knocked about and scratched, dented and worn, is a time capsule for his world. It's a world long gone now, and Nick is spot on: I am glad I didn't have to break my back or clot my lungs working gruelling shifts down a pit. His voice reminds me that things have changed, but it also nags at me not to forget where I've come from.

When Christianity slowly started spreading through Northumbria from the seventh century, the masses began to witness intricate Gospel books for the first time. Writing on their reputation, Eleanor Jackson says that they 'were the most important Christian books of the early Middle Ages [...] some were made for special devotional or ceremonial purposes [...] and lavished with the utmost attention and creativity'. Jackson adds that 'even among this group, the Lindisfarne Gospels stands out as exceptional'.[1] Such works of scripture, painstakingly copied out and held in reverence in the monasteries in which people huddled, would have inspired awe and devotion. With their zesty carpet pages, shimmering lumens and detailed knotwork patterning, they would have at once charmed and humbled the ordinary onlooker. Upon first seeing them, many must have heard the pious calling intended by their creators, an invocation to forget their petty pagan beliefs and heed a higher calling: *Here is the word of our Lord God made manifest before you: Join him.*

The Lindisfarne Gospels book is composed of over 250 leaves of vellum and written in Latin. Made by one man, Bishop Eadfrith, and created as a gift to honour God and his noble follower Saint Cuthbert, the Lindisfarne Codex has become the most salient symbol of Northumbria as the Christian crossroads of Europe. Inspired by the Celtic Christianity imported to Holy Island by Saint Aidan (a missionary from Iona, the Columbine monastery itself an island off the west coast of Scotland) and alluding to a global palette of theological influences – Rome, Greece, Constantinople – the Gospels are a Northumbrian icon *par excellence*, a bright star burning through the so-called Dark Ages.

Then night fell. The marauding Vikings landed on the beach, their pitchforks glinting, their mouths salivating. The Gospels were swiftly bundled into Cuthbert's coffin along with his portable altar and comb, and supposedly the ragged heed of the Northumbrians' martyred king, Oswald.[2] Then they all fled from the island, relics intact. Or so the mythology has it. What follows, according to the cult that was engineered around Cuthbert after his death, is akin to Moses wandering the desert. The disciples of Cuthbert spend a century in exile. For seven itinerant years they make their way around the north of England, zig-zagging through the present-day Anglo-Scottish border. The Lindisfarne Gospels falls into the Solway Firth but is retrieved completely intact and dust-dry. Eventually the monks settle (for a century) at Chester-le-Street, where another priest, Aldred, translates the

Latin script into Northumbrian-inflected Old English. After that they shift one final time a few miles down the road and build Durham Cathedral, making a mountain around their man.

Like all great epics, the cult of Cuthbert and his final journey as recast in the bardic tradition is subject to exaggeration, corruption and fabrication. Each successive storyteller has embellished the edges, but the core remains the same: our martyr found safe haven at last, and heavens, how we're thankful. We now understand that these monks, complicit in establishing the Danelaw by elevating Cuthbert to Super-Saintly status, were following the prevailing currents of power and prestige. Parading their relics was a deliberate strategy: a way of whipping up support for Roman Catholicism, a grand pageant that signed up new believers and converted sceptics as it roved from monastery to monastery.

Haddaway an' shite! I hear Nick howling. *What does aall of this have to dee with a little lamp used by a working-class bloke on Tyneside, like?*

There was a time not very long ago when an item such as this would have been so commonplace as to have not warranted pause or observation of any kind. The very ubiquity of mining – and the associated cultures and labour union practices that bloomed around it – meant that to someone like Nick, the whole idea of this book would seem daft. But now these items are relics. Occasionally I'll see them in the background of someone's Zoom screen, polished and gleaming on bookcases. Or I'll see them for sale at flea markets: tactile emblems appealing to some Venn diagram overlap of Blitz-spirit Brits and steam-punk hipsters. When I was viewing a house for sale recently, a Davy lamp caught my eye, prominently displayed on the hearth. In a trendy Newcastle bar I once chatted to a girl in her twenties wearing a Metallica t-shirt and Doc Martens with a lamp tattooed up her arm. She proudly told me the artist had copied her grandfather's model and that he used to work the seam at Rising Sun, the colliery that inspired Geordie blues rock band The Animals.

Like the miners' lamps, the Gospel books have become vestiges. Aestheticised – exoticised, even – and in many ways coveted. But redundant. Just as those lamps once guided people in subterranean graft, the Gospels once functioned in a similar way, guiding with tunnels of light a path from drudgery to salvation. In a post-industrial, multifaith society, what residual stories from these and other items might now tug at the region's compass? The Lindisfarne Gospels spends most of its time covered in Styrofoam, sealed in a box and held in darkness in a temperature-controlled archive at the British Library in London. And yet, every seven years, back to the North East it shuttles – *gannin' hyem*. For a few months at a time, we are blessed to see them, before once more the lid is closed, and they're left to dream of the road.

Now that I have this lamp, I want to use it. A relic from the North East, it seems fitting that it should follow the expedition of the region's most famous relics: a lantern parade illuminating a path from the coast to the cathedral. Starting at Holy Island, where in the seventh century the Lindisfarne Gospels book was crafted by Eadfrith working by sun and candlelight, I'll carry Nick home. Like me, he's an auld County Durham lad, forged in the place where the Gospels once sat on the high altar, even though his place, beneath the bowels of Britain, was literally and figuratively beneath: the base of the economic pyramid which sent coals from Newcastle to the world.

In religious, occupational, artistic and more broadly cultural terms, the crucible of this region can be traced back to the pragmatism of the lamp. A person finding fuel to burn and using it to illuminate a task – be it a monk copying scripture, a miner hewing coal, a submariner scouring oceanic depths, the lighthouse keeper oiling the flame ashore, or a poet crafting verse – all needed beacons. Our first known texts were etched onto cave walls, figures showing human struggle and sacrifice, but also wonder and celebration. In the North East, wooden tablets found near Vindolanda off Hadrian's Wall show the prosaic writings of everyday people living in garrison settlements during the Roman occupation: the shopping lists they made, notes from the edge of empire sealed for centuries in the peat below us.

When paraffin combusts and the flame ignites, silhouettes grow and dance from their source, casting the long shadows our first footsteps grow from.

Here, let me hold up my lamp, let me tell you a little story.

REMEMBER BEFORE GOD
THE DURHAM MINERS WHO HAVE
GIVEN THEIR LIVES IN THE PITS
OF THIS COUNTY AND THOSE WHO
WORK IN DARKNESS AND DANGER
IN THOSE PITS TODAY

HE BREAKETH OPEN A SHAFT AWAY FROM WHERE MEN SOJOURN
THEY ARE FORGOTTEN OF THE FOOT THAT PASSETH BY. JOB 28.4

Introduction: Lights of the North

He breaketh open a shaft away from where men sojourn. They are forgotten of the foot that passeth by.

Job 28:4

Twelve pilgrims gannin' to Durham. The cathedral an apparition, floating weightless in an eggshell sky. The worm-bent river cradling the mound where it would be perched and consecrated. On the hill, a dun cow, its docile head of tussled fringe, snout and horns turned back to its cow-girls, guiding the party of monks on their last leg from Chester-le-Street.

Apostles carrying icons. One holds a candle, one holds a lute, one holds a book. Words in motion, a peripatetic congregation, a mobile mass, a carnival with no fixed address. Until they get to the outskirts of Dunholme, the coffin suddenly stops, as if clamped by an over-zealous parking attendant. Inside their reliquary: the bones of Cuthbert, Oswald's bonce, and their most precious text: the Lindisfarne Gospels.

Word is, a herding lass appeared, asked if they'd seen her stray dun cow. Then another came, a milkmaid, her eager arm pointing to the hill above the river, at which point the coffin again became weightless, legs started drifting. Cuthbert satisfied after so long in transit that his final place of rest was now in sight, his *Dunholme* — Durham. *Here*, he said, *here lads and lasses, we're hyem.*

Through the Rose Window, rainbow light is tumbling down in colonnades. Spokes illuminating the shrine. On a simple marble slab beneath is an inscription: *Cuthbertus*. This is where the disciples washed up with their figurehead.

Just beyond the south transept, beside the entrance to the cloisters, is a wall-mounted wooden memorial. A different kind of shrine, this is for the Durham miners.

At first sight these two dedications to martyrs and miners would seem to have little in common. But I can think of something – both were carried by their *marras*.

Marra is a dialect word, forged by the shipbuilders, colliers and farmers of the north, referring to one's comrades. Marrows growing in the soil of allotments, ripening to feed hungry bellies, grew as close together as men and boys toiling beneath. The emphasis was always on equality: you're my marra because I'm yours. This was the 'we're all in it together' mantra, before it was corrupted by austerity and co-opted by Conservative dogma.

What is in the marrow is hard to take from the bone, as the Irish proverb goes.

At the western end of the cathedral, in the smaller Galilee chapel (a nod to Christ's western entry into Jerusalem from Galilee in Israel) is the tomb of the Venerable Bede. The patron saint of scholars, Bede was Northumbria's most important biographer. A fellow South Tynesider, Bede lived and worked between the twinned monasteries of St Peter's and St Paul's, churches on the banks of the mighty rivers Wear and Tyne, where I come from. A polymath, he wrote the first history of the English people. Without him, we'd know far less about Cuthbert, Oswald and other northern saints. You could say that Bede carried his marras' messages.

Introduction: Lights of the North

Northumbria is the heart of England's soul. What we have come to understand as 'English' history was first outlined on the banks of the rivers Wear and Tyne, in the scriptorium led by the Venerable Bede. At one end of the cathedral, the north's most famous saint, at the other his devoted annalist. In the middle, a monument to the ordinary lives lost in pursuit of black diamonds. From Cuthbert the miracle worker, whose body remained incorrupt after death and for whom the cathedral was built, to Bede, fount of knowledge and medieval Northumbria's Wikipedia, to the coalminers who risked their lives at the bottom of the economic pyramid so that Britain could boom. All of them lights of the north.

Beneath the miners' memorial is a biblical inscription: lines from the Book of Job. I'd been thinking a lot about this passage. Breaking them down into four memorable parts, I'd roll them on my tongue, recalling them the way I memorise a poem. Why are they standing out to me now?

> He breaketh open a shaft
> Away from where men sojourn
> They are forgotten of the foot
> That passeth by.

In the summer of 2022, making my annual pilgrimage from Sunderland to Durham Cathedral in memory of the poet Bill Martin, whose work often cherished the social and intellectual life of coal-mining communities, I found myself in front of the miners' memorial, offering a small pebble. The intention, according to custom, was to place the pebble at Cuthbert's coffin, making a symbolic link back to the coastal community where he'd been Bishop of Lindisfarne. But fate intervened: his tomb had already been cordoned off, closed for a private party of Australian tourists. No matter, I'd go with plan B for Bede and deposit it at the Galilee chapel. After all, Bede was an old mate of mine from the shores of the Tyne. But alas, Bede's gaff was also shut. So, I had to go with plan C for coal.

Sometime earlier, on a beach walk at Marsden Bay with my wife and kids, I'd pocketed a small selection of pebbles. Little chippings of magnesium limestone, I'd carried them on walks along the Leas and over to Whitburn, rolling them in my fingers the way I roll questions on my tongue, the way I repeat words to memorise poems. I placed this little custard-coloured one in front of a wreath of flowers, where it was looked upon by a pair of cherubs and, in gilded relief, the most monumental icon of the north: a miner's Davy lamp. Off to the side, hanging above a book of remembrance, polished and glinting in the same colonnades that touched Cuthbert's flags, was a real one, a black torch forever suspended to give form and substance to the lines from Job.

Lights of the north. The phrase stuck with me. An hour later in the pub, the charming Victoria Inn on Hallgarth Street, I was in the queue ordering packets of crisps and pale ales when another image came to mind.

I used it as the basis for my description at the start: Doris Clare Zinkeisen's 1932 *Durham, Pilgrims*, an old railway poster advertising LNER services stopping at the cathedral city. I'd first seen the picture earlier in the summer, when it was on show with other posters at the Golden Age of Travel exhibition at Ushaw College, a former Catholic seminary five miles west of Durham city.

It depicts the dun cow legend, a foundation tale in the mythology of the North East, telling of how Cuthbert's incorrupt body was eventually ferried to Durham after its long peregrination around the present-day Anglo-Scottish border. Twelve disciples follow their messiah. Their leader – playing an oboe, clarinet or bassoon – takes the guise of Cuthbert's spirit, guiding them to where his earthly remains should lie. With their instruments primed, their wreaths bedecked and ready to be lain, their testimony would have sat as touchpaper on the end of their matchstick tongues.

Carrying clinking pint pots back to the table, we debriefed on the day's walk, toasting glasses to Bill. We'd only come a short way, fifteen miles or so from the foot of Tunstall Hills, the former home of Bill Martin, who'd been walking this route since the mid-1980s. Sadly Bill had died in 2010, his pilgrimage fading into memory. But in 2016 I revived it, and every year since, bar the interruptions of childbirth and a global pandemic, a group of us have strapped on our boots and taken to the byways. As ever, our party of half a dozen was chaperoned by the poet Peter Armstrong, who intoned 'Next Year in Jerusalem', a favourite saying of Bill's indicating that, after having walked to Durham Cathedral, the only higher pilgrimage point could be the Holy City itself.

It was then that I thought: how often do I, tongue half in cheek, refer to this place as 'the Holy Land'? Joking with exiled marras on the Northern Line, speeding through Charing Cross and Leicester Square where we'd act out our roles as token Geordies and Mackems, we'd nevertheless be sincere in our appreciation of the land of three rivers, the territory at the top of the country, a place set apart, between the North Sea, the North York Moors and the Scottish Borders.

I've a theory that, because the North East has experienced so much loss and change, because its brain drain and economic precarity continue to suck talent to the south, people who are from here are especially proud. It's true that this can manifest in the worst ways – jingoism and myopia are sad truths of the area – but most often it comes across as pride in place: a belief that whether it's to Middlesbrough, Sunderland or Newcastle you *belang*, there's nowhere like the North East; no people as canny and clever; nowhere more welcoming and more eager to exclaim its distinctiveness.

Suddenly I got it: this is why lines from the Book of Job speak to the plight of the Durham miners. A class who dreamed of self-determination and whose altruism was built on self-organisation, they were forgotten by the establishment. They were, to foist a religious link, unorthodox. To the forces of globalisation, role-played by the Thatcher government and its neoliberal acolytes, the miners were obsolete. These people and their descendants were left to wither on the vine. *They are forgotten of the foot that passeth by.* How often, I thought, do we walk past the overlooked and small? In our haste to reach a glittering destination, we can neglect the many minor jewels along the path.

> He breaketh open a shaft of light away from where men sojourn.

In the Victoria, we're all sharing photos taken on the hoof. The picture at the opening of this chapter was taken at the end of the walk. I supped a hoppy gobful, chased it with an ox-flavoured crisp, swiped to this image. Looking at the Davy lamp by the miners' memorial where I placed my pebble, it clicked: I hadn't been doing this walk just for Bill, I'd been doing it for myself, to better understand my own complicated feelings towards the place, the constant push and pull I feel about coming from a port town at the mouth of the River Tyne. There in gold, the miners' tool, and back home on my mantlepiece, in burnished bronze, my great-grandfather's lamp. Now that I held a light of the north, I had to break open a shaft of my own.

Introduction: Lights of the North

A few years ago at Hospitalfield, an artists' centre in Arbroath where I'd been staying for a symposium with other creative researchers, the poet Linda France told me that I was a chronicler. At the time, I didn't know what to make of her comment. But a few years into the Marratide pilgrimages that I'd reignited in Bill's name, and having published a collection of poetry steeped in the particulars of South Shields and its promontory, I realised she was spot on. I had been hoarding things from the place I know and love, even, or perhaps especially, when it deeply frustrates me. Along with the talismans – the lamp, coal and pebbles – I'd really been spending thirty-five years hoarding something more nebulous: stories, tales, sagas. I suddenly had an imperious idea: I'm a bard, I'm like Bede. This is my role: to hoist my light like a pit-lodge banner at the front of the procession, picking up accounts as I go, making my way to Durham with my cabinet of curiosities.

That night, back at home, feet bathed and pumiced, and a large tea eaten, a back-of-a-tab-packet idea began to form. I sketched out a rough map of the lands between Lindisfarne and Durham: those beacons of the North East. I realised that there were three nodes that could be plotted geographically, waystations bookended by a crumbling abbey and a mighty cathedral. The old and the older. But what of the present, what of the future? In the spring and summer of 2023, and then into the winter and early spring of the following year, on a series of journeys totalling eighty miles, I'd make it my mission to find out.

The first and most distant of these nodes is Lindisfarne, the Holy Island. A tidal isle a few miles from Berwick-upon-Tweed, it was here in the seventh century that Irish missionaries led by Saint Aidan consecrated a new monastery near the royal seat at Bamburgh. Aidan came from Iona, a monastery off the west coast of Scotland, from where he was requested by King Oswald of Northumbria to become bishop for his people, newly converted to Christianity. After this, Cuthbert, noted as a spiritual healer, visionary and miracle worker, became the island's lodestar, his followers carrying his uncorrupted body and relics off the island when they came under sustained attack from Vikings.

The middle node is the one that means the most to me personally: the twinned monasteries of St Peter's, Monkwearmouth, and St Paul's, Jarrow. This sliver of land, this hinge between Geordie and Mackem, where the mighty rivers Wear and Tyne jostle, is where I come from and live. In the nineteenth and twentieth centuries this was the shipbuilding epicentre of the world. But in the seventh century it was known for its influential abbeys. From here, wily priests developed trade networks and imported vast libraries and innovations from continental Europe, filling their scriptoriums with the sun-soaked words and worlds of the Mediterranean. Under the auspices of Benedict Biscop, then under Abbot Ceolfrith, and most famously under the wing of Bede, the Wearmouth–Jarrow monasteries became the most important seat of learning in early medieval England. From here, Bede calculated tide times, plotted astronomy and chronicled the lives of saints. He also reported on the Synod of Whitby, the meeting in 663/664 at which church leaders decided whether to follow Celtic or Roman rules, including those setting the date of Easter. The Northumbrian king at the time, Oswiu, decided in favour of Rome.

The third node is Durham itself, the compact university city whose grand cathedral and imposing castle set high on a leafy hill are enclosed by the sickle bend of the River Wear. As ships were being caulked and rivetted further up the river,

Introduction: Lights of the North

around its adjacent villages mine shafts were being sunk, Durham becoming the heart of the Great Northern Coalfield. Christianity and coal, the two pillars of the North East, converged along this route. As Roger Garfitt, writing on his friend Bill Martin, said:

> The primitive Christianity of the monasteries had surfaced again in the close community of the pit villages and their long political struggle.[1]

If Durham is our Cathedral de Santiago de Compostela, Cuthbert our Saint James, then the sites between his origin and end points are our holy way. Pilgrims travelling through Galicia in north-west Spain follow the famous Way of Saint James, greeting each other with 'buen camino!' I ventured to trek a North East English Camino, altering the European salutation to a Northumbrian equivalent: 'gan canny!' Following a filigree of northern saints' trails ribboning back to the so-called dark ages and now bisecting a place steeped in post-industrial mythology would bring me into deeper touch with the faith of my forebears and provide a greater understanding of the contemporary concerns of the people I live among. Most people walk *to* Lindisfarne, some of them tracing Cuthbert's Way from his birthplace in Melrose in the Scottish Borders. But I would follow the opposite path: crossing the famous causeway at low seas, seeking the peculiar spirit of Northumbria.

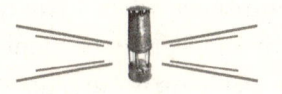

On a shelf by my writing desk, I keep a white Cartwright & Edwards Ironstone English mug bearing the coat of arms of my hometown, South Shields. The crest at its centre depicts a lifeboat at sea with the town's motto 'Always Ready' above four rowers at oars, a coxswain and a presumably rescued passenger. A rope-lined anchor is flanked by two union flags, on the left of which a sailor in a square rig cap and neckerchief holds a plotting compass; while on the right a regal-looking woman – the Queen Mother, perhaps – in a mural crown and white dress carries the caduceus, Hermes' staff symbolising peace. Together the lifeboat, sailor and queen represent the town's 'courage, humanity and commerce'. On the mug's reverse, the words 'South Shields Corporation 1850–1974' are printed. My nana, who was a nurse on the children's ward at South Tyneside Hospital, was given a set of them in 1974. I often fixate on those dates and wonder what those 124 years, when the town was a corporation, now mean.

Following the Local Government Act of 1972, county boundaries were redrawn, creating five urban districts in 'Tyne and Wear', a new metropolitan county historically dived into Northumberland and Durham and bounded naturally by the River Tyne. I was given this mug by my grandparents a few years ago, and for a while I'd fill it with coffee and take it into the English and Creative Writing seminars I teach. Since part of its handle snapped off, I've used it to store stationery. I like that it's faded and broken – its transformation evokes the sometimes-arbitrary interactions between time and space. The metropolitan borough in which I currently live, South Tyneside, has existed only fourteen years longer than I have. Did it become real as a consequence of the 1972 Act, or is it made real each month now, when I pay rates for my wheelie bins to be emptied and flowers to be planted in my village?

The Camino of the North East doesn't officially exist. You won't find any signs on stiles or fence posts; there's no guide book to buy, no TripAdvisor guidance, and certainly no *credencials* to be stamped in a passport. If you turn up

Introduction: Lights of the North

at Durham Cathedral and tell them you're a pilgrim who's been following the Camino of the North East, they'll think you're off your *heed*. There's a Camino Inglés, connecting Finchale Abbey near Durham to Escomb Church near Bishop Auckland. Walkers of this route can claim *credencials*, the distance counting towards the 100 km required for a pilgrim to have officially walked the Camino to Santiago de Compostela. So my North East Camino, semi-fictitious as it is, does integrate into a wider network of pre-existing routes. There's St Oswald's Way and the Northumberland Coast Path, both opened in 2006. A decade earlier, St Cuthbert's Way was formed. Then there's Bede's Way, created in 2004. The nodal points of these routes have been here a lot longer: Durham Cathedral was built between 1093 and 1133, while the twinned monasteries of St Peter's and St Paul's at Monkwearmouth and Jarrow have existed since 674 and 685, respectively.

Does it matter that a singular Camino of the North East is not a formally recognised walking path? Does it matter that a county is apocryphal? And what of that more nebulous appellation – a country? I don't mean the modern-day sovereign nation state, but more that idea of an ill-defined territory around which a set of ideas and customs has clustered: a cultural imaginary which persists and attaches significance to a geographic area via a famous figure from sport, music or literature. When I drive into South Tyneside from adjoining Sunderland or Gateshead, I'm met with a large sign showing Sandhaven Beach in South Shields on a sunny day. In 2012 the council deigned to erect these generic markers, replacing the more poetic designation 'Catherine Cookson Country', which for twenty-five years had greeted motorists visiting the place which had birthed one of England's most successful novelists. Cookson, who sold over 100 million books, depicted poverty and hardship around her native Tyne Dock. In a drive to attract investment, the Cookson Country epithet – which, for many, conjured russet rivers, polluted skies and industrial strife – was ditched. Which in a sense is fair enough: times have changed. But the altering of the signs raises interesting questions about collective memory, identity and civic branding, and says a lot about how literature can be deployed, and removed, instrumentally. This is not inconsequential in the thinking that has gone into my Camino of the North East, which I found exits somewhat ambiguously between the three-dimensional places people now inhabit and the terrain of the mind they think their places belong to. As the cliché goes, the map is not the territory.

As I began to literally and figuratively interpret this route, making links on the map and joining dots on the ground, I realised that in creatively inhabiting it, it very much came to life. It didn't matter that I'd fabricated the route: the space it held open for contemplation, conversation and lateral thinking became paramount. I made it meaningful by beating its bounds. Whether or not this North East Camino ever appears as a dotted line on the Ordnance Survey is less significant to me than what it represents today: a new way through the old North.

In his 1992 study into the origins of North East regionalism, the historian Robert Colls says by 'walking the land and looking at it, and by writing and reading about it, the New Northumbrians rediscovered their region'. In the 'reconstructed' prose of Colls, drawing on styles popularised by the likes of the late-nineteenth-century rambler and writer of illustrated north country guidebooks, Edmund Bogg, Colls gives a fictive account of their endeavours:

> It does not even matter that not all of us are Northumbrians by birth – for we have read our Border Ballads and the

Introduction: Lights of the North

Proceedings of Newcastle Lit. and Phil., and all good patriots are welcome to join in our walk. In spite of our historical interests, our real destination is with the present. As we travel the land, so we traverse our minds. In each sacred place where a reverie is induced, the past is fused with the present to form a unity, a unity which the better-read among us recognise as the 'personality' of place.[2]

In the summer lull between the first two Covid-19 lockdowns in August 2020, I met up in Durham with two friends from Wrexham. Mike, who matriculated from Collingwood College as an undergraduate, had brought his partner, Emma, for her first visit to the city. Walking out the back of the cloisters at the cathedral and down to Prebends Bridge, we took to a wooded path high up above the River Wear. A little way along the track, we suddenly noticed a distinctive bright yellow scallop shell on a fence post.

In the same year, six Northern Saints Trails were launched. With Durham Cathedral as their destination, these routes aimed to position the region as the Christian crossroads of Britain, drawing on ancient pilgrimage ways. Jonathan Miles-Watson, an anthropologist at Durham University who has been involved with the project from its earliest stages – 'when I walked these Trails without the slightest thought of the possibility that I was engaging in an act of pilgrimage or research' – notes how the Northern Saints Trails transform 'the Cathedral from a static place of endings into a dynamic terminal of emerging possibilities'.[3] I like that.

What does it mean to inhabit a place where so much seems to have faded into history, yet remains tantalisingly close to hand? Conversely, what new stories might be stemming from Durham and its hinterland in the wake of Christianity and coal? Miles-Watson writes eloquently of the 'sense in the region of two lost pasts: one industrial and one medieval'.[4] Colls, meanwhile, reckons 'this sense of loss has turned the region into a company of historians'; that in 'the North-East, so many people and places *used to be* that the region is hardly discussed without reference to what went before'. A pilgrimage, if it means anything, must involve a reckoning with the present. Riffing again off Colls, who describes men who 'name themselves by occupation – a fitter "by trade" – even when no longer in that occupation', I come to this Camino of the North East as a writer, a lyric poet by trade.[5] With my personal and professional identities overlaid, I think of this as at once a poet's peregrination and a stride down the strandline of the place I hail from. I have skin in the game. While so much in the North East does seem to have withered into communal memory, the thing that does stay close at hand is family and a deeply felt sense of community. Much of this Camino is new to me, but much of it is familiar. I have trodden some of these miles many hundreds of times already: cross-referring them now, I'm keen to see how the plot might thicken as I join one known path to its lesser-known neighbour.

In practical terms, this is how I'll *gan*. In Part I, partially following St Oswald's Way and the Northumberland Coast Path, I'll set off from Lindisfarne and make my way down the coast to North Shields. Referencing the poet James Kirkup, I'll be guided by 'the sea on sanded feet', thinking about England's most northerly littoral, where the brine swells around old castles and the sea still simmers with the psalms of saints.[6] In Part II, Stringing Bedes, I'll figuratively connect the venerable polymath's legacy to the after-image of 'coalstalgia' in the Bernician heartlands: the rivers Tyne and Wear, where I grew up and live, walking adjacent to my home and picking up the pulse of the modern-day region. The journey culminates at the cathedral in Durham, where the book concludes the post-pilgrimage experience by thinking

Introduction: Lights of the North

through how that hub connects to its spokes and what it means to have faith in the region.

Along the way, I plan to meet up with a number of people – poets, artists, musicians among them – whom I will ask to bring totemic items to put in dialogue with Nick, my battered auld lamp. I believe in being chaperoned through areas I'm unfamiliar with, deepening into place in the company of local experts. But I won't be walking in company all of the way: much of the journey will be a solitary one, affording me space to figure out my small part in the grand, unfolding drama of Northumbria. Finally, I'll walk in a troupe of thousands at the Big Meeting – the Durham Miners' Gala – the political carnival at the heart of the former coalfield where I'll once more pay my respects to the living spirit between the salt and the ash.

Part I
The sea on sanded feet

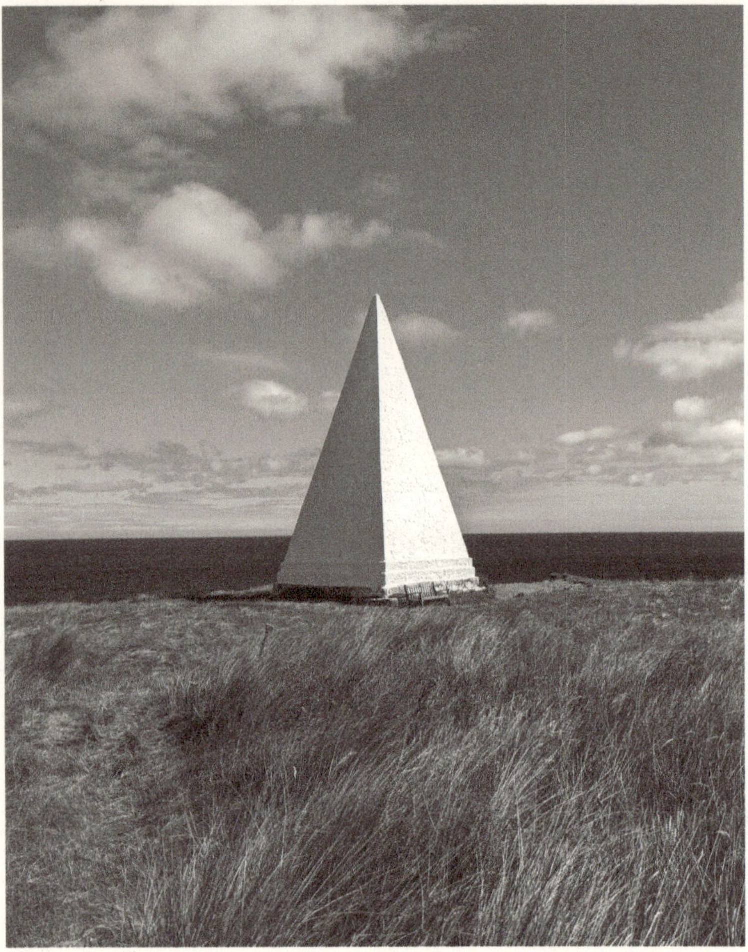

Chapter 1

The compass takes its weigh

As the tide ebbs and flows, this place is surrounded twice daily by the waves of the sea like an island and twice, when the shore is left dry, it becomes again attached to the mainland.

    Bede[1]

Between mainland and island, in neither sway,
a nodding of the needle as the compass takes its weigh.

    Matthew Hollis, 'Causeway'[2]

I wanted somewhere to muse, a place I could ponder. I wanted skies and seas that melded into each other like solder. I wanted to feel the ascetic's appeal, melodious seabirds strumming the shore. What I get is bus-loads of tourists and ice-cream vans. What I get is tat. It's June so the half-mile road to Lindisfarne Castle, backdrop to a thousand portrait photographers, is chocker. I push on round the island – the North East's north-east – passing valerian tinselling the battlements, passing upturned keels, pebble cairns and Gertrude Jekyll's garden. I jog on round the bridleway, mindful that the tide is due to shut in less than two hours. Grasses thick with sea thrift, clover, buttercups. Then there it is, jutting from the coast like a counter in a board game: the Emmanuel Head daymark. Not a soul aboot. Beaut.

Waves fizz like radio static. Little else to be heard. Few venture this way, likely afraid they'll miss the day's last crossing. Lindisfarne won't let you linger long: unless you've booked one of the handful of B&Bs, you need to make it off before the tide's *sneck* closes. I reckon I've got an hour, so I'm not going to be copying the island's lodestar, Cuthbert, and settling in for weeks of isolated prayer. But I do want to feel Lindisfarne's balm: the way it has of reminding you that quiet places of contemplation can still be found in the British Isles. I've come here to Cuthbert's sanctuary, where miracles were performed by him even in death, because lately I've been feeling a malady: weird psychosomatic symptoms causing me anxiety in a vexing kind of feedback loop. I'm not sure how far I believe in the 'sea cure', but I am hoping some of Lindisfarne's elixir might rub off on me.

Lindisfarne is the first Durham lodge. Each July when thousands gather at the Miners' Gala, coming from outlying former pit lodges to converge on the city, the congregation echoes on a grand scale that first symbolic transportation: when the soul of Northumbria was resprung from its tidal enclave to its new site high on a hill above the River Wear. In the summer, I'll walk with the masses at the Gala once more, paying my respects to the lodestars of Holy Island where they now lie in state. But reaching that destination writ in stone involves starting from the sea, leaving from Lindisfarne and marching behind a metaphorical banner brandished with

Cuthbert's cross, Oswald's ragged heed and the light of Aidan behind me.

Paggered. Goosed. Wiped. Shot. Knackered. Half deed. That's how I remember feeling when I was here last summer, but I tried to keep it all in. As in Hollis's poem, I was 'in neither sway'. Don't get me wrong, this isn't a pity narrative, nor do I want to set off claiming this Camino of the North East will soothe all troubled souls, but it's true to say it had been a tough few years. A domino line of life events – completing a PhD, having a first child, buying a first house, launching a book of poetry, having a second child – had been accompanied by the great restraining, the Covid-19 lockdowns. An outrageous stress response was triggered, leaving me with debilitating waves of anxiety. Leaden legs, pounding head. I found it difficult even to walk through my local park.

Poetry as a kind of 'nodding needle' came to be part of ... – I don't want to say my cure, but perhaps a salve for the post-lockdown world of my early thirties. Adjusting to new fatherhood and a fresh job, I reacquainted myself by – to paraphrase another poet, Basil Bunting – plotting the stars I steer by. Scotswood-born Bunting, who fraternised with literary heavyweights such as Ezra Pound and W. B. Yeats and who spent time in Persia as a translator before returning to the North East to work as an editor on the *Newcastle Journal*, is associated with Northumberland chiefly because of his modernist epic *Briggflatts*. It's a poem which infuses memory and myth, with the author's adolescent love in idyllic northern uplands juxtaposed to the sagas of the tenth-century Norse king Bloodaxe. Today, though, another poet is on my mind as I sit at Emmanuel Head: my old friend Degna Stone. I'm recounting lines of her pantoum 'At Snook

Tower', whose haunting atmosphere seems to encapsulate Holy Island's *genius loci*:

> Base notes of wood smoke play on the breeze,
> cover his footsteps, obliterate all trace.
> As timber markers wait to drown at high tide.³

Stone's poem contains a refrain which I say aloud again today, sat beneath this upturned exclamation mark at the far corner of Northumberland: 'The edge of your feelings wears off by degrees'. It has become a mantra. I've been on Lindisfarne only ninety minutes, but already its milky estuary, mudflats and wild dunes are shivering into an odd sensation. Not a peace, exactly, nor even a real tranquillity, but some perception that the world is bigger than I am – than we all are – and that the perma-crisis we seem to be living through, well, it too shall pass. As surely as the tide begins to flood, it soon turns to ebb.

In a sense, then, I guess this journey will be traditionally pilgrim-focused in that I will be trying to figure out some things about myself. But, again, I want to usher my own ego to the sidelines, for the real star of this show is the place itself – the coastal terrain and city edgelands, the suburban villages and small towns I'll pass through on my way to Durham – and the people who inhabit it. When Saint Cuthbert's followers carried his body off Lindisfarne and set about finding a permanent resting place for it, they were taking the first steps along a route which laid the foundations for the North East of England as it is known today. As I place my feet loosely in their indentations, I do so because, along with wanting to better understand my station in life, I want to better get to know this place I call *hyem*.

If poems are my constellation points, then Nick is my solid worry stone. Laid on its side, the lamp resembles a submarine.

With its rivets and indentations, its soldered name plate and all its imperfect metalwork, I see it as a craft sent down into the deep, a submersible carried far into the earth, into nooks and crannies which no human should ever really have had to witness: those damp spaces held up by wooden stakes, where barely half a man could squeeze, to hew fossilised plant matter into troughs. Talking about 'relic logic', writer Ed Simon says that our 'residual attraction towards relics is an attempt to rediscover something that we've lost'.[4] What might I rediscover along this way, led by my helmsman? I see Nick as a genie, a wraith in the lamp whom I'm conjuring into a spirit guide. A thinned sea glitters, birds hover and jive, and I gulp geet big lungfuls of Holy Island atmosphere. I put my back to the obelisk, its stonework reassuringly cold. I wait to feel my internal compass settling.

Built between 1801 and 1810, Emmanuel Head is a daymark – a guiding post for ships – one of the first to be erected in the country by the Newcastle-based Trinity House, a guild set up by the city's seafarers in the sixteenth century. Responsible for making the River Tyne navigable (the guild received a Royal Charter from Henry VIII in 1536) so that it might more safely and lucratively receive and send out trading and merchants' vessels, Trinity House built the precursors to the High and Low Lights lighthouses at North Shields. Such beacons and watchtowers all along the shore testify to both the dangers and the prospects of the North East coast. They remind me that in making journeys along this stretch of England's neckline, I'm paying homage to the mariners and engineers who worked in tandem to make it a more benign place to berth.

I love its simplicity. Where Ancient Greek obelisks were frequently placed in pairs at the entrance to sacred temples, and were intricately adorned in hieroglyphs with gold relief testifying to sun gods or earthbound commanders, there's something much more austere about the Emmanuel Head. Shorn of any decoration, it has a singular purpose: exclaiming to people out in the boats – *you're hyem*. This, of course, is the constant paradox of the sea – one I'll be thinking about as I make my way down the coast – that it's simultaneously a place of sanctity and hazard. The littoral regions are where we've historically found food or set off for (or arrived at) new lands, but the shoreline can also be sinister and uncompromising: a place plentiful in water but not safe to drink; where you can often see *terra firma* but not quite make it. These guideposts – and there are two other fabulous examples to the south of the island, the Guile Point and Heugh Hill Lighthouses – have emerged to stake our claims to the land, filling me with a weird kind of confidence. Even though, like the lamp by my side, they're totally vestigial now thanks to advances in GPS technology, there's something poignant in their symbolism: the way they continue, literally, to stand in for our absent presence, holding up torches so that we might join the dots of a trail landward.

Sober in stripped-back stone, finished in a whitewash and this morning reflecting the sun lifting over the Farne Islands, it is one of my favourite parts of the Holy Isle, and even better for being relatively little known. I note that it makes the perfect dropped pin to locate my 'A' in this A–B sojourn, and I turn to put it at my back and head for the castle and priory, where I've a different kind of stone to look at. I jog back for a few hundred yards, keen to feel my heart drumming in its chamber, then settle into the walk. I know I'll be back and don't have to do it all at once, but I take five minutes to divert down to the beach, pocketing several pebbles. The pebble-carrying tradition is a well-known aspect of the Camino routes through France and Spain. One of these will be deposited at Durham Cathedral soon. I pick a cautious path across seaweed-strewn rocks, knowing that if I roll my ankle here it's going to be a painful mile's hobble back to the car. I make it back up to the grassed verge without doing any damage, one or two *alreets* offered to the gathering morning walkers making their way with chunky Nikons to the dunes, where no doubt they'll know the names for the birds and the wildflowers.

I walk on to the village centre, passing the castle and harbour, upturned keels and fishing boats anchored in the horseshoe of the Ouse. Ringed plovers and sandworms mark the finer details of myriad romantic watercolour paintings, the vista a backdrop to countless sunrise portraits and doubtless witness to many a marriage proposal. There is an ebullience to the island today, as I'm sure there is most days, even in the depths of winter, which must stem from its cut-offness. Arriving here, as some do on foot but most do on wheels, there's an instant feeling of otherness: of being entirely elsewhere. People get stranded here. Each year, without fail, a dozen or so people get caught short on the causeway, having attempted to make the crossing when it was too late. To avoid this, you can pay to stay on the island in one of its guest houses. I can think of worse places to be marooned. The film-maker Daniel Draper, whom I'm planning to meet in Sunderland later on my travels, once told me that he'd been up here in late 2021, at the cusp of Storm Arwen. Draper recalls not a desolate place, but that haloed sensation which has now become cliché: the calm before the storm. He just made safe passage back across, taking a taxi to Berwick for an emergency stay in a hotel there following the closure of routes south on the East Coast Mainline.

In the grounds of Lindisfarne Priory, on a raised plinth, is what looks like a giant squashed bowling ball. *Feather Star*

Mantle is sculptor Russ Coleman's homage to Saint Cuthbert. Set here in February 2023, it's the first time since the Reformation that a memorial has formally marked Cuthbert's first burial site. The monument replaces a cenotaph which once stood on this spot, but was removed in 1537 when the priory was closed. Its triptych name connotes aspects of Cuthbert's life and stardom in death, not least his association with the eider ducks, which, through his association, became known by the wonderful colloquialism 'Cuddy Ducks'. Coleman's sculpture marks out this interplay between the earth- and sea-bound, between the past and the present. Something placed on a mantle – like my lamp, Nick – is usually set there for some reason of reverence or showcase, so there's a pleasing synergy to Coleman's three-word lyric poem, which in a way tessellates Cuthbert's reputation succinctly.

Saint Cuthbert, patron saint of northern England. But who was he? Woven into the fabric of the region – the name featuring on school jumpers, shopping arcades, care homes, street signs and, of course, churches – the Cuthbert brand is ubiquitous, but how did we get here? To start, we need to turn to another saint, Aidan. An Irish monk who had settled at Iona (the monastery founded by Saint Columba on the west coast of Scotland), Aidan accepted King Oswald of Northumbria's invitation to travel to Lindisfarne to convert the pagan English to the new Christian faith. In 636, a monastic community was established on Lindisfarne. It makes sense that Lindisfarne was established in the sightlines of Bamburgh Castle: better to bind the souls of your people with benedictions forged locally. Aidan's missionary efforts saw him travelling widely throughout the Northumbrian countryside. Going from village to village, speaking with people and gently persuading them to convert to Christianity, Aidan became the most famous apostle of the new Northumbrian-inflected Celtic Christianity. Often depicted with a torch and a shepherd's crook, Aidan was known to converse with people on their own level, meeting them on their own terms.

Witnessing the flame of Aidan's soul go up in smoke and ascend to the angels, Cuthbert, high up in the hills minding sheep at this point, is said to have felt the urge to the holy calling. After spending thirteen years with the Melrose Monks (Aidan had established the monastery in the Scottish Borders), Cuthbert moved to Lindisfarne in his early thirties. Following the Synod of Whitby in 664, in which King Oswiu decided to break from the Irish monks' traditions and instead turn to Rome's way of doing things (including, famously, calculating the date of Easter), Cuthbert spent ten years running the monastery on Lindisfarne. In his forties, following the extreme ascetic custom, he retreated to the Farne Islands, where he believed a life of hermitage was what God had in mind for him. However, in his fifties, he returned to Lindisfarne. Persuaded by the new king, Ecgfrith, and the Church, he became a bishop. Cuthbert was known for his spiritual healing in life – he would frequently be visited by devotees on Inner Farne – and is often depicted as a kindred spirit to local wildlife, but the reason for his fame is his abilities in death, as in many a saintly fable.

After his passing on Inner Farne on 20 March 687 – torches lit telling of the news – Cuthbert was brought back and buried on Lindisfarne. People who came to the grave to pray reported miraculous healing. Eleven years later, during which period the Lindisfarne Gospels were made, Cuthbert's coffin, in anticipation of his 'elevation', was opened and, to everybody's great surprise and confirming his saintliness, his body had not deteriorated at all. Thus began the cult of Cuthbert: the man who had been a spiritual guide in life was now the possessor of an incorrupt body in death. His relics became a focal point for pilgrims, who hoped that proximity to the saint would allow some of his godliness to rub off on them. One hundred years later, under sustained Viking attack and following murder and marauding, the Lindisfarne community, carrying the relics of their idol, along with the great Gospels book made in his honour and the head of their martyred warrior Oswald, left the mainland. For several years they were itinerant around the north of England, before they settled at Chester-le-Street, again for another century. Following a brief sojourn to Ripon, they finally set down at Durham, where eventually the cathedral would be built.

How do we know all of this? Well, from 'A' for Aidan to 'C' for Cuthbert we have a significant joining: 'B' for Bede. The Venerable Bede enters this story more comprehensively in Part II, when I reach Jarrow, but for now, suffice it to say that in his famous *Ecclesiastical History of the English People* of 731, Bede gives us the gen on Aidan's evangelising. Here he is, looking like a door-knocker in high campaign mode for a kind of medieval socialist party:

> For he neither sought after nor cared for worldly possessions but he rejoiced to hand over at once, to any poor man he met, the gifts which he had received from kings of rich men of the world.[5]

I walk round the grounds of the priory to where the statue of Saint Aidan now stands. Sculpted by Kathleen Parbury in 1958, Aidan is shown in customary gait: crook in his right hand, torch raised high in his left. It's a salient image: one which resonates with this old collier's lamp in my possession, now stuffed back into my rucksack. I unzip the bag and pull Nick out again. The light of the lord and the light of the collier. I think of the famous nineteenth-century allegorical painting by William Holman Hunt, *The Light of the World*, which depicts the figure of Jesus, lamp in hand, about to knock on an overgrown door. For those more literate in Scripture, John 8:12 might come to mind – 'I am the light of the world. Whoever follows me will never walk in darkness, but will have the light of life' – but my mind is drawn to a different painting, one I first learned of thirteen years ago.

Holding Nick in front of Aidan, eclipsing the saint's conical stone torch with my battered brass icon, I'm suddenly back in Durham Cathedral in 2010 for the premiere of *The Miners' Hymns*, a rich multimedia show which overlaid Jóhan Jóhannson's dramatic electronic and brass score over Bill Morrison's film. Reading the programme afterwards, which featured Sean O'Brien's lament for the mining industry – 'There are miners still/in the underground rivers/of West Moor and Palmersville'[6] – I was unsure of the reference to *Going Home*, but when I did a bit of digging, I found a well-known image by a totally different nineteenth-century artist, Ralph Hedley. *Going Home* depicts two colliers walking home from Blaydon Main pit – an older bearded figure and his younger apprentice – the latter foregrounded. Over his shoulder he hauls his pick. The older *gadgie* smokes a baccy pipe. The younger man is dressed in shorts, owing to the heat in the mines. Both carry gleaming safety lamps. In the far background, colliery winding gear and chimney plumes are fading from view as the men head down a tatty ash path following their gruelling shift. A sole tree suggests that classic nineteenth-century dichotomy: the encroachment of industrial life into the countryside. Hedley became an important documenter of working life in late nineteenth- and early twentieth-century North East England, his own family riding the crest of burgeoning industrial activity, moving from North Yorkshire to Tyneside in 1850.

When I look at the sculpture of Aidan here today, shepherd to a mass of peasant infidels lining the bracken from Kyloe to Detchant, Roxburgh to Rothbury and back to the king's court at Bamburgh, and I look again at Hedley's prints, it's tempting to read my own situation as a kind of pastor. The man who would be a bard, carrying his lamp through England's edgelands, gathering the fragments, making flint from sea coal and firing it through the heart of Westminster. I can easily conflate the face of that young man in the Hedley image (he'd be, what, 150 years old now?!) with my own great-grandfather, and I can certainly envisage him as the even-older visage of Aidan, superimposing a mish-mash of Christian missionary work and union-led labour. But what would I be doing, really?

Alluring as it might be to see myself roaming the pre-industrial drovers' roads of Northumberland or witnessing the blast furnaces at Consett burst into life, there is a damaging narrative there which I must resist. No shepherd, no saint, no 'hi-ho, hi-ho, it's off to work we go', but a man with a battered old lamp, working out what it means to walk and think with these towering figures. Aidan was noted for travelling on foot and, of his many virtues, Bede lists discretion as chief among them, so it makes sense to me to try to heed his message and listen in attentively as I go.

A panel within the Priory grounds tells me that the base of the Cuthbert memorial sculpture is made of Swaledale fossil limestone, quarried near Durham. Jurassic-period crinoids can be seen flattened into the plinth. The modern-day counterpart, the feather star, is a comparable sea creature which might be seen drifting along the seabed. The main memorial itself is a basalt erratic from Northumberland: a boulder which was once at the earth's molten core but, over millions of years and following periods of glacial drift, slowly surfaced, travelling across the land, making its own unhurried pilgrimage. The gilded design, backed on to a circular cut of Frosterley Marble (which comes into this story again later), features Cuthbert's pectoral cross. Discovered in his coffin and held in the treasures exhibition at Durham Cathedral, the emblem of the county still looms large, featuring on everything from the university's crest to county council branding. I imagine the coxswains of Hatfield and Josephine Butler Colleges donning it on evening glides down the River Wear; and I imagine it on the bin wagons of Bishop Auckland and Beamish, alive in its firmament, a north star for our northern saint.

The first time I came here I knew none of this. I was probably six or seven. We made a two-car expedition with my grandparents, driving up from Shields. It was the early summer holidays and someone had decided we'd go to Holy Island. The name lodged in my head and slowly inflated, resonant with intrigue, adventure, risk and, well, holiness – whatever that meant to my young self. I don't remember much of what we did on that first trip, but I do recall the approach: the first sight of the island as we pulled off the A1, like Atlantis risen from the North Sea, then that surreal drive over the causeway, the fear that water would start seeping up through the bottom of the car. I remember the grocery stall selling island-grown vegetables and jars of jam, the trestle tables of mussels and crab sticks. I don't remember anyone talking about Cuthbert or the Lindisfarne Gospels, but the gravity of the place lingered on. An island, which is holy, just up the road from us. *Mint.*

I place the lamp down by *Feather Star Mantle* and think of Nick, hewing coal from the earth, sixty years away. And I think of Cuthbert, reciting psalms off these shores 1,300 years ago. And then I think of the stone comprising this memorial and the coal my great-grandfather worked his arse off to shovel, all of it here millions of years before we had any concept of religion, saintliness or England. Bede writes about these people – Aidan, Cuthbert, Oswald *et al.* – with a reverence that I find compelling. Thinking about the people who would come here – who still, in fact, make the causeway crossing barefoot, often with large wooden crosses on Good Friday – I am struck by our human desire to be beside relics. Clearly, on one level we can understand now that being beside a corpse is not going to cure our ills. Just as I understand that this lamp means nothing in practical terms. But there's something transcendent about being kept in check, of holding communion with these objects, which brings us out of ourselves. Gustav Mahler supposedly said that 'tradition is tending the flame, not worshipping the ashes', and I think that's absolutely what those pilgrims must have been doing when they came across to Holy Island to be with Cuthbert – his shrine wasn't where they saw themselves; rather, it presented them with a continuum, a great looping Möbius strip turning back behind them into the murky depths of time, which would also spool out in front of them infinitely.

From geet big stones to tiny fossils, I want to try to search the strand for Cuddy's beads, but time is against me. The beads are portions of the fossilised stems of crinoids – marine echinoderms, as are modern sea urchins, star fish and sea lilies. The coast of Northumberland, and Holy Island in particular, is known for them, appearing on its beaches like rustic rosary beads. When we drove up here last summer, I had in mind that if I could find some of them – even just one – and string a rosary of my own, it would somehow act as a kind of ointment. Packing a picnic the night before and waking early enough to fill the flask with hot tea and ply the kids from their beds, we drove the hour and a half up the Northumbrian coast. It was one of those windy days when, even as an adult, you don't especially want to dwell on a tidal island, but for small people it must have felt like a real hoolie. We spent half an hour or so unsuccessfully searching for Cuddy's beads. I realise now that, even had I found any, they would have been palliative at best. It was in the act of digging around for them – in rolling up our jeans and taking the kids' Crocs off for the first time to imprint their tiny toes into the sands – that I found my balm. If Cuthbert's spirit now means anything, if the Northumbrian soul has a purpose beyond drawing tourists to the region, then surely it's in irreplaceable moments of family connection like this, when your bairns' laughter lifts you faster than the Holy Island causeway.

When I was researching the history of my lamp, I went down a rabbit warren. First, I contacted the Durham Mining Museum in Spennymoor asking if they could tell me Nick's age and place of manufacture. They shared a photo on Facebook and I began receiving messages from associated coal-mining groups. Several enthusiasts contacted me and before long I was learning about hinge pins, asbestos-laden gaskets and Kanthal wire. I learned that Nick is a Protector SL (side lighting) and was used for gas detection. Known as 'workman's lamps', they were carried by miners trained to read flames underground and identify levels of methane. These lamps would not be relightable underground: an electrical current would be used on the surface to relight them. I learned how to date Nick; that he was made in the year 1958 and manufactured in Eccles, Manchester. This annoyed me at first – I thought there's no way Nick could have been made anywhere but the North East – then I was told that after the 1950s the National Coal Board only used protector lamps. Prior to this, there had been three main manufacturers in the region: Patterson of Gateshead, Laidler of Durham and J. Mills of Newcastle.

I'm aware that the origin of the miner's safety lamp is contested and that there are competing claims on its invention. While the chemist Humphrey Davy was working on his design in 1815, it was claimed that he was heavily influenced by the Sunderland-based physician William Reid Clanny, who, two years earlier, had presented a paper to the Royal Society outlining the design for his own lamp. Northumberland-born George Stephenson also declared that he had come up with the first safety lamp, but Stephenson's design was different to both Davy's and Clanny's. As Andrew Lacey has written, 'it is possible to arrive, contemporaneously, at very similar ideas or designs independently and by different means, which serves as a reminder that claims to absolute priority should be treated with caution'.[7] I am less interested in who invented the first miner's safety lamp and more pleased that, through a combination of scientific enquiry and determination to save lives, it was invented at all. Throughout this book I generally refer to my protector lamp as Nick, while elsewhere I refer to Davy lamps and safety lamps, doing so in a nonpartisan way. Thanks to Baz Mollett, who helped me date my lamp, I learned that in the 1950s most colliers in the North East would have referred to theirs as Geordie lamps or protector lamps. Nick: the protector at my side, reinvigorating my stride through the soul of Northumbria.

I was told initially that the lamp could not be relit. Then, someone else told me that it would be possible, and detailed instructional videos walking me through the process appeared in my inbox. I was sent pictures of similar lamps – restorations that had been done as passion projects and which drew me into the garage workshops of men in Peterlee. Photos showed grand glass cabinets containing dozens in a collection: Stephensons with outer gauze, inner glass and copper perforated cap; Davys with single gauze; Mueseler lamps with chimneys, which came later in the nineteenth century. I learned that in Scotland some called them 'Glennies'.

Everyone addressed me as 'marra'. One bloke, upon learning I was in South Tyneside, told me that Bede's Well used to be in the fields that ran down from the back of his house in Jarrow. I felt a fragment of the kinship of the pit. For now, I like the symbolic power of the closed-off lamp: the protector whose fuel is story and myth, which will be powered by motion. The bronze plaque on the front brandishes Nick's tally, the number 222. I hadn't heard of Angel Numbers before starting out on this journey, but in an undergraduate lecture I was giving last year, I showed a picture of the lamp and a student told me that triple-two is very lucky. A cursory Google into numerology suggests that I can expect collaboration, unity and spiritual alignment.

How long the monks must have waited for alignment, planning their crossings, waiting for the right time. Staunch observers of the coast, I see them working it out – how long it takes for the tide's tendrils, the duration of their release. Coming at day or night, no doubt, torches lit, a procession of devotees crossing to come and be kissed by Cuthbert's glow, to come and bask in his after-image, to be healed or forgiven or given another chance. And then their leaving: the bier packed, envoys sent out in advance, to give clear warning – *Cuthbert cometh*. Another chance. A second home in death. If making a pilgrimage is meaningful precisely because you follow it in the footsteps of all of who've come the same way before, it's doubly poignant when you know you can still enact change. Here you are, still walking, your skin being sun-bleached, the raging thirst you feel, all of your fickle muscles working and your brain churning to process the headlong rush of it all; you know that you can take all this with you back into your life, altering your outlook. A second chance. The road has risen for us. Were we walking, we'd do it in an hour and a half, the geet big wooden stakes leading us as way-markers. In the car, it takes five minutes. Each crossing an echo of the pilgrims' journey, each person carrying a remnant of the *Haliwerfolc* – 'people living within the county palatine of Durham, and by extension the land they occupied, being under St Cuthbert's special protection'.[8]

Lindisfarne itself has become a relic. People come, as I have done, to be near the origin-point of Cuthbert, but his remains are in Durham Cathedral. So, I wonder what people are really drawn here for. For some, it must be the low-key jeopardy: the feeling that they could get marooned. For most, though, it's got to be the atmosphere of the island, a feeling that you're stepping back in time, perhaps to a simpler, more rustic way of life. Celtic Christianity talks of 'thin places', where the membrane between our world and the transcendent is poignantly slender. Often high mountain zones, hills and valleys are seen in this way, as spaces where it feels more likely to be touched by the grace of God. For me, the whole ambit of Lindisfarne puts it into the 'thin place' category: as I meditate on the point where the sky stops and the sea's salt-tang begins, I feel my ego and worries start to drip away. I feel centred.

I said I'd hoped some Holy Island elixir would rub off on me. I wasn't expecting to be coated in dozens of little prickles. I pick pirri-pirri burrs from my socks and shoes. This New Zealand native plant, which looks like a miniature firework, is thought to have been brought to Britain on the fleece of sheep which were imported to nearby Berwick. A small part of the Northumberland coast is now stuck to my trainers.

The compass takes its weigh

When they're all picked from my shoes, I start the car and make for the crossing. Looking across the causeway, its own thin place, the Northumbrians' royal seat at Bamburgh is bidding me over.

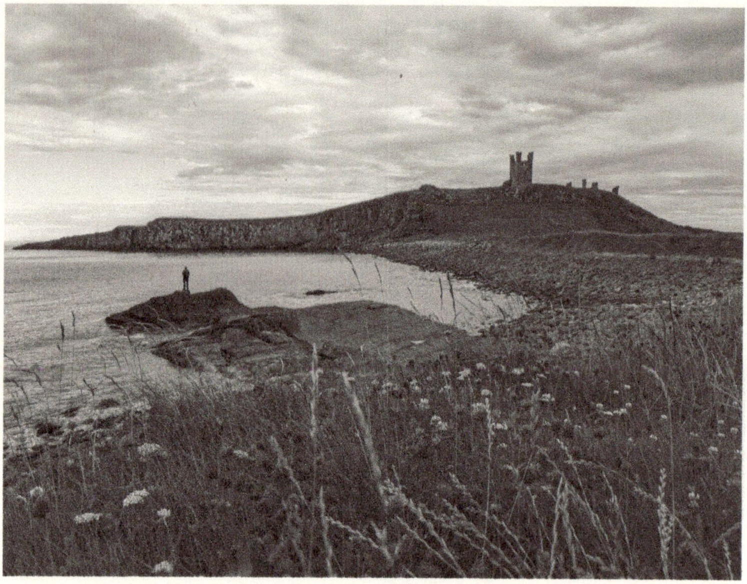

Chapter 2

Coastline of castles

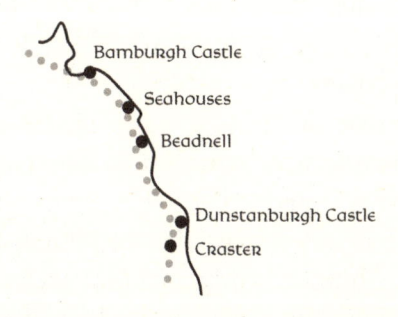

```
· · Bamburgh Castle
   · Seahouses
    · Beadnell

    · Dunstanburgh Castle
    · Craster
```

Early on a Wednesday morning in mid-July, I pick up my old friend Matt from his parents' house in Whitburn. He's come from Norwich to walk a stretch of the coast with me. We've booked two nights at the recently opened Premier Inn in Alnwick. Pilgrimage purists will say that I'm cheating – that I should have walked over from Holy Island and stayed the night at Bamburgh – but I'm no perfectionist. So, the journey resumes at seven in the morning in my VW Golf and takes in the morning rush of northbound Tyne Tunnel traffic. By eight thirty we're changing into walking boots in the car park of the Premier Inn, then briskly hiking to Alnwick bus station to catch Travelsure's 418 service. The price cap for single-ticket bus journeys has been extended, so even though it takes us another hour and a half to reach Bamburgh, it feels like incredibly good value at two quid.

Through all the villages on the coast, the bus wends its way. At a Victorian infants' school by Boulmer, a TV crew are setting up. We think *Vera*, but later learn it's the crew for *The Red King*, a folk-horror-inflected mystery thriller currently being shot in Northumberland. The bus gradually begins to fill with a mixture of walkers and locals, more so as we near Seahouses. By the end of the journey, I'm champing at the bit to be off, so seeing Bamburgh's imposing fortress round the bend is a relief. We alight and use the facilities, before making our first stop, at St Aidan's Church just off to the west of Castle Green.

In the summer of 2021, I was commissioned to write a poem responding to a remarkable aspect of this church: its ossuary. Myself and eight other poets wrote works in response to what was dubbed the 'Bamburgh Bones' project, in which over a hundred early medieval skeletons which had been dug up along the beach at the foot of the castle were reinterred.[1] With wide skies and miles of untrod beaches, the Northumbrian coast is celebrated as a place of pilgrimage and as a beguiling holiday destination, but it's also a place where the sands of time occasionally uncover their ghosts.

Bamburgh Castle was once the seat of power in the Kingdom of Northumbria, and archaeologists' work on these Anglo-Saxon remains showed that people had travelled widely to be at King Oswald's court. Between 1998 and 2007, excavations in sand dunes at the Bowl Hole, a few hundred metres to the south of the castle, revealed a graveyard consisting of dozens of individuals. Analysis of strontium (a plant mineral captured in tooth enamel when people eat) showed that, far from being a remote outpost, Bamburgh 1,300 years ago was a thriving cosmopolitan centre. People had come here from the west of Scotland and Ireland, but also from as far away as Scandinavia and the Mediterranean, including a nine-year-old child whose teeth reveal origins in North Africa by way of time in France.

This was what was known as Northumbria's Golden Age, a period from around 650 to 800, when its wealth and influence attracted knights, bishops and other noblemen to hear Aidan preach and to be gilded by association with King Oswald. But the record also tells of skilled craftspeople such as metal workers and weavers, all of whom were drawn by the intellectual, artistic and spiritual crucible fomenting in Bamburgh during the seventh and eighth centuries. Contemporary populist slogans like 'Stop the Boats' and the heinous 'Breaking Point' 2016 UKIP poster, not to mention violent disorder by the far-right witnessed on British streets in the wake of the Southport stabbings in summer 2024, look even more contemptible when you consider how long people have been traversing the bounds of statehood to come and enrich life on our shores.

King Oswald, amalgamating the previously warring Anglian kingdoms of Deira and Bernicia, ruled over a unified Northumbria, one whose present-day iteration is being governed for the first time in the modern period by an elected North East mayor. While the challenges the mayor faces are entirely different to those of a seventh-century Anglo-Saxon king, in her chairing of the first meeting of the North East Combined Authority, in May 2024, Labour mayor Kim McGuinness spoke of a similar unanimity of purpose: of being 'unified in our drive to make things better for the 2.1m people who live right across our region'.[2] The historian Dan Jackson notes how 'Using the more inclusive term "Northumbrians" avoids bogging us down in the imprecise demarcation of Geordies and Mackems, the two feuding tribes of Tyne and Wear whose modern rivalry has obscured how much they share in common'.[3] This harks back to Oswald's integration and, for me, points beyond the region's parochial fault lines.

At Ad Gefrin in Wooler, fifteen miles inland from here, the Ferguson family are pivoting to the same 'spirit of belonging', advocating for the 'rich culture of the Northumbrian court; a time of welcome, celebration and hospitality'.[4] A border market town might not seem the most obvious place for a whisky distillery, but the owners have played on recent archaeological finds at nearby Yeavering, once the summer house of Northumbrian royalty, to connect ideas of kingly hosting to the fermenting of grains.

After a quick look around the empty twelfth-century church, we make our way into the ossuary. Crouching down behind a newly installed wrought-iron gate, it's possible to see some of the many ossuary boxes which now house the Bamburgh Bones in their final resting place. It felt important to visit today and to start this leg of the Camino here. When I wrote my poem[5] in response to the project, my daughter had just arrived, and so perhaps understandably for the very tired father, I was having a lot of odd teeth dreams. It doesn't take a great deal of psychological association to connect this kind of subconscious image to waking anxiety, and this is exactly what I ended up writing my poem about, not the bones in the boxes, whose lives seemed so distant as to be totally abstract. But coming down here today and then walking along the coast where these people worked and prayed, I feel suddenly quite privileged to have had a small role in helping to keep their legacy going, to understanding them as real people whose association with Bamburgh has been permanently imprinted upon it, and who finally got the dignified end they deserved.

By now it's after eleven and we need to get to Beadnell, so we hot-foot it across the green, where eager young tennis protégés rally in the morning sun, to stand on the west of the castle in the dunes. In 2015, the folk-punk troubadour Frank Turner shot a video for his song 'If I Ever Stray' on the beach here, while further down the coast, Lloyd's Bank made a global financial instrument look more folksy by having their famous black stallion gallop the sands of Beadnell Bay. A less well-known image is the stag rock, a white deer painted into the cliffs at the headland of Black Rocks Point. Folklore stemming back to Aidan's time tells of the saint once saving a stag from a pack of hounds by making it invisible, and now each time the lighthouse on the cliffs above is painted, so too is the stag, which is reminiscent of the 17,000-year-old Lascaux cave paintings in the Dordogne. From the beach we can see the whitewashed obelisk of Emmanuel Head glinting a few miles up the coast. High up to our right, the mighty fortification of Bamburgh: the supreme Northumbrian castle. King Penda and his Mercian army once tried to burn it down, but Aidan, who was on Inner Farne at the time, performed another miracle and saved it. As Bede tells us:

> When he saw the tongues of flame and the smoke being carried by the winds right above the city walls, the story goes that he raised his eyes and hands towards heaven and said with tears, 'Oh Lord, see how much evil Penda is doing.' As soon as he had uttered these words, the winds veered away from the city and carried the flames in the direction of those who had kindled them, so that, as some of them were hurt and all of them terrified, they ceased to make any further attempt on the city, realising that it was divinely protected.[6]

Not for the first time, I think of the sheer elemental scale of the Northumbrian coast. All the way down now, from Bamburgh to Dunstanburgh, down to Warkworth and beyond, I'll see castles where the pulse of flame echoed off the waves, and where messages encoded in fire were sent to ward off, protect or inform. Take the death of Cuthbert, signalled with torches by the monks of St Cuthbert's hermitage to the monks of Lindisfarne. In a miniature illustration from the twelfth-century Yates Thompson manuscript, freely digitised and browsable online thanks to the British Library,[7] we can see death's relay being completed by torchlight, a valedictory parade booming between the salt and the ash.

This is what William Martin dubbed the 'Tideroad', writing in that sequence: 'I am over rock and across sand/An exile white beyond the bar'.[8] Up here, things can seem fuzzy. I'm trying to reach back into the medieval past, but it's out of focus. I've got one of Martin's books in mind, *Cracknrigg*, its back cover adorned with a lino-cut image, Bill's impression of a Viking longship, or perhaps a coble – those traditional open wooden fishing boats, found between Flamborough Head and Berwick, with flat bottoms and sharp forefoots enabling safe landing among sandy havens. When I look at Bill's image now, I can't tell whether there are saints or marauders on board. Captors and captives, all of us running and failing the hurdles of time.

Once Matt and I have pressed on a bit round the shingle, the full scale of Bamburgh Castle can be properly taken in. We find a whacking great driftwood trunk to perch on and pull out the flask. The forecast has warned us of thundery showers, but the weather is serene. The air has the full hit of seaweed sweetness, the ivory sands stretching for miles north and south. No wonder people feel close to whatever form of heaven they believe in when they stroll here. The sense and scale of the light here are incredible: it feels like we're being charged by the solar power of the Northumbrian coast, and we'll need it to get down to Craster before the last bus. Bamburgh Castle is imperious, the type of structure which would make most attackers say, 'you know what, let's not'. And there's something metaphysically alluring about that humanmade statement to power squaring off against the sea – a 'we'll fight anyone' mantra.

The tide is still a way out, so we push on along the beach, gradually coming in line with, and then passing, the Farne Islands. Billy Shiel's Boat Trips, one of the tour operators taking passengers to the Farnes, is sending a vessel out from the harbour at Seahouses to show people Cuthbert's hermitage and a huge, and now sadly sickened, colony of seabirds. Seahouses comes into view quickly and we, still feeling energetic early in this three-day walk, bound up the dunes, taking a bench overlooking a rocky plateau known as The Tumblers. We have our bait here amid the ragwort, gazing at Inner Farne, to Big Harcar and Little Harcar rocks, Longstone Lighthouse and the treacherous seas where the lighthouse keeper's daughter Grace Darling performed her famous rescues.

At this point I realise that in our haste to see the ossuary, we missed Darling's grave, which is in the grounds of St Aidan's. Lines from Hector Gannet's epic song 'The haven of Saint Aidan's'[9] fill my head, reminding me of the resilience of this part of the coast. In 1838, on its journey from Hull to Dundee, the boilers of the paddle-steamer SS *Forfarshire* failed. Using a makeshift sail, the captain tried to seek refuge, but the ship began to drift dangerously in Staple Sound, eventually crashing into Big Harcar. Twenty-two-year-old Grace and her lighthouse keeper father, William, leapt to action, rescuing nine people from the sixty on board. Grace's early death due to tuberculosis five years later may have only added to her lustre (think now of the notorious 'twenty-seven club') but she's still remembered as one of England's greatest heroines. I'll meet with Hector Gannet (aka Aaron Duff) later on in this part of the book, but, for now, again, a line of his 'The haven of Saint Aidan's', recording Darling's courage, rings in my head as we set off for Seahouses: 'Echoes way out to the lighthouse'.

Aidan follows us along this coast, just as in life he took to the drovers' roads to preach the word of God. The first time I came properly to Seahouses was a decade ago, for my twenty-fifth birthday. My wife, Kate, and I stayed at Saint Aidan's B&B in adjacent North Sunderland, a converted chapel where, having taken one of the boat tours to the Farnes, we proceeded to drink a lot of Lindisfarne mead. Now the hostelry is closed, and in any case we don't have a lot of time to linger in Seahouses today, but we do stop briefly at the southern end of the harbour, where a pair of whalebones set in sculpture frame a good view of the boats coming and going.

Seahouses is regarded as the gateway to the Northumberland Coast Area of Outstanding Natural Beauty, and it is not difficult to see why. North Sunderland (the 'north' added to avoid confusion with Sunderland on Wearside) was the original separate settlement south of the old parish of Bamburgh, a place of rigg and furrow farming providing victuals for the monks' offshore dwelling. As the settlement was set a short way back from the coast, villagers would be briefly protected from invading Norsemen. The fishing industry began to take off in the eighteenth century, hence North Sunderland's 'sea houses' bled one village into the other.

The remains of large limekilns can be seen down on the harbour, where today we could have had an unusual souvenir, a lobster pot for £25, suggesting where trade now lies. The National Trust manages the Farne Islands site, which is a wonderful place to see guillemots, shags and, famously, puffins. On Inner Farne, where Cuthbert had his hermitage, a thirteenth-century chapel welcomes visitors from the mainland to bask in the same spiritual surroundings as the holy man. Seahouses is the place to set off on such a journey and this accounts for a large proportion of its visitors. The rest of the village is dominated by the kinds of shops from which one purchases needless tat. I once bought a porcelain puffin from the National Trust shop, along with a red and yellow Northumberland iron-on fabric patch, and we sat in the car eating overpriced fish and chips. It's that kind of place. It does have a great pub, The Olde Ship Inn, where Kate and I once spent a fantastic evening knocking back the bitters surrounded by nautical memorabilia.

Round the headland south of Seahouses, we walk for a while on a golf course, before briefly joining the B1340 road for a quiet mile into Beadnell. Along the foreshore, people work on converting and extending sea-facing properties. A team of sparkies, plasterers, brickies and joiners are modifying at least three houses within a few hundred yards, presumably to add to the area's already vast stock of second homes and holiday lets. Earlier in the morning the bus took us through the slightly set back Beadnell village, its Church of St Ebba (Oswald's sister) an arresting centrepiece, but now we carry on down the periphery to the limekilns by the old harbour.

The first thing to know about Beadnell is that it feels a bit like a film set, or at least it does at two in the afternoon on the Wednesday in July we approach it. There's an excellent puzzle-based video game called *Everybody's Gone to the Rapture* in which the player, assuming a first-person vantage, directs some unknown, possibly spectral, presence around a fictionalised village in rural Shropshire. Gradually it becomes clear that some cataclysmic event – a nuclear strike is implied – has seen everyone off, and the player is left to assemble a series of clues as to what the community was like in the before times.

Beadnell is nowhere near as apocalyptic, but it is a tad surreal, and it certainly now exists in the after times. By the limekilns, in rain that threatens but never bothers to properly show up, we meet the poet Katrina Porteous. A few years ago, I was asked to interview her for the poetry journal *Prac Crit*; since then, I have familiarised myself with her work, which is rooted to the Northumbrian coast she's called home since 1987. Porteous is sprightly and unassuming. She's a much-revered presence in North East poetry, having spent a career making books and, famously, radio broadcasts capturing a lyrical mix of fishing dialect and ruminations on the changing tides of time. Minding a poorly cat back at her late parents' home sixty miles away in Shotley Bridge, she can't stay long, but has graciously come back up to meet us and explain why there's more to Beadnell than first meets the eye.

Katrina's family ties to the village stretch back to the 1930s. Her father inherited his parents' house and wanted to keep it for holidays. Struggling to make a living as a writer, Katrina begged her parents to let her live there. Their acquiescence was a boon for her emerging writing: it allowed her to come to intimately know, and in time poetically render, Beadnell's fishing community. She speaks passionately about feeling a sense of responsibility for recording their stories and documenting their shared place and a desire to give something back in turn. It's a sentiment that resonates with me, carrying this battered old miner's lamp as a kind of conduit for collective memory. The support I've received from family adds to the duty I feel to faithfully capture my ancestry; whereas as a nascent poet, the encouragement I've enjoyed from other writers, including Katrina, confirms the need to inhabit an imaginative space – connecting my own cove of poesis to wider currents.

Katrina has brought along two artefacts connected to the coast. The first is a netting needle, made by Charlie Douglas, one of the fishermen she shadowed upon arriving in Beadnell in the 1980s. Its design goes back a couple of thousand years, but it is based on a slightly simpler design which pre-dates the written word. Katrina tells me that remarkably similar designs have been found as far away as Indonesia, a strong rebuke to Western-centric view of design and technology. Acting as a shuttle for making the nets needed to haul a catch, it speaks to the fishing trade's status as the backbone of the economy until the early 1980s. By the time Porteous arrived here, the trade was on the decline, bigger trawlers from far-off ports devastating the seafloor and scuppering the local fleet as small boats became increasingly economically unviable.

The second item Katrina shows us is a fishing heuk – a tiny dagger on the end of a frayed twine. Some 1,400 of these would be attached by what were known as sneyds to a long line, and each fisherman would take to sea in his coble for the winter fishing season between October and March, aiming to catch as much cod and haddock as possible. The women of the community went out onto the beach each morning, baiting each heuk with a mussel and a limpet. From the liberal perspective of the twenty-first century, you could argue that these women were little more than indentured servants – tied to the shore and pressed into the rote work which pre-figured their husbands' perilous voyages – but a more charitable view might take it that this was something of a circular economy: a place in which, women and men, working in tandem, used the local resources available to them, each applying their skills to the best of their abilities to make a sustainable living.

Either way, fishing like this, until the middle of the twentieth century, hadn't changed much since medieval times. Katrina's research[10] and reading has shown that Durham Priory's cellarer's account books record Holy Island fishing boats being used to catch the white fish requested by the prince bishops as far back as at least 1333. Which all makes perfect sense, when you think about it: the monks who had left their island community wanted to still be feasting on the freshest Northumbrian fish.

Katrina's latest collection of poetry, *Rhizodont* (named after a 350-million-year-old fossilised fish found on a limestone ridge at Cocklawburn beach by Berwick-upon-Tweed), sees her work reckoning ever more with deep time. The fossil record in this part of the world, stretching out into the North Sea, reminds us that we are a mere blip when compared with the geological scale, a humbling reflection captured in Katrina's titular poem that pays homage to the three-metre-long fish whose tusks and huge teeth gave it its name: 'The rhizodont/Dragging itself out of water./The old world sinks and slips//Beneath its tilted strata'.[11]

I put it to Katrina that the themes she's now grappling with – a disconnection from land, the loss of tradition, global extinction events – speak to the zeitgeist, and I wonder aloud whether that marks her work out as political. She's quick to tell me that she doesn't see herself as being politically motivated – she has more questions than answers – but it does seem to me that, in its capacity to pay close attention to both the very local and specific, while at once recognising the stratum of time we all find ourselves fossilised within, her work is more than just fashionably flirting with 'eco poetry'; it is eco poetry – that is to say, poetry which is entirely mindful of its capacity at once to capture the ineffable and to reflect the material realities of living on a highly volatile ball of matter.

I take some photos of the old herring yards – a building which looks like a sort of compacted Disney castle – while Matt and Katrina muse on selkies and sea shanties. Katrina has captured, on video and in numerous sound recordings, the dialect of the Beadnell fishing community, a tongue which, as she says, is now totally gone. As extinct as the fossils imprinted onto these Northumbrian beaches, this north Northumbrian vernacular was entirely particular to Beadnell. Two miles further north, at Seahouses, the dialect would have differed. When she arrived here and started talking to people like Charlie Douglas, his sister-in-law, May, and all the other fishing folk, Katrina was seen as a bit of a curiosity. But, quickly realising that she wasn't some fly-by-night, they soon almost forgot she was there and continued about their business as usual. This allowed Katrina privileged first-hand accounts of the dying end of a centuries-long tradition, and she was often out at sea on cobles after the crab or on small boats after trout in the bay. 'After a while, they didn't see me as a woman', Katrina says, as we both again acknowledge the gender disparities involved in the labour.

Having earned their trust, Katrina began to make films of the fishermen, eventually working verbatim dialogue into her poems. Much of this is documented in *Two Countries*, her 2014 volume. In it, we get a sense of a writer thinking through the global and the local: the whirr and hum of the Northumbrian as it is slowly engorged by the English, or else clings on resistant, finding new forms. The late poet and academic Bill Griffiths was inspired by Katrina's work, particularly in her long poem 'The Wund and the Wetter', which was an important source for his *Fishing and Folk: Life and Dialect on the North Sea Coast*, the last in a trilogy of North East dialect books. But Katrina has always had a suspicion of the academy (as did Bill Griffiths), and both books speak to the uneasy tension that sometimes exists between hard-won anthropological research and universities' cavalier absorption of it.

It makes sense that Katrina is a poet, because poets can do things that other people can't do – that other writers can't do. We are shapeshifters, bending language and warping time with our will. Suddenly millions of years come crashing down and we're stood on a beach with primitive sea creatures, the type all tetrapods, ergo all humans, are derived from; but then, click, we're in the nineteenth century as the limekilns fire up, or we're at St Ebb's Point, where linnets can dash from the twelfth or thirteenth century to now, then back, to when this grassed-over mound was a chapel, the place where followers of Saint Ebba would have prayed, with views back to Cuthbert's hermitage on the Farnes and to her brother's throne at Bamburgh. Poets snap us back or pull us forwards. Katrina recalls the skulls and bones of Victorian children being uncovered here – the remains of unbaptised infants whose final creche was nevertheless a spiritual place. We measure out the size of the chapel from the rectangular mound still visible, as a colony of bees clings to a thistle and more linnets shake the centuries from us.

We're back down onto the beach at Beadnell, now only one or two fibreglass replica cobles still going out to fish, and around the bay to Long Nanny, the bird sanctuary at Beadnell Bay. Warnings all along the coast have advised us of avian flu, which seems particularly distressing given Cuthbert's fondness for birds, but here's a promising sign as a cordoned-off section of the beach to High Newton is protecting the breeding sites of species such as ringed plovers and Arctic terns. Conversation soon turns to social media, which Katrina is sceptical of, as I tell her I'm torn between thinking it a useful tool for finding interesting people (several of the encounters in this book came about directly because of it) while agreeing with her that its ephemerality, an imperative of the capitalist motives now driving it, is antithetical to the slow work and consideration required of poetry and literature.

At Newton Steads, Katrina leaves us, but before she does I express my gratitude for being shown around her patch. I might have been a bit unfair on Beadnell when I first arrived here a few hours ago, but now that I understand it on a bigger scale, I can see the double bind of tourism. I certainly can't imagine having had a life of baiting fishing heuks ahead of me, and would have seized any opportunity to spread my wings and take flight. I hope that when the second-home owners and holiday-let guests come here, they treat it less like a theme park and more like a real place rich with history. They'd do worse in that endeavour than to be furnished with a copy of Katrina's new book, whose rooted teeth, beyond all else, tell of persisting through tough weather.

Speaking of, it's turned into a glorious afternoon. We come over a big rise in the land at a quarry by Newton Point, and eventually reach a lookout with a wonderful view down to Low Newton-by-the-Sea, the remains of Dunstanburgh Castle silhouetted in the distance. Again, a place of ghosts. A pint of lager at the Ship Inn awaits. We could cheerily spend the rest of the afternoon here – the pub is uniquely set at the back of a village green framed by the beach at its eastern aspect – and with homebrewed ale and crab sandwiches available, the temptation is a strong one. Before supping our pints, I take out the next OS map: Explorer 332. We've moved onto a new sheet now, marking, in cartographic terms at least, the middle of our trio of treks. A retired southern family on the adjacent picnic table are discussing range anxiety, worrying about whether they'll get their hybrid car back to the Home Counties in one run, which I think says a lot about the territory we find ourselves in.

Around the bay towards Embleton, we drop down to the beach once again. It's absolutely roasting now and this stretch almost feels tropical. I can see the idyllic appeal of this 'unspoilt' corner of Northumberland, especially to the metropolitan-bound south-easterner (or, indeed, to the metropolitan-bound north-easterner), and Matt and I very diplomatically run through both the cons and pros of tourism, deciding that, were it not for the visitors (ourselves included), that four o'clock pint of glorious homebrewed lager would have been another flask coffee.

We round the bay, dog-walkers with labradoodles thinning out as we stupidly carry on sand-side rather than taking the easier path on Embleton Links as the map suggested. The tide is coming in now, the going like trudging through treacle. But Dunstanburgh Castle is clearly in view, and after a couple of miles of gruelling effort (and not much talking) we emerge parallel to the golf course, plonking down for five minutes among the ragwort. Fuelling up on flapjacks, we press on for the final few miles, now right below the castle, which sits on an escarpment of Whin Sill rock, coated in guano. We watch a golfer drive down the fairway then we start speaking to a bloke from the West Midlands, who's hobbled along here from Craster, despite a dodgy knee and back, to see the oystercatchers.

Rounding the western side of the castle, we come out on a slope of grazing sheep. Dunstanburgh occupies a unique position on the headland. Built in the fourteenth century by Earl Thomas of Lancaster, it was probably intended to be a fortress against King Edward II's forces, in the event of the political situation turning sour. It eventually passed to John of Gaunt, before being the focus of fighting during the Wars of the Roses. In its present state of disrepair, it's still an imposing sight, presumably intended to rival Bamburgh in some sense. Its half-fallen-down state seems to me to fit the Northumbrian narrative of border reiver skirmishes very well, though it could more generally represent humanity's hubris at the tidal zone, where eventually all will crumble into the sea or be desiccated by the magma beneath.

From here to Craster it's about a mile and a half. The rain is back with a little bit more gusto this time, so we find the final gear to make it to The Jolly Fisherman. Before entering, I clock the shape of a ship made of fragmented stone in the wall of a cottage opposite. A lovely nautical addition. But we're dithering: we've missed, by five minutes, the bus back to Alnwick. Pity us, having to stay in the pub until the next one arrives at ten to eight.

We find ourselves at the bar-room equivalent of slack tide: the hubbub of late afternoon giving way to a trickle of early-evening diners, in their finery and fine accents. They're counterposed to the Northumbrian locals propping up the end of the bar, supping on pints of Shipyard Pale and talking about the ethically dubiously owned football club forty miles to the south that they insist on supporting. I spot that the barmaid has travelled in from Shilbottle, ten miles away, while the gadgie at our end of the bar with the local accent is wearing a Warkworth Harbour polo shirt. It's not *Guardian* gastro fare, that's for sure, but it's a fiver for a pint of Tim Taylor's and we're in Northumberland. One more pint and we resist the luscious smell of boiling mussels, to board the top deck of the x18 back to Alnwick. Robson & Son's fishmongers bellows out smoke – the famous Craster kippers being prepared – as our shiny new Arriva bus takes the express route back to the market town.

We arrive and check in just before nine. Too late for food. So it's a mile's further hike, on top of the fourteen we've already done, into Alnwick, where the best – nay the only – option ends up being a visit to Pizza Royale for a chicken wrap, some cheesy chips and onion rings. We eat them in the market square as the streetlights start popping on and two men in a Transit van arrive to begin assembling the stalls for the next day's trading.

Alnwick is an odd place, not unlikeable at all, but certainly not the most welcoming of towns. Its castle and grounds became famous when the *Harry Potter* films used them for Hogwarts, and at one point Alnwick Garden claimed to have the world's largest tree house. To many locals it's the home of the excellent second-hand book shop Barter Books, which has a model railway running along the rafters, nodding to the building's history as Alnwick's original train station. But there's also something of a down-at-heel quality to the place – its paving rickety, some of its older buildings losing roof tiles – which sits at odds with the amount of tourist money that must rush through it. Many market towns are like this, of course, and we're visiting it midweek, but it certainly seems that a long baker's dozen years of austerity have begun to wrap their tendrils around the alcoves.

We stop at the excellent Ale Gate micropub on our way back to the hotel for a night-cap, where conversation is dominated by local accents of mainly middle-aged men and women supping modestly priced pints of cask ale. We take a £3.70 pint each of Double Maxim, decompressing on the long old day we've had. On our way out of the pub, in the shadow of the Tenantry Column topped by the Percy Lion, we resolve to dig further into Alnwick's curious half-charm, but before that we've got big piles of sand to empty out of our boots, and some shut-eye to get behind purple curtains of the Willowburn Industrial Estate.

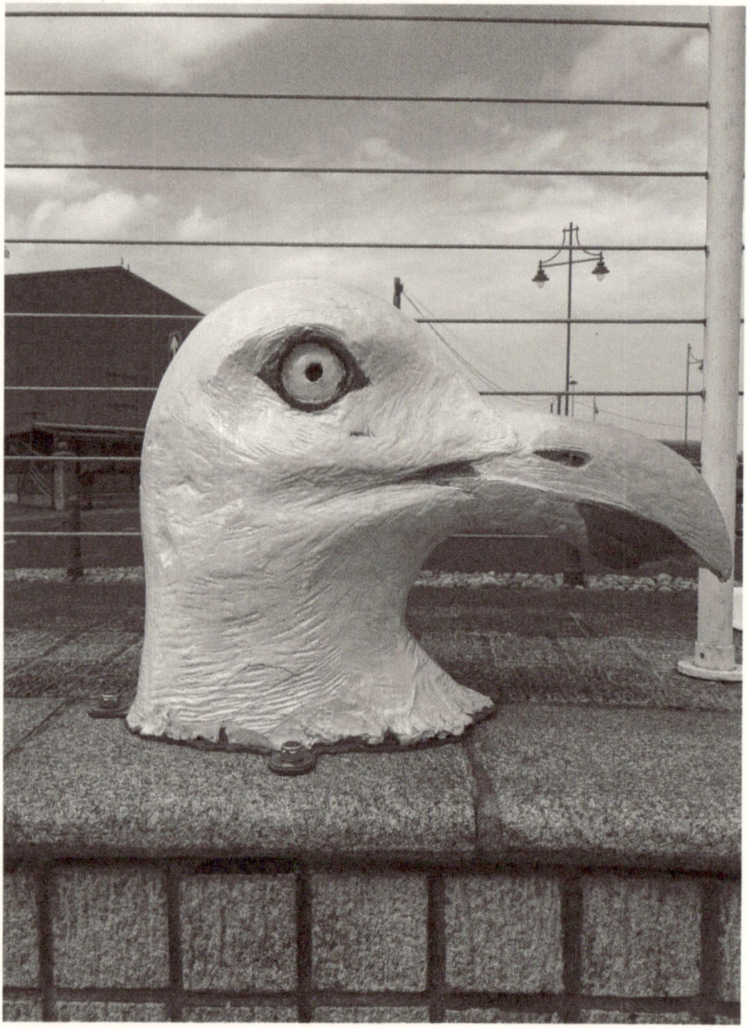

Chapter 3

Salt pans and sand dunes

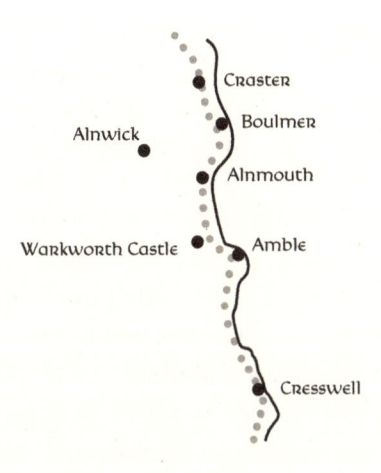

```
            • Craster
            • Boulmer
  Alnwick
     •
            • Alnmouth
Warkworth Castle •• Amble

            • Cresswell
```

After finishing our fried breakfasts and refilling our water bottles, Matt and I are waiting in the car park of the Premier Inn. We're fortunate to be getting a lift from artist Katherine Renton, who's offered to take us back to Craster to pick up where we left off. We stick our rucksacks in the back of her Dacia Sandero and drive out of Alnwick, last night's supposition that the lion on the column was something to do with the Percy family fresh in our minds. It seems to Katherine that the Duke of Northumberland's estate effectively still operates along feudal lines: she thought that to have even a shed put up in a garden on land belonging to the Duke's estate, one has, essentially, to pay a tax. Katherine told us that a neighbour of hers paid thousands to have a new porch erected.

While researching for this chapter, I came across differing interpretations of the Duke's benevolence. The story goes that statue was erected in 1816 by tenant farmers working the land belonging to the second Duke, Hugh Percy, in thanks for his reducing their rents during the depression following the Napoleonic Wars. The third Duke of Northumberland, supposedly seeing that the people were doing well enough to fund a monument, then raised their rents again, leading to a backlash and the monument being known as the 'farmers' folly'. In a myth-busting 2018 article in the *Northumberland Gazette*, however, it is claimed that 'local writers at the time did not record any increase in rent'.[1] Misrepresentation seems to quickly follow representation in small towns like Alnwick. Nevertheless, common sentiment seems to have won out, at least as reflected in the views of Katherine, for whom the lion represents an outdated system of power stretching back 700 years. Katherine claims that, as a symbol, the Percy Tenantry Column is still is held in contempt by what she calls the 'proper Alnwick locals'.

Which neatly, and inevitably, brings us to the fraught issue of class as applied to North Northumberland. This large, rural area is now a parliamentary constituency in its own right, represented at the time of writing by the Labour MP David Smith, who at the May 2024 general election replaced the Conservative Anne-Marie Trevelyan in what was then the constituency of Berwick-upon-Tweed. As England's most northerly constituency, the North Northumberland seat runs from the Scottish border down the Northumberland coast to Amble, to where we'll be walking today. It voted 55.5% in favour of leaving the European Union. England's most sparsely populated county, Northumberland has only approximately 320,000 residents. Most of them cluster in towns such as Ashington and Blyth, where the urban fringes of Tyneside overlap with the south-east of the county. There are no cities.

As a very basic demographic summary, this should set the backdrop for the place I'm walking through. Popular imagination, fuelled in recent years by TV programmes such as *Vera* and by the actor Robson Green's various peregrinations of the territory, will have had impressions of the place as wild, striking, rugged. The county's official tourist website puts it thus: 'Northumberland is a land of big adventures, breathtaking beauty and unlimited possibilities. Discover romantically ruinous castles, barely visited beaches, bunting-strewn market towns, and enjoy unlimited experiences.'[2] I want to see how that official presentation holds up along the Camino of the coast.

We've parked up in Craster, at the site of a former quarry, where Katherine's father would occasionally berth his yacht in the harbour. She explains how whinstone dug out of the earth here would be sent down on an overhead wire to boats docked at the harbour. That was when Craster had some industry remaining beyond smoked kippers and gastro-pubs. 'My boys used to play on the tank traps further down the coast at Alnmouth', she says gleefully. 'Northumberland is so defensive. I told myself, *I'll never paint the castles, it's too obvious!* But, then I found a valid reason to paint them using paints I'd made from local rocks such as sea coal and bricks washed up on the coastline.' Katherine is scanning the coast, her mind wheeling through family and artistic memories. 'Then there's RAF Boulmer, and all the pillboxes.'

We spotted a few pillboxes yesterday, looking like that internet meme of the concrete Rod Stewart, marram grass on his heed. Maybe that idea of being on the defensive connects to the class issue: if you're on the side of landed wealth and in with the dukes, you're more likely to praise the people who erected geet big phallic columns in your honour; but if you're skrimping and saving, trying to earn a living from farming or fishing or mining, you're more likely to take a critical stance on the duke and his vast wealth. According to the *Sunday Times* Rich List, Ralph Percy, the 12th Duke of Northumberland, has an estimated wealth of £509 million. At April 2023, median weekly pay in the North East was £614, the lowest average in the UK.[3]

Part of the draw of painting using natural materials, Katherine explains, is to challenge ideas of ownership, power and hierarchy. Constructing symbols of the elite using working-class building materials reclaims Katherine's sense of agency. Recently, she has started using sea coal, yellow ochre and brick to create images of the coast, including its castles, but also featuring less obvious landmarks such as boardwalks and harbour walls. The sea coal connects her to her grandfather, a Shilbottle miner who we'll hear more about soon, while the yellow ochre speaks directly to the littoral: in beaches all along this coast, there it'll be in striated rock shelves, a buttery mark at the place where the tide laps the land. The brick is more typically class-loaded, reminding me of the Northumberland-born poet Paul Batchelor's ode: 'O root and seed of boxed-in lives! O token of dissent!'[4] I sent the poem to Katherine before we meet. It resonated. We both agreed that something about the ubiquity of the brick – its 'faithful service in a pit village terrace'[5] – decries the accruement of gargantuan wealth, speaking to a more egalitarian lifestyle, while also, paradoxically as the poem implies, being a complicated marker of containment. *Divven't gan oot of your lane, laddy.*

The day before Matt and I travelled up here, I had coffee with a neighbour's son, Daniel Schmitdke, a psycholinguist at McMaster University in Ontario. Danny was back in the area for a summer break to see his parents and we met to catch up. As men comfortably in our mid-thirties, both back on home turf, conversation turned to our formative years in the early 2000s, and what it meant to complete our GCSEs and A-levels and then go to university under the twilight of the Blair government. While growing up in the South Shields suburbs was mostly fine, we both remember acts of wanton violence and a feeling of anomie – the 'charvers' who'd get off the Metro to smack the skater kids for no apparent reason – with pockets of deprivation being only a few fields away from where we grew up.

In year 11, Danny's school was visited by our town's then MP, David Miliband, Tony Blair's heir apparent. Danny remembers an extremely polished and confident man (as prefect, Danny had been sent to greet Miliband and his aid at the school gates), a presentation which was totally at odds with the apathy of many of the students, who seemed to have absorbed the residues of resentment and recession from generations past, the overriding sentiment being, *that'll never happen here*. Like Danny, I left the North East to pursue my undergraduate degree, charmed, I suppose, by the Blairite/Milibandian vision to drive and strive. Now, of course, I wonder what motivated (or didn't) those lads who made dope bongs on the upstairs of the E6 bus. With reports coming out that 30,000 children were persistently absent from North East schools in 2022,[6] I suspect that setting fire to your own hair with a can of Lynx Africa still holds more appeal to many of the urban youth of Tyneside than anything New York-dwelling Miliband might intone, however well intentioned.

Craster is certainly monied, though quite how much of its wealth regularly fills the coffers in Northumberland is questionable. Key boxes and plaques with holiday cottage web addresses are everywhere. There are some beautiful new houses, but as with Beadnell yesterday, very few people actually about. We see one man pushing a baby in a buggy and a couple of houses where al fresco breakfasts are being taken by the holidaymakers. It's all very tranquil. Unlike Katherine's accounts of arriving here in thick fog and trying to find safe passage into Craster harbour in a small boat. Or the tragic outcome of the *Tadorne*, a French trawler which ran into trouble in thick fog off Howick in 1913. The Craster rocket brigade managed to save all but five of the ship's crew. The ship's boiler can still be seen at low tide on the beach by Howick.

Although she works in paints, in essence Katherine is a poet who looks for the stories that aren't being told. Matt and I are like sponges, ready to absorb. From the harbour mouth looking back, Craster looks beautiful (which Saturday broadsheet supplement wouldn't want to cover it?), but it seems eerily quiet and hollowed out. Sometimes you see the postcard image of a place and while you know there's more to it, it won't easily be summoned. Maybe it's because all of Katherine's stories about Craster are in the past, and so it seems to suffer from that wider North East affliction of the 'used-to-be' place. Certainly, there is a tourist industry here, but I'm left wondering where people actually are. As an outpost to Alnwick Castle and Gardens, that honey pot frequented by tourists, I'm left worrying that Craster might have become a kind of coastal theme park which opens only after midday

From Craster to Howick it's quiet, mostly easy-going walking. At Cullernose Point, a man with a border collie has stopped with binoculars to watch the seabirds. He looks totally enraptured by his observations, and I want to commit similarly: to tune in as much as I can to the swirl and swell of the sonorous sea, to be present and feel the pendulum of my legs crunching at the gravel beneath my boots, to note the birds and the butterflies. But then the real-world comes bleeding in, my phone ringing in my pocket, a call from my estate agent. I let it go to voicemail and we carry on round the coast.

The path begins to get a bit windy, all ups and downs, through gorse bushes for a bit then back out, but after a mile or two we draw up alongside the Bath House, once the coastal residence of the second Earl Grey, Charles Grey. Yes, he of tea-brewing fame and our one-time prime minister. The Grey family home is still at Howick Hall, a mile inland, where today there is, according to Katherine, an excellent arboretum and equally excellent cake. The Bath House is so named because Earl Grey had bathing pools cut into the rock, supposedly to encourage the outdoor learning of his fifteen children. Like so many other properties in the area, it's now a holiday let. At the time of writing, the price for you to stay in it (along with five other guests) for a week starts at £1,349. If accommodation in that price bracket is unaffordable, you might consider the Mesolithic House at Howick – well, you could if the replica that was built hadn't gone the same way as the rhizodont. Radiocarbon dating showed that the house was constructed in about 7600 BCE, leading to its title, at the time in the early 2000s, as Britain's oldest house. Katherine told us to keep an eye out for the imitation, but it seems to have totally vanished. Again, what stays afloat and what descends into the pit of time sometimes seems arbitrary.

The next few miles are glorious. Casual tourists have by this time in the morning either been suckered to Craster proper or they're further down the coast at Alnmouth. At Sugar Sands – now there's a poetic-sounding name – four or five people are filming what looks like a romantically inflected music video. A couple mock embrace by the waves. Locals' dogs yap. I try to commit to memory and not my Google cloud an image of the strand, all russet flowers and marram grass. At Howick beach we see the remains of the *Tadorne*'s boiler, and tank traps are starting to become more frequent. Craster harbour used to have a tall wooden gantry at its top, but that was taken down at the advent of the Second World War, as it was too obvious a target for the Luftwaffe. The defensive coast at work again.

We're soon down onto Low Stead Links, a little concrete bridge crossing the burn to take us onto Longhoughton Beach. For some reason, the video game *The Last of Us* comes to mind. While it's known as a postapocalyptic survival horror narrative, the game's richly envisioned 're-wilded' North America features scenes that could have taken this stretch of coast as their basis. This really is the Northumbrian beach with nobody on it.

Up a bit of an incline, legs beginning to pull slightly, we reach Boulmer. Pronounced 'boomer', it's the site of a Royal Air Force station, which provides surveillance of the UK's airspace. Threats to Northumberland might now come in a different form, but this is still a strategically important defensive area. The base is about a mile inland, so what we see is a very pleasant-looking, almost archaic, seaside village, where an agrarian landscape seems to merge seamlessly with a low-lying coastal plain. There's a wonderful 1920s tinplated memorial hall, which I've been eager to get a closer look at since yesterday when the bus zoomed through. Down onto the beach itself, an old tractor catches my eye. Fitted with a trailer to haul what appears to be a small fishing boat, it suggests a cottage industry of sorts still operating from this part of the coast. A sign warns us that digging for any fishing bait within the area shown on the map is prohibited. Much of the coast here is designated a Site of Special Scientific

Interest, meaning conservation efforts extend to limits on recreational fishing.

Fishing on and around Holy Island and the Northumberland coast has become a hugely contested political issue of late. In February 2023, the UK's Department for Environment Food and Rural Affairs (Defra) rowed back on plans to instate a Highly Protected Marine Area (HPMA) around the island – plans that had angered t the local fishing community. In a decision which was welcomed by the former MP Anne-Marie Trevelyan and was no doubt cheered by many a Holy Islander, there are, as usual, medieval echoes going back to Cuthbert. On the way home from a preaching expedition far from Lindisfarne, one of Cuthbert's novitiates, sensing that the monastery was still a way off, that no inns were present and they were without food, began to worry. Cuthbert, noting an eagle soaring overhead, cautioned his young disciple not to fret; the eagle would feed them if it was God's wish. Sure enough, when they approached the bird, it had caught a massive fish, which they took back to broil up for the whole community to be fed. There are many such food-based miracles in Bede's *Life of Cuthbert*, but this one seems to me particularly pertinent to the plight of the Lindisfarne fisher-folk, caught as they are – as we all are – between centuries-old traditions and the imperatives of ecological stewardship amid the climate emergency.

Through the yarrow and the birds-foot trefoil, we come across the candy-cane markers for Boulmer, before making our way through a decrepit caravan park at Seaton Point. More true to the tone of *The Last of Us* than the beach we've recently walked, this certainly isn't the place of wealthy tourists. We trudge along a barely used path, beating down ferns and avoiding nettles. Nearly all of the caravans look like they've been shut up for some time. Wooden picnic benches sprout weeds. Curtains are drawn. It's a frankly depressing place, but it soon gives out, its ends marked by a newly built farmhouse and barn conversion, presumably yet another luxury holiday let which will soon see the area revitalised, or whatever marketing speak is artificially applied.

A couple of shepherd's-hut-style cottages do appear to be in use, with a series of kayaks piled up by a VW Transporter at the northern edge of Foxton Beach. We drop down on to another wide expanse, tank traps at its western flank, twisted wrack and hunks of brick mingling in the dry sand. I'm keen not to overstress the vastness and sparsely populated nature of these Northumbrian beaches – not because I want to keep them hidden from Southrons – but because it almost becomes prosaic, walking along here, to encounter another tremendous beach roamed by little more than a couple of couples walking hounds. In fact, the appeal of Alnmouth becomes irresistible, and not just because we've decided today to slightly lessen the load and leave the flask at the hotel. After a few hours of not really seeing anyone else – bar the cursory 'good morning' here and 'alreet' there – we've started to feel the pull of chatter, the friction of land. Rounding the beach over Marden Rocks, where gutweed and purple laver give the rockery an effervescent sheen, we turn south-west on to Alnmouth Beach, where the first of the trip's beacons comes into view on the dunes overlooking the estuary.

Rounding the golf course – England's oldest nine-hole links, apparently – we take a piss in the auld pinfold, a grotty embarrassment to public toilets everywhere, before marching up the high street to the Old School Gallery to meet Katherine again. As the name implies, the place was once a Victorian primary school, but is now a hub for local and national artists, selling original works, prints, pizzas and, as we find, delicious cake.

Alnmouth was once described by Methodist leader John Wesley as 'a small seaport town, famous for all kinds of wickedness',[7] presumably because it was, then, an active port with ten pubs. Alnmouth today is a little oasis of calm, cut off by the river Aln, which in 1806, following an almighty storm, changed its course, cutting off the southern end of the settlement where a church once stood. The village was once a thriving export market for grain and wool from the nearby agricultural industries, but the arrival of the East Coast Mainline brought wealthy Victorian tourists, and it looks like the demographic has changed little since. You rock up in your Tesla, golf clubs in the back, play nine holes, then eat some deep-fried sea bass and drink a gin and tonic.

At a picnic table outside the gallery, I take Nick from the bag – he hasn't had much fresh air yet, to be fair – and Katherine has a hold. We begin talking about her grandparents – her grandfather John Tully, who was a coalminer in Shilbottle, and her grandmother Sarah Dixon, a rural labourer from the Breamish valley. Where the greenery meets the sand, the fossil meets the flock. Then, coffees supped, we head off west out of Alnmouth, the marshland that used to be flooded now grazed by cattle and full of bullrushes. We're heading along the cycle path to Warkworth.

At the lowest of low tides, you can cross the Aln estuary and scramble up the hill above the ruined mortuary chapel, where a wooden cross marks the place where supposedly Saint Cuthbert agreed to become Bishop of Lindisfarne. We're not in favour with the water and, in any case, have had enough of the dunes for now, so observe it from a distance. It's an arresting sight: this modest wooden cross, much like the one on Cuddy's Isle, speaking to the after-image of these northern saints, plying the dunes with a spirit writ in sand. Skirting Hipsburn, we begin gaining height, with fabulous views back to the milky estuary. Flanked by alabaster dunes and wheat fields weaving in the breeze, Alnmouth really is in a beautiful spot. It's views like this that leave me unsurprised to learn that, in 2022/2023, Northumberland enjoyed the greatest increase in holiday let income across the UK.[8] Two further miles of bike track take us to the outskirts of Warkworth. We haven't time today to take the rowing boat across the Coquet to the hermitage built into the cliffs, but I'm told it's well worth a visit.

We stop just before the old stone bridge – a view of which Katherine's father, Arthur Rousselange Young, painted – before entering St Lawrence's Church, a twelfth-century stone structure which replaced an eighth-century timber one. The pulpit shows various gilded scenes from Northumbrian martyrology, including a wonderful image of Cuthbert in a coble being guided to Coquet Island by an otter, and Saint Hilda and the poet Caedmon.

According to Bede, Caedmon, a cowherd, asleep one night in his shed, had a vision. When he awoke, he remembered a song he had sung in his dream, astounding everyone at the abbey in Whitby with his magnificent verse. Caedmon, Bede tells us, had previously been incredibly shy, but this divine intervention changed all of that. Abbess Hilda, who was instrumental in unifying disagreeing factions at the Synod of Whitby, was impressed by Caedmon's capacity to weave beautiful poetry around challenging theological concepts. All of Caedmon's poems are lost, but Bede did describe one of them, 'Caedmon's Hymn'; Bede also described several Old English manuscripts containing glosses more suited to the vernacular than the Latin of Bede. This makes Caedmon the first named English poet, and Bede his amanuensis. Adding a note of caution, Bede tells us that 'this is the sense but not the order of the words which he sang as he slept. For it is not possible to translate verse, however well composed, literally from one language to another without some loss of beauty and dignity'.[9]

As a poet myself, and as someone interested in the intersections of folkloric transmission and the official record, that 'Caedmon's Hymn' reaches us as a corrupted translation does not mean it loses any of its power. On the contrary, I think this very fractured history of the poem speaks to what I'm doing here, carrying a knackered auld lamp down the coast, trying to catch and set down half-remembered snatches of songs from the briny breeze.

After a quick pit stop for a rum-and-raisin ice-cream from the village Post Office, we make our way through the burgage plots on a narrow *chare* running between them. A chare is a North Eastern term for a lane, and the burgage plots are long, thin parcels of land running down to the river, in which locals could grow vegetables and strike up small cottage industries such as beekeeping, woodturning and masonry. A result of the Norman Conquest, the burgages allowed land to be easily managed and revenues to be regularly collected by the burgh, the township. Some of these burgage houses, which front onto the main street, today a place dominated by the cream tea brigade, had two entrances: one for cattle and another for people. As we emerge behind The Sun Inn, with its gaudy dragon and suit of armour, Warkworth Castle dominates the view. Home to the Percy family in the late Middle Ages, it featured in Shakespeare's *Henry VI*, Harry Hotspur and his wife making a number of appearances. Like the hermitage below it, there's scant time to visit the castle today, but I'm assured by Katherine, who lists it at the top of her favourite Northumbrian castles, that I should come back and tour it.

Katherine tells us that you can draw a line beneath Warkworth: that south of it, everything changes – the landscape flattens, there are fewer trees and the people are a bit different. I sense another class rift opening. We're parallel to the River Coquet now, the town of Amble in view. Along the riverbank, a recently installed public art trail begins with what can only be described as a butt plug. It's part of the Amble 'Bord Waalk' project, an app-based tour of a dozen newly commissioned bird-related sculptures encouraging people to consider the area's marine birdlife. Carcasses of old coal barges left to degrade in the river can still clearly be seen, telling of a time when Warkworth Harbour used to ship coal. The vestiges of small shipyards are also on view, but Katherine, growing up here in the 1970s and 1980s, recalls a depressed place: a small-town environment of poverty, dog-shit-covered chares, men riding horses into the Co-op, and people trying to steal puffins' eggs from nearby Coquet Island. It has all the small-town energy of a place that once boomed – a classic North East 'used-to-be' town – but one which, in recent years thanks to regeneration and investment, seems on the up.

Amble feels like a blessed relief: a real place. A bit bleak, absolutely, but the type of town, not dissimilar to Shields, if smaller, where people are doing everyday things, trying to get by, working hard, eating, caring, praying, smoking tabs, drinking, fishing, walking their dogs, mending their boats. It's true that there are still the giveaway key boxes by the doors of some properties (even the most modest stone terraces down here aren't immune to the creep of gentrification), but overall this is the first place I've come to where I could actually imagine living.

Once we've rounded the marina – a row of attractive, Danish-looking new apartments towering above it, suggesting the way things are going – we stop to look at the fire beacon. I think of the torches being lit announcing Cuthbert's death, and all of the fire beacons marking a semaphore down the coast. Before a postal service was invented and the limit of travel was what could be achieved by horse in a day, a volley of flaming messages would have carried news of peril or alarm quicker than a rumour. Leaving the marina behind, we carry on over The Gut, a burn that runs along the edge of Amble to the River Coquet, to the corner of Wellwood Street. In what was once a hair and nail salon and is now empty, Katherine proudly shows us the results of her work with Amble Links First School.

Katherine speaks proudly of an invigorating project at the First School she had previously attended. In her work on the project, called 'Northumberland's Colourful Coast', Katherine took the primary-school children on a number of painting expeditions to the Farne Islands and on to the local beach, so that they could learn about how art might connect them with their natural and social history. She notes how the children, in observing and then painting the birds, had gone from barely knowing what a puffin looked like to being able to identify dozens of species. The young people came out of their shells, telling her that they'd never considered being able to paint, or that they could draw or make images of the wildlife on their doorsteps. Projects such as this aren't only vital for the creative aspirations and educational attainments of the children who participate in them, they allow people to see their communities afresh. A display of the children's work was mounted in an empty retail space, transforming it into a public gallery. In the window of the shop, clay models of eider ducks, Canada geese and gannets are shown alongside pebble patterns, images of birds from the Lindisfarne Gospels and photos of the school group's boat trip to the Farnes. Amble feels like somewhere which understands how the social fabric of a town can still be harnessed to inspire new visions and understandings.

On the way back down Queen Street, Katherine bumps into John Young, proprietor of the long-established decorator's shop where some of her parents' early work was first exhibited in a makeshift gallery upstairs. Around here, we're used to the saying 'you dee what your daa did', but normally that means, or meant, miners following their father down the pit, onto a trawler out at sea, or into the same factory or trade – the old *& Son* moniker. It's refreshing, then, to hear about a Northumbrian woman who was able to follow *both* of her parents' vocations.

Both Katherine's mam, Eleanor Mary Young, and her dad painted, often sailing their yachts – first the *Eriskay* and then the *Buccaneer* – up the coast to make watercolours of Holy Island or Alnmouth. Her dad had escaped the grinding poverty of Benwell in Newcastle's West End, while her mam had left behind her own mother's detail, that of the hired farm hand. But, as Katherine tells me, these connections to the land run as a deep seam through her work, her own painting practice being the site from which she can ask difficult questions of access, ownership and xenophobia.

We're heading down to the beach, stopping to admire blacksmith Stephen Lunn's amazing peace sculpture – a wrought-iron weave of poppies and doves – before taking a moment to stop on the high bank, from where a railway line to Broomhill colliery would have once taken coal wagons to load onto ships at the staithes below. Amble was known as the friendliest port. In 1935, on her final voyage to Rosyth to be broken up, RMS *Mauretania* sailed past Amble, whereupon she sent a message to the clerk: '*Mauretania* to Urban Council, Amble, to the last and kindliest port in England, greetings and thanks'.

No doubt made true by repetition, it is in any case a more salubrious image than the macabre scenes of 1907, when the

Ina Mactavish ran aground at Warkworth beach to the north side of Amble Harbour. The volunteers used their breeches buoy in an attempt at rescue, but despite saving the master and his mate, the cabin boy, who had been lashed to the rigging for safety, died of exposure. On a beautiful summer's evening in a town like this, you'd be forgiven for thinking that death is something that happens distantly, but the truth is it always threatened these communities, whose lives were reliant on the sea's bounty, but who were also subject to its jeopardy.

Katherine points out the remains of the old brickworks, at the back of the attractive new Scandi-styled flats. Soon this site will be bulldozed and more trendy apartments will go up. The fish bars will be visited by ever more prestigious chefs (the Hairy Bikers cooked here recently) and, who knows, there may soon be a boutique bookshop and apothecary. In the square by Andrew Burton's cartoonish seabird head sculptures (I enjoyed the giant herring-gull), a pleasing sign that yuppification hasn't got out of hand arrives in the presence of a donut van – and not the kind knocking out artisanal nuggets dusted in agave nectar and almonds, but a proper jobby, serving up geet lumps of NYPD stodge to queues of people in Newcastle United strips.

We cross to Amble Harbour village, where 'Gazza the Gull', made of recycled plastic, advertises trips on the Puffin Cruises. Avoiding the waves at the south jetty, we head past Paddler's Park down to the salt panner's beach. We're due to meet Jim Donnelly, who lives in one of the cottages above, but first Katherine shows us where she collects her materials. I smudge some yellow ochre into my notebook and pocket a soap-shaped piece of sea coal. In Jim's house up on the point, one of five small terraced properties, three of which made up the original salt panning factory, he and his partner Kate give us a whistlestop tour of Amble's history of salt panning.

Salt panning, Jim tells us, was probably done here by monks originally, but really got going in the seventeenth century. Small vertical shafts were dug to mine coal to heat the furnaces that boiled the pans (this largely before coal was extracted for direct commercial purpose, that is, to be sold on elsewhere). In parallel to this, and still visible on the rocks below their house, pits would be cut into the rocks so that the receding tide would leave behind a collectable pool of saline. Coal, salt, bricks, fish. The economy of Amble made a lot of sense. Clay would be mined and turned into bricks; furnaces needed to heat the bricks required coal; coal was copious and could be traded as a commodity; and salt from the German Ocean was abundant, which, when panned and made edible, preserved the fish which was caught by the keel boats operating from the harbour. Then the bricks built the terraces, the terraces were populated, their pans frying the fish, their grates burning the coal; then the coal and ships withered away, the fishing trade was usurped by industrial trawling, and old punks were able to move in and tell me about it.

Jim and Kate's house is the factory where this activity peaked in the late nineteenth century. He shows me a black and white image, he thinks from circa 1895, showing the site, but maps detail it going back to about 1840. By the early twentieth century, Eastern European exports of rock salt had knackered the trade, and now Jim and Kate are able to live here, surrounded by a wonderful collection of sci-fi novels, records and prints. Jim is a widely travelled photographer who has shot iconic rock and punk groups like The Fall – he and Mark E. Smith are both from Prestwich in Greater Manchester.

We finish our cuppas – mine in an excellent Amble Puffin Festival mug – express our thanks and make to leave. On our way out, I spot a Davy lamp on the mantlepiece. I grin as Jim holds it aloft beside Nick, which somehow seems perfectly fitting in this house, with all its history. 'Where you off next, then?' Jim asks, and I say that we were thinking of getting a beer. Reading my mind, he says 'Brewis? It's brilliant'. Kate asks if we want a lift down. With sixteen miles in our legs, we definitely do. Five minutes later, on an industrial estate to the south of Amble, we're tucking into wonderfully hoppy pints of pale ale. Katherine shows us the picture of a flint axe head, now in the Bailiffgate Museum in Alnwick, which her grandmother Sarah Tully found in a field at Acklington Park.

Katherine's great-great grandmother Eleanor Heron died in a snowstorm in December 1863 while attempting to cross the moors from Alnham (source of the River Aln up on the Northumberland Moors) where she worked as a farm servant, back to her home at Hartside in the Ingram Valley. A stone at the spot in the Shiel Bog where Nellie, as she was known, perished can still be seen, and Katherine has made pilgrimages of her own there, following the course of the River Aln as it flows through her maternal inheritance. Her own mam painted scenes of old salters' tracks up in the Cheviots, and her father-in-law said that one of his ancestors had carried Cuthbert's coffin. This chimes with Charles Eyre's nineteenth-century account: 'in after ages many persons in Northumbria were accustomed to boast of their being the descendants of those who had served St. Cuthbert so faithfully'.[10] So, the salt road that carried mineral wealth from places like Amble, up the Coquet Valley and into the borders, was also the same place where Cuthbert's bier might have been ferried. It seems a leap, but I'm willing to indulge it.

What is certain is that, at Low Buston where Katherine now lives, surrounded by huge potato fields owned by the Park family and sold to Walkers for their crisps, her grandfather, working for Low Hauxley colliery and cycling eight miles to and from work each day, would have tunnelled coal from beneath where her house now stands. Adjacent to the 'Tankie Track', once the most northerly colliery line in England, Katherine recalls her granddad bringing home fossils found frozen into the seams he was working. We think of an epoch as being capable of connecting us a few generations either way, but when you speak to Katherine and consider her family's ties to the land and the sea, the distances spill out to dizzying degrees of abstraction. I hold the piece of sea coal I've just acquired like a paper weight, thinking about this in geological terms. It stratifies, and will continue to do so. Our lives might be ephemeral, but the poetry they imprint onto the future makes its own ongoing music: a sense if not an order.

We have tea at the hotel then stroll into town. The West Midlander we met at Dunstanburgh yesterday recommended the John Bull, which we find about two miles away. It's basically the living room of someone's terraced house, unchanged since the 1970s if the décor is anything to go by. Well-kept pints of Fyne Ales are served, but the Leek Show honours board and a passive-aggressive notice on the door are the highlight:

> Within these walls
> resides a latter-day
> Luddite and
> perhaps, the last
> Bastion of the Coin
> Of the Realm.
> So a warning to all,
> we only accept
> cash.
> Don't do plastic.

Who knew Alnwick's old-school boozers would provide such a fine specimen of a found poem? We're knackered but take a final libation again at The Ale Gate on Bondgate Without, spending a minute to check prices on the estate agent's window next door. Suffice to say we won't be moving to Alnwick anytime soon.

The next morning, Katherine is back to drive us to Amble so that we can complete the last leg: nine miles to Creswell. She shows us a few prints from the boot of her car – entrancing images of sandcastles and boardwalks, a beautiful greyscale of Craster Harbour – and then we're dropped by the old East Cemetery, its ramshackle spire and field of wildflowers our starting point. I've really enjoyed wandering around Amble, and I now understand what Katherine meant by that invisible line. Lindisfarne and Bamburgh might have the rightful claim to Northumbria's spiritual ancestry, but Amble is where it gets on with workaday tasks. It's canny and has a sincerity I admire, a minerality rising from the shore up through the jocularity of its people.

Before leaving we stuffed four sachets of Kenco into the flask. Within two miles we take a pew overlooking Hauxley Point, fixing our morning buzz. The view over to Coquet Island is superb. It was here, in the company of her brother William, who had become the lighthouse keeper, that Grace Darling caught a chill. Four years after her great rescue, she died of tuberculosis. The island was bought by the Duke of Northumberland in 1753. The battlements of his London residence, Syon House near Brentford on the River Thames, are made with stone extracted from Coquet Island. Readers from the North East will no doubt be aware of the long-standing campaign to reinstate the Lindisfarne Gospels back to Holy Island, or at least to somewhere in Durham or Newcastle. Notwithstanding the technical difficulties such a feat would involve (the 1,300-year-old codex requires carefully maintained atmospheric conditions, its delicate pages having to be turned regularly to avoid overexposure to light), popular sentiment holds that *they're ours and they should be brought hyem.*

When the Lindisfarne Gospels did last come hyem in autumn 2022 for an exhibition at Newcastle's Laing Gallery, I was commissioned to write a poem marking their return. I'd wanted to try to avoid the trappings of this debate, which often falls prey to regional insularity, and instead to focus on its mobilisation. My poem, which has the Gospels stopping at Scotch Corner services for a late-night Americano so the conservator can fuel up for the final leg of their journey, ended like this:

> We've been given our toy back for three months,
> 'til once again it's packaged and sealed.
> The travelling funfair leaving its halo on the grass.[11]

Of course, the Lindisfarne Gospels should be in the North East as a perennial halo. But at present, they yo-yo every decade, shuttling between London, where, following the Reformation and their being acquired by Robert Cotton in the seventeenth century, they entered the care of the British Museum, later the British Library. They've been there since. Over the years, several North East politicians have called for the Gospels' repatriation, including Kim McGuinness when she was the Northumbria Police and Crime Commissioner in 2022; the former Durham City MP Roberta Blackman-Woods in 2013; and former Gateshead East MP Joyce Quin in 2004. In 2006, the *Sunday Sun* campaigned to have them put on permanent loan in Durham Cathedral,[12] while a failed 2021 campaign to 'Facilitate full return of exhibits historically stolen from North East England' showed the ongoing strength of feeling on the matter. In 1998, the Bishop of Durham, Anthony Turnbull, spoke passionately on the matter in the House of Lords:

> I seek the mind of the Government on an issue which is causing considerable public interest in the north east of England. But the questions surrounding the location of the Lindisfarne Gospels are far from being of interest to only one region of the country. The issue touches on matters religious, cultural, social and commercial which help to shape the whole nation. I hope, therefore, that your Lordships will not interpret my question as a piece of special pleading from the north east but will seek to understand the wider implications of the principles at stake.

Of particular interest to this North East Camino, Turnbull added:

> The concept of pilgrimage is undergoing a contemporary revival. Cathedrals and other religious sites are often the focus of such pilgrimage. Durham Cathedral alone has almost half a million visitors per year. The juxtaposition of St. Cuthbert's tomb and the gospels, which was created in his memory so shortly after his death, would be a powerful and magnetic attraction for modern pilgrims who seek to recapture the holiness and values which Cuthbert made central to his life and legacy.[13]

I'd love it if this journey could culminate in witnessing the Lindisfarne Gospels once again proudly mounted at the high altar in Durham Cathedral. Funny what can be taken to London but cannot be taken back.

Through gentle dunes at Hauxley, we tread carefully through a patina of Viper's-bugloss and Bloody Cranesbill.

There are wall-brown butterflies and other wildflowers and creepy-crawlies we can't identify. An urban man who's never really been taught to look at things like this, I can only piece together information later, cross-referring my photos to records online and in my wildflowers guidebook. We crack on into Druridge Bay Country Park, greeted by Rodney Harris's brick tree, the most southerly of the Amble Bord Waalk sculptures, and probably the most sympathetically designed and placed, with cuttings made for sparrows' nests.

At seven miles, Druridge Bay is the longest on the Northumberland coast. In a travelogue, the writer can either try and spice things up, or can be honest. The truth is that, with thirty-five miles already in my legs from the past two days, and with Druridge Bay being (whisper it) a little bit monotonous, this final stretch is a slog. My left Achilles' tendon has really started pulling, and I'm keen to get to the finish, to collect the car, get gannin' and see me bairns. Nevertheless, we crack on. Much of the final three miles is spent negotiating badly marked paths through steep dunes. We go the wrong way for the first time in three days, which should probably be considered decent going, and eventually sit on some concrete ballast by a burn to have, in the words of my son's CBeebies heroes *Sarah & Duck*, a sit and think.

Past a sign for beachside farm weddings, a row of wooden chairs and the frame for a floral archway positioned by the path waiting the next bridal party, we find our final wind. We've now left behind St Oswald's Way, which six miles earlier had taken its westward diversion along the Coquet to Felton and Rothbury. But the Northumberland Coast Path is still figuring on the blue signs, ditto the yellow England Coast Path markers. St Oswald's Way is waymarked with the symbol of a raven (according to legend, a raven was the companion and messenger to the saint) but what could symbolise my wider Camino of the North East? A Cuthbert's bead, perhaps, or one of the otters that warmed his feet following his praying in the icy sea. No, it has to be the lamp. I take it from my bag, setting it against the lime grass and the tickling ocean. On my imagined badge, lining stiles down to Durham, would be a render of a Davy lamp, but maybe I'd also add some spokes of light around its cap, so it looked a bit like a lighthouse. This coaly coast has always been illuminated by beacons, so it would make sense to draw on that iconography, using the lamp as sign of benevolence and contemplation to the rambler, recharging the figurative Northumbrian fluorescence with each passage of their feet.

The Pele Tower at Creswell comes into view and after a half mile on the packed wet sand we emerge up the steps into the village. We get Lucozades from Creswell Ices and phone a taxi to take us back up the coast to Alnwick. Sometimes you've got to go back to go forwards. We pay the driver then transfer into my car. Matt nods off until we approach the Tyne Tunnel, and then I drop him back in Whitburn, as if the last three days have been some kind of fever dream. That night, I tuck myself into the bed covers at half past seven, and like a kid discovering the sound of the sea whirring around a cup placed to his ear for the first time, I fall asleep with the tide *cush-cushing* me as jetsam.

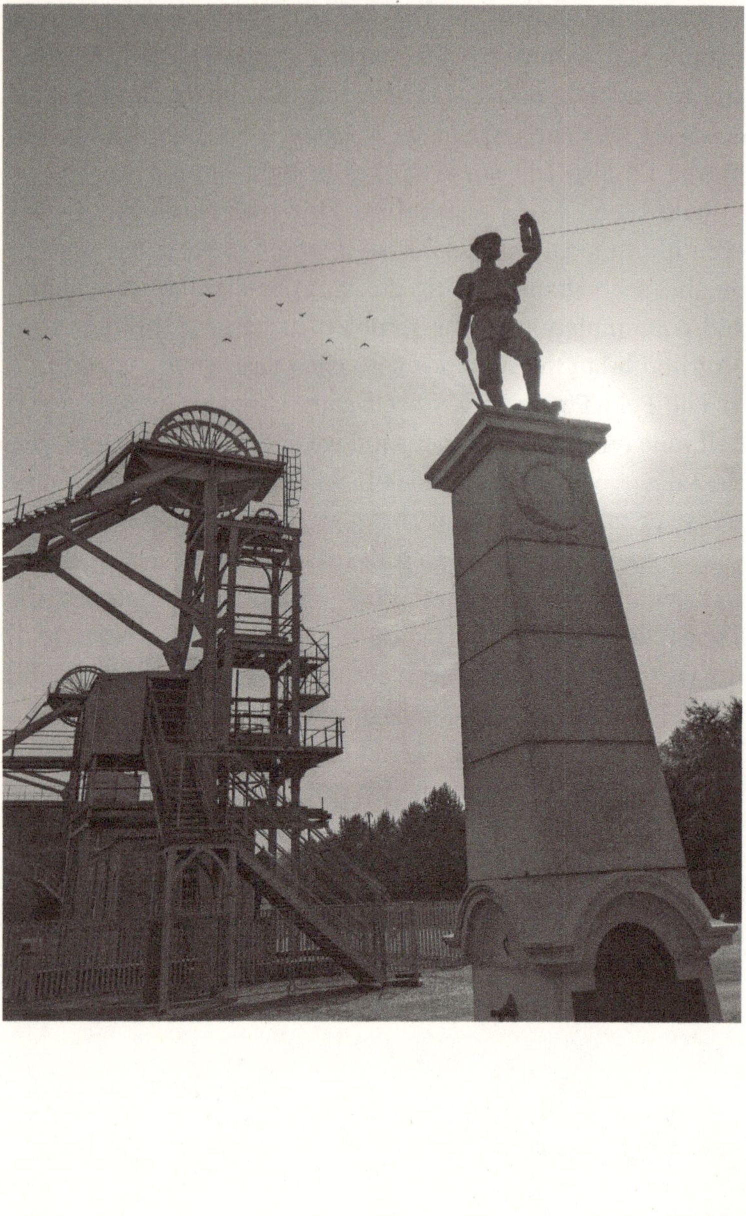

Chapter 4

The Spine Road

let them sketch this: this street of ghosts,
& smudge the windows of imperfect pasts.
let them use rulers, & only three colours:
a dirty red, a gloss slate grey,
the carbon black of detail.
let them learn from a wall of clay.
let them watch as it disappears.

    Paul Summers, from 'art lesson'[1]

I'm driving out of the Tyne Tunnel again, heading north past Holystone and Killingworth to Moor Farm, a serviced roundabout on the outskirts of Cramlington. Beefeater. Premier Inn. Petrol. I hook a right onto the Spine Road, the A189 dual carriageway which connects this part of Tyneside's periphery to the outlying towns. Constructed from the 1970s to open up employment opportunities in deindustrialised south-east Northumberland, the Spine is a dozen miles of tarmac spanning the rivers Blyth and Wansbeck. It might seem counterintuitive according to the logic of my pilgrimage to be heading north again, more especially so in a car, but this part of the route is difficult to navigate on foot, and in any case can't really be fully understood without some serious meandering.

I'm making three stops in this chapter: first, I'll visit Woodhorn Colliery Museum; then I'm meeting the artist Narbi Price in the middle of Ashington to get some scholarly context; finally, I'll make a detour to Cambois near Blyth, where an old miners' hall is being repurposed by the playwright Alex Oates and his wife, the dancer Esther Huss. From there I'll dog-leg back to the coastal Camino proper, preparing to head for the Tyne.

Sea fret mires the coast. It's one of those days. I miss my turning for Woodhorn at first, and end up at Lynemouth. The cooling towers of the power station intermittently come into view through a shroud of mist: it's as if some alien starship has suddenly appeared in earth's atmosphere. If it was a clear day there'd be a canny view here back up to near where Matt and I finished at Creswell. Coast-dwellers know that as quickly as it arrives, sea fret can burn off. A mile back inland, as if to open a curtain of mist on the past, the Queen Elizabeth Country Park is dowsed in sun.

This is my first visit to Woodhorn Colliery Museum, so on the gate I'm asked all of the usual details in order to Gift Aid my ticket. I hesitate when asked for my title, then give it as 'Dr'. I don't know if it's imposter syndrome or a more generalised English modesty, but it's rare that I use my academic title. Today, though, I hear the voices of family in my ears, and I go for it. It feels weird, with Nick stuffed in my bag and knowing that all the thousands of men and boys who worked beneath here who would never have had such educational privileges, but to not acknowledge it now would seem like erasure.

Woodhorn Colliery was operational between 1894 and 1981. The museum opened in 1989 and in 2006 it was given a new annex, the Cutter Building, the design of which reflects the giant steel-cutting apparatus used in later mechanised pits. Now a scheduled monument, Woodhorn is the most well-preserved example of a late nineteenth-century colliery in the North East of England. It feels important to come here to get some deeper sense of the working conditions Nick would have known. The museum's walk-through illustrates the significant twentieth-century events which formed the local, regional, national and global backdrop to the workaday chorus of life in the town. And while all of that social history is beautifully captured in great detail – right down to the sash worn by Miss East Sleekburn, pageant winner from a 1970s Bedlington Miners' Picnic – my motives for visiting are more artistic than they are industrial. Up on the first floor of the Cutter, having walked beneath a display of Northumberland miners' banners, I reach the Ashington Group Gallery.

Better known colloquially as the Pitmen Painters, this group of Ashington miners-turned-painters started as a Workers' Educational Association art appreciation class in 1934. In October of that year, Robert Lyon, a lecturer at Durham University's Armstrong College (now Newcastle University), was sent to help the group get going. Quickly realising that this wasn't his usual detail – his attempts to show the men slides of Michelangelo's work were met with mystification – Lyon set about getting the group to experiment themselves. They began with lino cutting before moving on to brushes on paper and board. Soon the class was painting regularly, each man bringing work to be criticised by the group the following week. Over fifty years they produced hundreds of paintings. Their subjects may have been quotidian, but their execution was remarkable. In their capturing of the commonplace realities of life in and around a working-class town, the Pitmen Painters documented the mid-twentieth century from seam to sky. The playwright Lee Hall would be inspired to write his own *Pitmen Painters* play about the group – a show that went on to be a runaway success on Broadway, where the men's frank attitudes and strong pitmatic dialects registered the universality of toil followed by rest.

Blissfully alone in the space, I'm able to take in the full scope and splendour of the work, as well as details that viewings online are never able to reveal. The Pitmen Painters' success in many ways comes from their plurality: the fact of them having been assembled in this way is suggestive of the democratisation of their medium, the feeling of comradeship that they shared beneath ground translating into an egalitarian spirit on the gallery wall. In this sense, it feels unfair to pick out favourites, but three images do keep me coming back.

In Oliver Kilbourn's *Half-time at the Rec (Welfare)*, c. 1937, two opposing football teams are being addressed by coaches. The Reds versus the Black & Whites might look, at first, like a recognisable sporting interlude, one that is still being practised on any given Sunday in countless British parks, but the vista as shown from the touch-line of the pitch reveals something now curiously out-of-time: four huge pit mounds. On one, a series of pullies used to remove colliery waste dangle like chair-lifts, but this is Ashington, not Alpe d'Huez. The train carriages at the foot of these northern pyramids are not taking tourists to Alexandria; instead, they attest to the pearls amid vast piles of grit, the extractive industry from which these twenty-two players are enjoying a brief reprieve.

In front of the wagons, a few clustered spectators are ready for an agonising second forty-five. One figure stands out. In a huddle for the Reds, a man a full foot shorter than his teammates – a feisty centre-half, the type your average football punter would describe as a 'terrier' – is holding his left hand to his mouth. He's whistling. I know he is because I've seen players taunt their opposition in exactly the same way. He's saying to the tall Black & Whiter opposite, the type a pundit would call 'strapping', and who's deflecting the hot air and bad advice doled out by his kit man, *Hew, I'm watching yee*. Little Red wants to snap some ankles if his team go another goal down.

Two other paintings take my eye. In Fred Laidler's *Fish and Chips*, c. 1948, people queue at the local chippy while bairns run around on the pavement off to the side. A little dog – a border terrier by the looks – watches the bairns inquisitively, as two boys row or play-fight. A third child – is she an older sister? – is hunched over the kerb, indifferent to the lads' antics. The door to the shop and one of its windows are open, suggesting the ferocity of Friday night frying, while inside we see the silhouetted figures of women rolling hot packets of cod, chips and batter. This is early evening at dusk. The family are about to enjoy a hard-earned fish supper, but the man's mind is drifting, his concentration already being pulled down from below the newspaper his haddock is wrapped in, beneath the table and floorboards, then much further down, through hundreds of feet of soil and clay, to the shift he'll start in ten hours' time.

In his *The Miner – Last Smoke Before Descent*, c. 1939, Jimmy Floyd shows us one of his marras, lit pipe perched in his gob, flask, shovel and pick propped by his side. His silver baccy tin is a gleaming talisman. The eye is drawn to his glowing Davy lamp, set between his boots. Soon he'll have a last blaa on his pipe and gan doon the shaft. When he squats to make his way to the seam, a fishy burp will emerge, and he'll know what it means to be netted.

On my way out of Woodhorn I stop to photograph the miners' memorial. Originally erected in Hirst Park in Ashington in 1923, it was moved to Woodhorn in 1991 and restored in 2002. From his prominent spot, a flat-capped collier holds aloft his Davy lamp like a figurehead on the bow of a ship. In his other hand he steadies his pick. The sun is still on its way up, so I manage to get the image perfectly back-lit. It's difficult, with this lamp of my own having accompanied me this far, not to see this as a form of corroboration. But, as I go on into Ashington and see the town of ghosts it's become, I do wonder whether the miner on the plinth is a patron saint, or whether he might not actually be a poltergeist.

I'm parked up in Bensham, waiting for the artist Narbi Price. On my lap are the crumbs of a fantastic bagel, bought from a kosher bakery round the corner. This part of Gateshead is home to one of the UK's largest Orthodox Jewish communities and serves as a centre for Jewish education, with Talmudic students from around the world coming here to study. It's also home to a thriving Muslim population – mosques and synagogues dotting the Edwardian Tyneside flats and corner shops advertising Evri pick-up points and the *Newcastle Chronicle*. Given also the white working-class Geordies, Bensham makes for a rich melting pot high on the hill overlooking the Tyne bridges. Narbi jumps in and we cut across the Toon on the A1 Western Bypass, before joining the Spine Road again and heading north.

Narbi and I first met in 2016. Both fledgling PhD students at Newcastle University, we'd attend the same research training classes. At an end-of-year conference, we realised we had a shared interest in working-class representations in painting and poetry. Narbi had just started his research into the Ashington Group, and I'd just done a micro writing residency at Newcastle's Mining Institute. We often talked about what it means to come from the North East coast – he from Hartlepool, me from Shields – and the weird ways in which the after-image of industry is still imprinted into such towns, even well after the removal of said industry. Years later we would bond over the punk poetry of Craig Finn and his rock band The Hold Steady. Following a Hold Steady gig at Camden's Electric Ballroom in March 2022, Narbi and I got chatting again. I outlined the early stages of my thinking for a Camino of the North East, and I heard more about the work he was doing as a trustee with the Ashington Group. I resolved to travel to the town and ask Narbi to show me around.

At the back of a car park, adjacent to the goods-in of Lidl, Narbi points to the site where the Ashington Group used to meet. On this spot was an unassuming shed where they worked on their paintings. I ask Narbi whether a plaque has been put up to signify the location. The brisque tone of his reply says more than the words themselves: 'Has there fuck'. We walk round the corner on to Woodhorn Road, where Narbi guides me into the former Co-op. Before entering, I clock the sign for the Ashington Miners Amateur Boxing Club (a group I'll encounter again soon) – a pair of red gloves tied beneath a pick and a hammer. Inside the local convenience store, I'm advised to look above its strip-lit counter of scratch cards, spirits and tobacco. Beyond the modern fittings, the old stonework of the Co-op's central stairwell can clearly be seen. Behind these boarded-up walls, adorned in jarring adverts for Chivas Regal and stock photos of Warkworth Castle, is a former ballroom – part of Ashington's once-rich cultural offering. Narbi describes a thriving operatic society and an active folk club. Back out on the street, the Central Billiard Saloon opposite seems to want to confirm former glories, but is thwarted by breezeblocks behind the glass on its third floor.

We walk west to where the new Northumberland railway line, axed under the 1964 Beeching cuts, will soon see passengers travelling into central Newcastle. This is a land of vape shops and greasy spoons with names like 'Collier's'. It's a place where the Istanbul Barbers is situated a few doors down from the Reptile Recovery store, and where the Rohan Kanhai Wetherspoons – named in honour of the Guyanese batsman who elevated Ashington Cricket Club to prominence in the 1960s – is chocker at two in the afternoon. At risk of sounding like I'm on an ill-judged poverty safari, it is true to say that Ashington looks and feels materially deprived, but I also think that to judge it solely on those terms is to miss the point.

'It no longer has a function', Narbi says, as we make our way to what he describes as 'Old Ashington', the rows of numbered colliery workers' terraces, flanked on their ends by the larger managers' properties. At the end of Seventh Row, Narbi points out The Portland, a coaching inn bearing the name of the Duke of Portland, who, in 1867, sunk the Bothal Mine Shaft, encouraging people to come and live and work in the town. Before this, Ashington had been a small hamlet of sparsely populated farmsteads set in rural surrounds – reflected in the ash-dene of its name, *Essendene* in the middle ages.[2] We make a circuit of Eighth Row, as 'classically

Ashington as it gets' according to Narbi. We stop to admire the ordinary architecture – an uninterrupted quarter mile of late nineteenth-century houses actually makes for quite the spectacle – and I think again about the half brick in Paul Batchelor's poem, its 'century of faithful service in a pit village terrace'.[3] Many of the old coal holes have themselves been bricked up, as the properties were converted to heating by gas boiler, but a few originals remain, their little black wooden doors standing like snapped-shut portals, black holes back to another era.

From here it's a short walk north to the old pit wheel which marks the site of the town's first colliery, on the corner of Rotary Parkway and Eleventh Row. The plaque informs me that this was once the biggest pit village in the world: by 1921, some 5,500 mineworkers grafted here. We're entering Ashington's Colliery Trail, an edgeland environment which starts between an Aldi and a Kwik Fit and soon becomes a thriving woodland. 'When I walk through here, I always have to remind myself that these trees aren't yet forty years old', Narbi tells me, as we reflect on the way in which the industrial past is remembered. In the middle of Northumberland Business Park, between the Powergrid stores and the Polar Krush factory, is an artificial lake populated by stainless-steel origami birds. To its northern end, a pagoda-come-bandstand has been erected. The whole atmosphere is stagnant but there are signs of work going on in a sort of weird twenty-first-century way – behind the nondescript doors of small manufacturing units and call centres – and we're soon crossing the fake oriental bridge to pass The Old Ash Dene, one of those pubs where you never know what time it is and you could as well be eating a doughy burger in the airport lounge of Abu Dhabi as be on an industrial estate in the North East of England.

Passing Asda – built on top of Portland Park, Ashington's former football ground and the setting of Kilbourn's painting – Narbi tells me it's now the largest employer in the town, before we reach a barricade at what has been wryly described as the 'Ashington Hole'. Officially the Portland Park development, plans for the site have been on hold since 2017, when the Conservative-led council announced that it intended to move Northumberland County Council's headquarters from nearby Morpeth to Ashington. The site has been derelict since, its colloquial name a quiet rebuke to the political tit-for-tat which seems to have mired the place. To me it seems to point to a more fundamental absence. I press Narbi on Ashington's loss of functionality, and he tells me that the place 'is hunkered around voids', like the one we're now skirting on our way to Spoons. In the bathroom, I catch myself in the mirror. My flat cap is still on. I've just realised that I've become a walking cliché. As I head back to the lounge, I notice the other men – some of them younger, in Newcastle shirts beneath puffer jackets – look like they've walked out of Ashington Group paintings. I ask Narbi how well the group is known in the town.

'Pretty well, certainly to older people' – he gestures at a few old boys at the bar – 'but part of my role as trustee is to keep them in people's imaginations, so that they're not just dusty paintings'. And what of Narbi's own work, I enquire. 'I've painted several scenes around the town', he answers, referring to the entrance to the Colliery Heritage circuit where he did a picture of the crumbling brickwork on a garage opposite Aldi. Narbi's works, in the blurb to his solo show 'The Ashington Paintings', themselves shown at Woodhorn between May and September 2018, 'depict sites rich with histories, some of them evident within the palimpsest of marks, but much of them hidden by redevelopment, repurposing, redaction'.[4]

Given that this pilgrimage is a multilayered traversal or tracing of a band of genies, it seems apt of Narbi to go on to add that 'the ghosts are what interest me'. On his website, he explains the rationale behind the show:

> These paintings are the product of many hours spent walking the streets of Ashington, at times in the footsteps of the Ashington Group, through a changed landscape that they would barely recognise physically, but in a socio-political climate that, increasingly, they might.[5]

Narbi pulls a book from his rucksack – William Feaver's *Pitmen Painters*. 'This is my de facto bible; the way I first got to know the group.' Feaver, a former *Observer* art critic, became acquainted with the Ashington Group following a chance meeting at Newcastle's Laing Gallery in 1971. His account of becoming a patron for the group, Narbi explains, allows their story to be retold more organically. It stands in certain tension to Lee Hall's play *The Pitmen Painters*, first performed at Live Theatre in Newcastle in 2007. Hall, whose best-known work, *Billy Elliot*, was not only a huge success in the UK, but went on to be a Broadway hit, took some flack from living descendants of Robert Lyon, the tutor who guided the painters' development. In the play, Lyon is portrayed as a plum-mouthed, Home Counties stiff, his presence a stark contrast to the miners' straight-talking pitmatic. But in real life, Lyon was a more down-to-earth Scouser. Still, the dramatic tensions created by an artificial class divide make for compelling theatre – I saw the play performed at Newcastle's Theatre Royal a few years ago – and it has certainly helped to raise the group's profile.

As we enter the fringes of the eastern district of town known as The Hirst, talk turns to creative practice and the UK's competitive and often bureaucratic arts-funding landscape.

It's a conversation I feel like I've already had with Katherine back up in Amble. 'You've got to pound the pavements', Narbi tells me, as we do just that, coming up on Hirst Park, where Jackie Milburn and the Charlton brothers honed their footballing skills. 'It's the opposite to this "parachuted-in" approach to using artists', he says. 'Over the years I've come to know Ashington and its people really well.' The parallels between Lyon, sent from Newcastle University, and Narbi, who now works at the same institution, are clear: both are well intentioned – to arrive and not patronise people, but to work with them and facilitate their own artistic views of the places they hold dear.

We reach Douglas Jennings's charming sculpture of Jack Charlton in the park, just as two teenage boys and their youth workers come past dribbling a ball, laughing. Behind it, on a recently repaved central square, Narbi points out another quotidian landscape which he has used as inspiration. On a small interpretation board off to the side, I see a black and white photo of the miners' memorial which I'd admired at Woodhorn. Now, it seems, even the replicas of the miners are moved off elsewhere. They may not exactly be sanitised, but there's something in the statue's absence which I find uncomfortable. This is one of those voids that Narbi spoke of earlier: a fissure in the urban fabric which the Sunday league teams might not now even register. As we leave the park, a wind turbine spins ominously over the roofs of the ex-pit terraces.

There's one more place Narbi wants to show me, but we decide to backtrack and get the motor to arrive quicker. Coming up on the car park, we pass a care home bearing the ultimate North East simulacrum: a fake pit wheel. Even in their dotage, the elderly of Ashington are reminded of what once was. We drive south for a couple of miles to the River

Wansbeck. Passing another void – a closed-down theatre now trading as a kids' soft-play centre – we cross the water and park up in Stakeford. Walking a short way down the hill to the Wansbeck, Narbi points out 'The Blacka', the old coal bridge that I've sped past on the adjacent Spine Road and which will soon see rail passengers travelling into the town. Narbi has painted the view of the massive steel stanchions directly below this bridge, along with the graffiti on the concrete pillars holding up the Spine Road. We're only a quarter mile west of it, so we can see individual vehicles speeding by. Ashington seems to be a place of transit and bypass: somewhere you go round on your way to the tourist gems further up the coast, or somewhere you leave each day to go to work in Newcastle.

This is why Narbi's concentrated expressions of life in the town are so important, and why I'm grateful to analyse them in detail now, cross-referring to my catalogue of Ashington Group images to trace the influence of painting from close observation. I can see the ways in which the minutiae of everyday life are recast under Narbi's eye. His is a painterly vision in which the overlooked is put under the microscope, in which the quotidian aspects of life in harsh, northern towns are deliberately brought into focus. He paints phone boxes, fence posts, garages, puddles, park benches and many other routine scenes, usually at close range.

There is, on an initial glance, a morose quality to these works, but they're so painstakingly rendered that further inspection gradually strips away this veneer, so you're left thinking of the human markings – the clearing through a copse, Northumbrian flags wrapped around a tree, names and dates carved into a bus shelter. In one of my favourites, indigo wildflowers dot the grass on top of a former colliery. Reminding me that at the peak of mining, Ashington never got fully dark thanks to the burning slag heaps, one of which was among the biggest in Europe, Narbi concludes by excitedly telling me about his plans to celebrate the Group's ninety-year anniversary next year, along with the work he'll be doing in nearby East Durham. We jump in the car and head back to Gateshead.

A couple of days later, Narbi sends me one of the paintings he was trying to recall as we walked around. It's Oliver Kilbourn's 1951 *Rainy Day, Ashington Co-Op*. He's right: little of the view down Woodhorn Road has changed. Were it not for the conspicuously mid-twentieth-century car and bus, Kilbourn could have painted the scene yesterday. And this is the odd paradox of the town: much of the civic infrastructure which was built to serve its booming monolithic industry remains (albeit often in a sorry state of dilapidation) decades after that industry folded. Ashington now might well be a town unmoored from its original purpose, but it's still somewhere people – 28,000 of them – live. And I'd argue that they live in ways that are recognisable to the majority of our population, certainly here in the North East, where the affluent second-home-owners of Beadnell or Bamburgh are the exception, not the rule. The coming together of these artists to elevate the prosaic nature of their work, habitation and leisure might offer us helpful clues as to how, to quote the writer and thinker Dougald Hine, 'a living culture carries its traditions, the only way it keeps them alive'.[6] Paraphrasing Hine, as we 'make good ruins', we might start by asking what values and morals can guide us forwards. The former miners' institute in Cambois, three miles away, is a good place to start looking.

> More and more now he thinks he hears them
> from the undersea shaft, long unworked,
> their tappings and callings: no fathers
> or grandfathers of his.
> Poor leavings, these,
> that keep a needy fire alive.
>
> Pippa Little, 'Sea Coaling (Lynemouth)'[7]

Once more up the Spine Road, the River Blyth glistening as I flick the indicators up and take the turning at East Sleekburn. I've arranged to meet Esther Huss and Alex Oates, stewards of the Tute – the former Miners' Welfare Hall in Cambois. Think 'Albert Camus' as pronounced by a Geordie and you've got the sound right. I'm early so I drive first to North Blyth, following the bend of the river as its cavalcade of warehouses give out to huge cranes at the adjacent docks. I park up near the end of a single-line railway track, in the shadow of the former Alcan storage silos. When the nearby aluminium smelter at Lynemouth was still operational, raw alumina made from bauxite was stored in these huge vats, which now jut out from the coast like giant upturned egg boxes. A few hardy retrievers are walking their owners along the strand below, where sea coal ripples through the sands.

Back in the car, I return the way I came, passing the huge steel turbine plinths being decommissioned in the river, to the Buccanneers car park by Cambois beach. Charltons Bar, owned by John Charlton, son of famous footballer Jack, is an inviting prospect, but so too is the wide expanse of sands, more sea coal glinting on its surface like those long unworked tappings in Little's poem. From here I can see round the curve of the bay to Newbiggin, and the other way back to the wind farm signifying Port of Blyth's position as one of the UK's premier offshore and renewable sites. I step onto the sands and for the first time doing this Camino I don't really know why I'm here. There's a one-horse-town feel to the place, which probably isn't helping. I decide to turn up early and head for the Tute, but on my way am waylaid by a giant red pit wheel, poking out from bracken and weeds behind a stonemason's and a metal basher's.

Broken beer bottles protrude from rosehip bushes. There is no signage or interpretation board, though somebody has taken the time to graffiti the area's postcode, NE24, in white paint on the tiled base of the wheel. I cross the road to the promenade. An approaching couple look like they might be old enough to be able to tell me more about the memorial. But that's a mistake. 'Ah divven't knaa, mate. Sorry. Ah'm not really lurcal', he says, in a thick Ashingtonian burr. He ponders some more, his wife none the wiser. 'Wey, I'm sixty noo, so I'd hazard a guess the early eighties? The tradition's aall gone.' They walk on and I'm left scratching my head. Left in a dilapidated state, flaking paint and surrounded by overgrown bushes, it's no real tribute to the work that went on here.

Fans of the hit Disney streaming programme *This Is Wrexham* might remember a poignant episode from Series 2 in which the Gresford colliery disaster of 1934 is brought into focus as a way of framing the longstanding camaraderie surrounding the football club. Hollywood actor and writer Rob McElhenney – who, along with film star Ryan Reynolds, purchased Wrexham Football Club in 2020 – travels to Gresford in Wrexham, North Wales, to visit the memorial which stands as a monument to the 266 men killed in the underground explosion — the worst in Britain's history. The celebrity owners' new plans for a redeveloped stadium include situating Gresford colliery's sister wheel on a pedestal outside the ground, where it will take pride of place welcoming supporters to matches. In Cambois, the spirit of the industrial past has clearly been neglected in its overgrown pit wheel, but down the road its echoes are ringing out in different ways.

Alex Oates greets me at the door. Born just down the coast in Whitley Bay, he's a playwright and, along with his partner Esther Huss, a German-Geordie dance artist, now also the custodian of 'the 'Tute' – Cambois Miners' Welfare Hall. Built in 1929 to service the welfare and recreational needs of local miners and their families, the building had stood vacant for fifteen years. Then, in 2019, it came up for auction, with Oates and Huss winning the bidding at £40,000. The pair met in London, where Alex was trying to make it as a playwright and Esther was fitting her dance practice around her role as a carer. 'I came to the conclusion', Alex says, 'that London didn't need me'. Esther nods in agreement, adding 'the move to the North East allowed us a different pace of life. We began making and sharing work and sharing experiences.'

I'm offered a cuppa, Alex retreating to the kitchen to brew up while Esther and I look out of the imposing windows, which frame a wonderful view of the dunes and its single-track railway line, the one I was parked up at earlier. I'm told that once a day a train will clatter along these tracks, usually late at night, on its way to ship Lynemouth's remaining bauxite to Norway for processing. The North Sea Link also joins the UK to Norway here, a 450-mile subsea power cable connecting the Kvilldal hydropower complex in Suldal to Cambois. I imagine the undersea miners' ghosts of southeast Northumberland puzzling over this cross-continental handshake, as the ocean floor prickles with a high-voltage current far exceeding the brutal forces the marauding Vikings a millennium earlier could have dreamed of.

I'm shown around the back rooms, where steel reinforcing rods installed in 2017 clearly show remedial works done to stave off subsidence. There is a marked difference between this structure and the new Cutter building at Woodhorn, five miles away. There, where material reality has been wrapped in a packageable mythology, there is recognition and funding. Here, the off-record history of south-east Northumberland clings on like flaking paint. The remains of the Ashington Boxing Club's dumbbells and training balls are gathered in a corner awaiting collection. So often these spaces which were designed for one purpose have ended up being used for something totally different, a juxtaposition highlighted by Esther, who remembers a boxing ring being set up in front of the stage. I take to it – the stage, not the ring – now and look out over a magnificent parquet floor and flaking walls painted saffron, imagining at once sparring young warriors from Ashington and interwar couples from Cambois coming here for dances.

We sit down for tea as I further take in the majesty of the space. I set Nick on the table as if at a campfire, Alex and Esther the masters of ceremonies. 'One of the things we're grappling with here', Alex says, 'is how to take people on a journey – how does a community that has not been exposed to contemporary art interact with new dance practices?' With an egalitarian approach – all events at the Tute are free for Cambois residents – the bigger question is how to draw them through the door in the first place. 'Do we give them what they want, or what we want?' Alex ponders. Esther adds that it's 'about pushing people out of their comfort zones. We don't want to give them *Strictly [Come Dancing]*, but nor are we here to say what we should programme.'

I'm asked about my first impressions of the place and can't help mentioning the phrase 'back of beyond', one they've heard before. There's a palpable rural/urban divide in this part of south-east Northumberland, where it can take up to two hours using public transport to travel twenty miles into Newcastle. Local residents leave hours ahead of hospital appointments at the Royal Victoria Infirmary or Freeman. At the time of my visit, Rishi Sunak's rowing-back on the HS2 rail link is getting a lot of media attention, but the real travesty isn't a high-speed line that in any case would never have connected to the North East of England, it's the appalling state of intercity and intercounty travel. 'We have friends in Newcastle', Esther continues, 'people connected to Dance City and so on, who when they come really can't understand why we're doing this. It feels like the middle of nowhere to them. The Newcastle crowd have much lower expectations of productions here, thinking it must be a bit crap because it's being done in Cambois.'

But to local volunteers, like Becka, who Esther tells me has been helping out with the Tute for eighteen months, and who grew in confidence following a period of seclusion during the Covid-19 pandemic, 'it has touched something deep'. In a few weeks' time Unfolding Theatre will bring *A Street Like This* to the Tute and, in an ongoing collaboration with local theatre producers November Club, they plan a spectacular promenade performance around Cambois next year. All of it taps into Esther and Alex's ambition to involve the local community in as many ways as they can – from baby and toddler playgroups to writers' workshops. Alex describes their house in North Blyth – 'the island' – as the place they chose to be isolated in, having felt pushed away by London, and to a lesser extent by Tyneside's theatre establishment. While Alex still makes work with the big players in Newcastle – he's about to adapt Tom Haddaway's classic tale of class migration *The Filleting Machine* into his own *The Filleting

App, a satirical comment on the often toxic overlap of social media and gig economy work in the post-industrial north – he feels like the relationships he's made here are more genuine, the work more imperative.

Funding is the elephant in the room. While they are now a charity and therefore able to apply for different grant and income streams, the ongoing austerity of the arts-funding landscape makes sustaining the enterprise a constant worry. In Baden-Württemburg, the south-western state of Germany where Esther comes from, state support for the arts equates to £12 of cultural spend per person, versus £1.50 per person in England. On a recent trip to Germany, the couple, travelling with their three-year-old daughter, whose upbringing in Cambois they admit is 'a bit of an experiment', visited Essen and Dusseldorf, post-industrial cities where the memory of such labour is translated into thriving modern metropolises which reclaim, not bulldoze, their industrial relics. UNESCO describes the Zolleverein coalmine complex in Dusseldorf as having 'a policy of sensitive and imaginative adaptive reuse [...] with significant items of the industrial plant preserved [...] their interrelationships remain visible in a clear and logical manner'.[8]

It's time to leave. Esther and Alex show me out, and I'm given a gift: *The Cambois Tales*, a collection of short stories written by members of the Tute's writing group which Alex organises. As I drive out of Cambois, I pass the Britishvolt site, where, until plans fell through following the company's collapse in early 2023, a gigafactory was going to be constructed. Using the site of the former Blyth power station, this site would become a linchpin in the electric car supply chain, providing the batteries needed for manufacturers such as Nissan nearby in Washington. In September 2024, however, it was revealed that the American private equity firm Blackstone had purchased the land following Britishvolt's collapse. The site will now become an artificial intelligence (AI) data centre, a move which the Deputy Leader of Northumberland County Council, Richard Wearmouth, said would put North East England 'at the heart of the A.I. revolution'.[9] The site, it is claimed, will become one of Europe's biggest AI data centres.[10] As a writer whose human creative endeavour is in jeopardy to the 'scraping' by large language models (plagiarism, by any other definition), I cannot agree with the site being used in this way, regardless of how many jobs it promises to deliver.

Alex had told me that locals feel a mixture of frustration and resentment at the site, which has been up in the air for several years now. Whether or not any AI data centre or gigafactory ever ends up operational at this place remains to be seen, but there is already vital work of another kind going on here. Alex and Esther are committed to the social and imaginative wellbeing of their community, and that, to me, seems like one of the most worthwhile things anybody could now be doing in a place like this.

AI has been touted by the new Labour government as something that Britian 'needs to run towards',[11] but in the North East an alternative narrative is emerging: one based on supporting nascent writers and investing in the creative industries. At the time of writing, plans were submitted to DCMS by a consortium of partners led by New Writing North to open a Centre for Writing at Bolbec Hall in Newcastle. In October 2024, I was pleased to be one of over eighty signatories to an open letter, 'A Creative Call to Arms', which ends on a clarion call: 'This investment can transform people's life chances, unearth talent, and ensure the North's creative voice is heard on the national and world stage'.[12] A sign above the exit of the Tute says, 'Inherit the past, look to the future'. I take my leave of Cambois thinking of those whose shoulders we stand upon, knowing that it takes only a few hands beginning to sway to start making bigger waves.

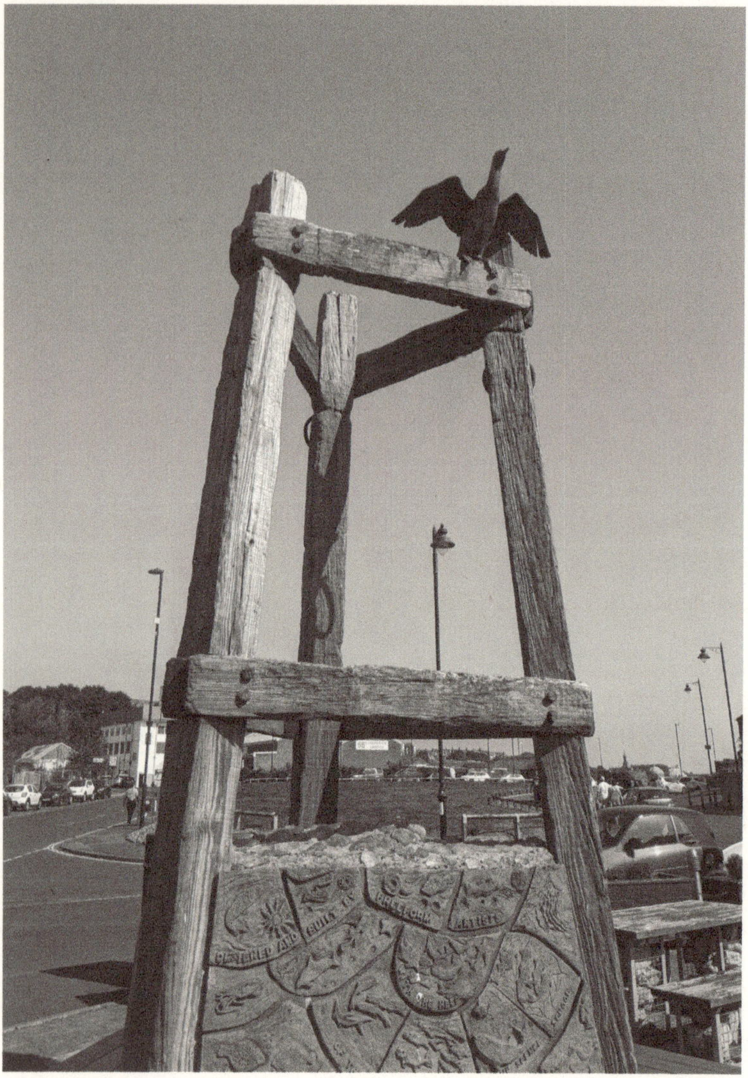

Chapter 5

Harvest from the deep

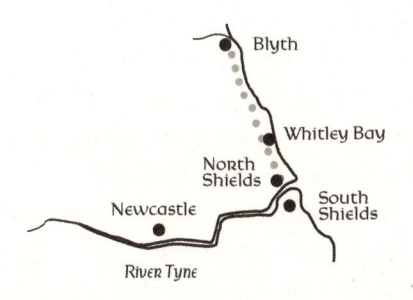

It's a murk auld day in Blyth. With my poet friends John Challis and Kris Johnson, I've just taken a taxi up the coast road from their house in North Shields. We dive into Ciccarelli's Gelato for cappuccinos, pull our hoods up and make for the beach. We start by the pastel-coloured beach huts, then take the view from the Battery – a collection of First World War artillery cannons guarding this stretch of coast since 1916. Through the mist, vessels come and go from Blyth's port. A squashed white lighthouse sits squat on the harbour wall. This is the worst weather I've had along the Camino but is the type the North East normally doles out. Down south along the wide expanse of Blyth South Beach we press on, catching up on the summer, on travels and new jobs.

The pair are recently returned from Washington State, Kris's home. Along with their five-year-old daughter, Fern, they've spent the past month there, and conversation soon turns to how and where we feel local or at home. John, originally from London, has lived on Tyneside since 2010,

Kris a few years longer. Their romance bloomed because of Newcastle's vibrant poetry scene, and both have published their debut collections with Bloodaxe recently. It's where I came into touch with them. Trying to make my own way onto the Newcastle poetry circuit circa 2010, I bonded with John in the beer garden of the Cumberland Arms in Byker, where I'd just given a reading of a handful of poems from my first pamphlet. Since then, we've gone on to share many fine nights of poetry and pints – poetry as a kind of social bonding agent and way of making sense of the world.

The tide is a decent way out, so we press on along the beach. South Blyth is about the limit of how far Kate and I can take the kids in the car for a beach walk before it begins to feel like too much of an expedition, so this feels like well-known territory. Up beyond the dunes to our right, Gruff learned to ride his scooter, and the whole stretch of paths wending down to Seaton Sluice seem imbued with a kind of comforting familiarity. Indeed, this is the joy of walking with marras – real pals who you don't first have to forge awkward small talk with. We've embraced the dreariness of the day – our whole left sides are already sodden, a mile in – and are able to talk freely. Of course, we ruminate on what it means to make tracks, deliberately set about a pilgrimage and all it entails, but the conversation is really an extended chance to catch up: on our respective kids' journeys through the education system, on what it means to be working for new universities, on what it's like having each of us launched books of poetry into the world.

On the outskirts of Seaton Sluice, we clock a dead gannet in the strand. Avian flu and its fallout have blotted the coast all the way down from Lindisfarne, but the remains of this gannet are the most staggeringly large I've seen. I think about Cuthbert's love of avian and marine life – of the otters warming his feet and the birds who'd scavenge him victuals – before experiencing the odd sensation that I'm in some way voyeuristically making the most of this scene: seeing the bird as it should never be seen, flattened down into the wet sand like this, a bent and lonely feather snagging the wind, its whole decrepit frame a sinister black question mark.

Climbing the high dunes, we've got a great view of Seaton Sluice: the Melton Constable pub, St Paul's Church, the famous Harbour View chippy. When it's a clearer day up here, it's one of the finest spots on the whole coast, I reckon, with great views back into the Cheviots. Seaton Sluice is so named because of the Seaton Burn – a small river – which wends its way from the west to the sea here. The sluice gates head a channel into the harbour, almost like a canal, and once allowed some small industry: glass works, salt-panning, fishing. We press on round the bend of the sluice, adjacent to The King's Arms, where a creepy doll hangs on a rope swing below, to look at the fire beacon on the cliff tops. The Delaval family's home – Seaton Delaval Hall, now managed by the National Trust – is half a mile inland, the Delaval family making their wealth here from coal.

Further up Holywell Dene (note that it becomes a Geordie 'dene', with steeper wooded banks), the ruins of the fabulously named Starlight Castle can be found in the overgrowth. This folly, supposedly completed in a day, was built for Sir Francis Blake Delaval in 1750 – a place where the young womaniser could keep his adulterous behaviour out of view. Fern took her first steps nearby, in the grasses at Seaton Delaval Hall, where John has recently been poet-in-residence. His collection *Hallsong* takes up pressing themes, writing the forgotten histories of the estate back into its narrative by weaving verbatim lines taken from grounds staff, cleaners and gardeners. John muses on what this place has given the world: 'much of the British empire was built on the stuff that came out of this region'. It's a sentiment captured lyrically in one of the poems from his residency about an archaeologist:

> We dig or else conduct a survey
> and bit by bit fetch up things
> born or created. Our work is time,
> time it takes to know the layers
>
> [...] We are not miners
> but disciples, and work to spread
> belief in land not as commercial.[1]

Having crossed back to an open area of parkland sewn with some of the most vibrant wildflowers I've ever seen, we take stock of the Pele Tower (now an art gallery), and note its Morden Tower vibes. Part of medieval Newcastle's city walls, Morden Tower in the 1960s came to be a sort of bohemian centre for poets. Local poets Tom and Connie Pickard invited international names such as Allen Ginsberg to read, and it's where the Northumbrian Basil Bunting gave the first performance of his modernist epic *Briggflatts*. With those poets' words ringing in our ears, we head for Collywell Bay, a small inlet of limestone stacks on the headland before St Mary's Lighthouse. Kate and I drove up here after the end of the first lockdown in June 2020, when Gruff was a baby, beginning to take his first tentative steps. It felt like a liberating moment: even though we were on a beach a mere ten miles from home, we'd somehow crossed into a more exotic realm. John and Kris have equally fond reminiscences about travelling out to Hexham post-lockdown – the summer fields of the Tyne Valley rolling into view for the first time in months. They admit to weeping at it all, to being overwhelmed at the release from physical isolation.

At Collywell Bay the rocks are too slippery to risk crossing further, so we make back up the bank, through the nettles and thistles, to join the road and the verge around the headland. At Old Hartley we pass behind The Delaval Arms – that name again – and a caravan park, on well-worn tracks where a group of retired ramblers have come out to head in the other direction. When Kate was nine months' pregnant with our daughter, Elma, we came up here for some last-minute fresh air. It feels significant to be back on this route, having not returned since twenty hours before Elma's birth. There's something about repeating a walk: about taking to the same tracks time and time again; the way memories accrete and overlap, the way the present butts up against the past, an echo held in the waves as they begin slushing up over the mini-causeway to St Mary's, all the seals round the other side frolicking in the shallows, the lighthouse badly in need of a paint, a smudge of muck flanking its side a bad advert for the nearby caravan park.

We're about to cross an imaginary boundary into North Tyneside. For the first time, the Camino leaves Northumberland, as we get to the fringes of Whitley Bay and a much more urban coast – a contiguous built-up area stretching south-west for twenty or so miles through central Newcastle to the far end of Gateshead. This is where, until very recently, John and Kris first set up home: in a flat two minutes' walk from the beach. Whitley Bay was John and Kris's first home as a married couple and where they lived for seven years. At their wedding in 2016 we danced to rock and blues music and drank tinnies from buckets at Earsdon Church Hall. In the cemetery at the rear of St Alban's, the headstones mark the Hartley pit disaster of 1862. Trapped below ground following an explosion, with only one collapsed shaft in or out, 204 people perished. As we danced to 'Get It

On' by T-Rex, the old bones of Hartley's pit workers might have felt the trembling of our feet on the ceiling of the turf: a stirring of the dead now captured and remembered by us as we pass nearby, thinking of all that comes from the earth, and all that remains sealed below it.

For even though this part of Tyneside feels to me like a place of low-key pilgrimage – family walks with the bairns, the short after-work constitutionals Kate and I would make before cooking tea – it's also the place where the queue to get into the church service was four miles long, comprising 60,000 people wanting to pay their respects. No wonder, when men and boys, hoisting their tin bait boxes and steel picks, walked one day to work and never came back. The Hartley colliery disaster led to a change in regulations that made it compulsory to have two access shafts to any newly sunk mine – a reminder that on any voyage, an escape route is not just a sensible backup plan but can be a matter of life or death.

As we press on to the beach at Whitley Bay itself, talk turns to politics. With John and Kris having spent some time in the liberal Pacific North West, their views are pretty broadly represented by the incumbent Labour MP, Alan Campbell, who has held this seat since 1997. But, as we heel back the sand, the three of us wonder what a progressive settlement might now mean in places like the Tynemouth constituency. Certainly there is doubt as to what – or whom – Keir Starmer actually stands for, and a pervading sense, if their cantankerous neighbour is anything to go by, of indignation bordering on apathy. 'Why would you come back here?!' he asked them, when you could be somewhere like America? It's true that they had considered the verdancy of the grass on the other side, but with Fern now in a local school and a house to their name in Shields, this is their home.

I think a lot about the push and pull, about whether my family could have a better life overseas, and in all probability we could. In the wake of the 2016 referendum on the UK's continuing membership of the European Union, there was a well-meaning but ultimately privileged draw, felt by a lot of middle-class people, to seek out tenuous Irish connections and apply for citizenship within the Republic. It was easy, the sentiment went, for an educated person of means to jump ship, but what about those less well-off, who had no choice in staying, whether they'd voted to leave or not? My wife and I still reflect on a pit-of-the-stomach sickness when the outcome became clear. We were about to leave Venice, where we'd just spent a week on holiday. David Cameron's resignation speech reached us from the overcrowded departure gate of Marco Polo Airport – a day that really did feel like the splitting of a glacier.

Perhaps in the years ahead a campaign to rejoin the European Union will gather momentum, but for now it seems that seeking communion with like-minded souls *and* finding some way of making peace with 'the other side' is probably the best settlement. Even though, clearly, I am journeying with people of a similar political persuasion, I like to think that what a pilgrimage of this kind does is hold open a space for respectful disagreement. It might also, following the inauguration of the North East mayorality in 2024, hold up a physical way for thinking through not what divides us, but the common grounds we share. I'd wager that even the most partisan would find harmony on a beach like this, in this little town by the sea, with its Spanish City dome boasting Tyneside's Taj Mahal and a little blinking light keeping time like a metronome.

It's midday. We head up to the foreshore for chips. In the queue, a man from Derbyshire, hearing about our quest down from Blyth this morning, extols the virtues of hiking in the Peaks. We don't have such inclines to follow, but there are a few miles on to Tynemouth, so we slurp at paper cups of tea to wash the salt and vinegar away and hit the trail again. Down the rampart there's a sorry-looking model boating lake, and on the breakwater wall a series of graffiti tags illuminating the space like the writings of medieval monks. It's suddenly all a bit Lindisfarne Gospels, as the tags of KOMR and JACKA ('the one and only') square off from stone arches with the North Sea, perhaps inviting communion with the waves, or more likely sticking them the Vs.

Round to the next bay at Cullercoats, we stop to discuss John and Kris's totem item: their brick. Kris had been here six or seven years and had started swimming in the North Sea. Coming back to shore from a dip in Cullercoats Bay, she picked up a half brick in the shallow waters. Marked into it were the words 'John And'. In the midst of the messy untangling of prior relationships at this stage, the romantic possibility proffered by the brick was tantalising. Now, it takes pride of place by their record collection, the real-life Kris standing in for the brick's textual absence of her name.

'It's something we've kept on to for years now and has moved with us through all of our homes', Kris says. 'I couldn't believe it at the time that when I was falling in love with John, suddenly his name came calling from the sea.' As if by inserting herself after the 'and' it would become true, the rest, as they say, is history. Now it's an important symbol of the new life they're making together here. 'We've bought into physical bricks and mortar in the area', John adds, 'And it was all foreshadowed by this discovery of Kris's'. It does seem too good to be true: a perfect moment of serendipity, a saline souvenir, the sea telling them – whispering it like a lullaby – that all will be fine, just trust the rhythm.

On Cullercoats Bay in the shadow of the wonderful watch house, a red ticker tape indicating pollution cautions against bathing. The miniature explosions our boots make in the sand seem to sound the alarm: we're shitting on our own doorstep. We walk past the caves where, of course, the smugglers smuggled and the pirates hid loot, and reflect not on acts of piracy but on how a small bay like this can work as a crucible, a point of origin and return. Cullercoats is the genesis point of John and Kris's relationship, but the whole coast up to Bamburgh, where many years ago they wild camped and to which they go back each summer, is a place where their love was kindled. As we walk and riff further on what it means to set up home in a place that you might not ever feel you can truly belong to, it strikes me as profound that the mysteries of the sea have had a big hand in germinating a marriage.

On the steps south of Cullercoats, in recently set cement, three artists have inscribed their names: Buster, Clyde and Cuddy. It seems that all the way down this coast, Cuthbert, 'Cuddy', is still looking out for us. We come up roadside in front of the imposing St George's Church before dipping down again onto our last beach of the day, Longsands at Tynemouth. Soon John and Kris will have to leave to fetch Fern from school, but we have this final mile together to walk along what I think of, frankly, as the most overrated beach in the region, but which is ultimately a very pleasant stretch of fine golden sands.

As all of the familiar landmarks have come into view from the strand – Whitley Bay's dome and the hotels and church spires of Tynemouth – I've thought about the subtle change in perspective you get from the beach. Normally when I'm coming into Whitley Bay it's from the west, in the car. During the first lockdown, when I was struggling with my mental health and finding the whole thing a real challenge, I drove out here to walk with John and Fern, taking Gruff along. It felt like a genuine boost to meet up with someone in a similar position, trying to parent through a global pandemic while also somehow trying to write. And likewise today, it's been a real blessing to walk with my fellow travellers and co-conspirators in poetry. I bid them both adieu as they walk hand in hand, a little half brick in their bag adding a glug of spirit to the lamp in mine.

'I grew up surrounded by tales of the sea', Aaron Duff is telling me in Tynemouth's Surf Café. On the table, he's placed his great-grandfather's binoculars. He can't be certain that they were used in Gallipoli, but he knows that his great-grandfather Jack lied about his age to become a Navy reservist. After that, it was the trawler's life, setting out from the Fish Quay at North Shields to make his catch.

Aaron's musical career took off when he adopted the moniker Hector Gannet a few years ago. The project has since morphed into a full-band set-up with two acclaimed LPs under its belt. Back in May, in a packed-out room at the Sage in Gateshead, Kate and I watched Hector Gannet perform a set which incorporated all of the musical explorations of the region that the act has become known for, but which also included incredible film footage: contemporary drone shots of the North East coast, combined with archive footage featuring Aaron's grandfather. It was this that led me to reach out and invite him along.

'I like to think of these', he waves the binoculars, 'as a way of looking through the past, wondering at the things they've seen'. Aaron came across footage of Shields trawlers making a voyage to sea in the 1950s. He suddenly realised that his grandfather was in the film, and, what's more, that one of his folk heroes, Ewan McColl, had written the score. 'Bloody Hell, I thought, Ewan McColl has written songs about me granda!' Realising what a gift this was, Duff approached the North East and Yorkshire Film Archive to write his own suite of songs in response, and that formed the genesis for the Hector Gannet project. The name is a reference to the vessel which was sent to rescue stranded crew of the Hewett A gas rig, which in 1968 blew up off the coast of Lowestoft. Aaron's grandfather was on board. As the *Hector Gannet* neared the rig, it listed and hit it, before capsizing and sinking. Three men died. Aaron's grandfather survived and, as Aaron says, 'the story has passed down the family since'.

An early September Indian summer. A marmalade sun blaring down, bathing Tynemouth in its pulse. When I came up off Longsands with John and Kris, I didn't know that somewhere beneath the sands lies a lion's head fountain dating back to 1862. In 1996, the Victorian Plaza which had stood overlooking Longsands burned down. Aaron's father, a firefighter stationed at Newcastle's Pilgrim Street, was on duty. Fire and flames are a recurrent theme of our discussions as we walk towards Aaron's home in North Shields – tales of combustion which seem to have symbolic roots in the medieval past, in the tales of the northern saints and this ransacked coast.

Rounding the bay at King Edward's – King Eddy's, to locals – a wondrous waft of cooking fish blowing up from the trendy Riley's Fish Shack below, we approach the Priory, burial site of three kings. Following his death in 651, King Oswiu of Bernicia, later known as Saint Oswin, was brought to Tynemouth for interment. In 792, the second king of

Northumbria, Osred II, who had been deposed and murdered, was also buried here. They were joined in 1093 by Malcom III, king of Scotland, he of *Macbeth* fame. I revisit my GCSE copy of the play, scanning the book to alight on a fitting line: 'We have met with foes that strike beside us'.[2] Today the place is swarming with Japanese and American tourists, two of whom, from Minnesota, we get chatting to. They're briefly off the boat, the DFDS *Seaways*, which landed here from Amsterdam this morning, and are touring the North East, having traced their Scandinavian roots in Sweden. The poet James Kirkup described the Priory as standing 'like a broken harp',[3] a simile which can really be understood only from the southern side of the river, from where its crumbling aspect reveals the shattered impression of beauty the poet was driving at. The sight of the harp pulls me into a reverie, characters and voices beginning to swirl.

A harp begins twinkling. Voices lift from the river-mouth, lilting on the rip-tide, baritones from the Black Middens. Five rafts carrying monks are being swept out to sea, their cargo of wood wobbling into the waves, blown suddenly by a Wallsend westerly. Their brethren in the monastery on the south side, desperate to assist but patently unable, are praying at the nearest rock for divine intervention. Cuthbert, standing on the north bank of the river with a growing crowd of peasants who are jeering at the imperilled monks, chastises the insulting party. Now, he says, wouldn't it be a better use of your energy to pray for the safe return of your fellows? But the braying posse, exhilarating in their schadenfreude, stand firm: their rebuke to the saint a result of their cynicism towards people's conversion from time-tested pagan beliefs to the new faith. Cuthbert, hearing their case, gets doon on his honkers. At the drop of a pebble, the wind changes direction. The castaways are borne safely back to the riverbank by the monastery, while the boorish unbelievers' cheeks gan scarlet with impiety. The voices are subsiding, the cries getting quieter. The harp's melody is quelled. The rafts have made it ashore....

'Something like that, aye', Aaron says smiling, after I've recounted a condensed version of the paragraph above. According to Bede, from whose record the mouth-of-the-Tyne miracle is traced, 'The man who told me the story, a worthy brother of this monastery, said he had often heard one of that very group, a simple peasant, incapable of lying, tell the tale before a large audience'.[4] To thicken the broth, the poet Alistair Elliot, writing in 1982, gives a geographic embellishment. In his account:

> Out rushed a squad of Brothers, with the Prior,
> And knelt, and sent up prayers – like mortar fire!
> I like your verse – while the whole show was guyed
> By local heathen from the South Shields side.[5]

To the partisan river-dweller, I can see why Elliot took the liberty of making out that it was 'them on the dark side' braying at the monks' misfortune, not the peasants of Tynemouth, as Bede has it. But that's just it – we only have the version of the story we're told to rely on, and it's up to us how we run with it.

Now we're trotting out a well-worn story: giving the Minnesotans the gen on Cuthbert Collingwood, second in command following Nelson's death, victorious at the Battle of Trafalgar. A Geordie, the big C's statue stands a little to the west of the Priory, overlooking the mouth of the Tyne. Those big mooths a lot of us have, gobshites, yapping on, but this is a statue that probably won't end up in the silt. Each Trafalgar Day, 21 October, crowds still gather to salute Collingwood and his maritime bravery. It's a celebration that was immortalised by the mid-twentieth-century artist Louisa Hodgson. She had a studio high up on one of the elegant Georgian terraces, from where she painted a scene that might have been nearly recognisable to Bede: a throng of people, lit by pyrotechnics, commemorating the triumph of human adversity over the vagaries of the ocean and its fearsome currents. I used Hodgson's image on the front cover of my first book. It's a *Dark Side of the Moon*-esque composition which beautifully captures the notional idea of light triumphing over dark. I said that Cuthbert was following me down the Camino: his mythology living on now in sculpture, oil paints and, best of all, fable.

A kestrel circles the Priory, below which a plaque on a bench for Tim Duff, a one-time Tynemouth mayor and Aaron's great-great-uncle, solidifies my impression that I'm walking with someone whose ancestry runs deep along these banks. Down to the riverside proper, Aaron has his *gegs oot*, eyeballing the waves. He spots oystercatchers, Sandwich terns and – I can see this one without the eyewear – a cormorant, fanning its span. It's a scene that Aaron describes as 'classically Shields', referring to the dolphin – a kind of wooden jetty, not the mammal – which used to attract resting cormorants and also featured on a painted pub sign for the New Dolphin Inn down at the quay. Along the little beach at the start of the quay, we come to the low lights. North Shields has two pairs of these; when lined up they provided a guiding line for safe passage through the harbour. Before the Tyne piers were built in the nineteenth century, their wooden precursors were set on wheels, so that as the tides shifted, so too could the guide lights, marking out the safest course into the river depending on the waxing or waning of the river line. The Tyne Improvement Commission, set up in 1850, also began to regularly dredge the river. They may be static now, and in the wake of GPS technologies redundant, but they are still wonderful orienting devices. I remember getting the DFDS ferry to the continent from Shields a few years ago, and it's certainly true that those high and low light beacons stand out, ushering the seafarer into a benign embrace.

We've reached Ray Lonsdale's *Fiddler's Green* sculpture, a wonderful cast of a trawler, tab in his gob, hand rested on his chin, looking wistful. Soon it will be joined by another Lonsdale: *Herring Girl*. Both pieces evoke the area's maritime past so beautifully, the 2017 *Fiddler's Green* alluding to the sailors' mythical paradise, where the women are easy and the rum is ever free-flowing. The *Herring Girl* sculpture acknowledges the gendered labour of the trade, a bit like up in Beadnell, where roles were often demarcated according to whether you were a woman or a man. Aaron speaks fondly of the herring lasses following the fleet, making their way down the east coast from Aberdeen.

Round at The Gut, where a few day boats are moored up, Aaron recalls his grandfather speaking of the trawlers being three deep. As I've encountered elsewhere along the Camino, fishing is highly politicised. It was a marker in Brexit and remains a complex and sensitive issue. Aaron reminds me that North Shields is still one of the UK's busiest prawn ports, and it's difficult, as it was in Amble, not to think of

Si and Dave, the Hairy Bikers, pulling up here on their road hogs to buy some fresh produce for surf 'n' turf. All along this quay, even in my thirty short years of coming here over on the ferry, the sense of the modern-day gentrification process creeps on.

Aaron laments the passing of Wright's, a ship's chandler and grocers which 'served the best bacon sarnies'. I remember it, too, a veritable Aladdin's cave of treats. It is of course now a fancy wine bar. Italian restaurant after barber shop after fish and chip shop flow into each other, and it is, on this baking hot late summer's day, a wonderful sight. Round the corner, where Aaron and his partner, Leigh, recently opened The Wheel House coffee shop, the new and trendy butts up against the old and established. A few old fishermen and dockhands, people who Aaron says are 'lost, really', come in for drinks, while across the street Harrison Ford in town filming *Indiana Jones and the Dial of Destiny*, was once seen enjoying a meal at The Ship's Cat.

Aaron's been down beneath the waves at The Gut, a place where 'time and tide have morphed the timbers'. Perhaps this is the best metaphor for what's happening to places like the North Shields Fish Quay: they're simply following the weft and warp of bigger currents. At The Low Lights Tavern, North Shields's oldest pub, recently made famous by being the place where the singer-songwriter Sam Fender nailed his Brit Award to a beer tap, we make a pit-stop. In the back room, Aaron points out a Scottish and Newcastle Breweries promotional photo, staged in the 1950s, which shows the crew of a Purdy's trawler being plied with booze. William Purdy was the first person to adapt steam trawlers to go out to sea and catch fish, in 1877. Aaron's uncle John, who's in this photo, was one of several men to be given free beer in order to, well, sell more beer.

I'm looking at them glaring out of the frame: John Duff has his arm around dutiful manager Aida Brownlee; Jack Reynolds ('Mopsie', the caption tells us) is laughing like a drain; Hector Mackie, his cap askew, fixes the pint being presented to him; while Geordie Skerr, scarf still wrapped tight round his neck, thinks of how good it is to be inside. All around them are foaming beer glasses and bottles of Newky Broon – Newcastle Brown Ale – and the men's *gansies* look thick and comforting, nearly as thick and comforting as the atmosphere that the brewery was trying to show off. Next day, Aaron tells me, the crew were so hungover they were unable to sail, and Purdy tried to sue the brewery for damages. The way pub folklore lives on in little details like this is beguiling to me: a window into the past as we finish our North Shields-brewed Three Kings pales.

On a little industrial estate comprising such establishments as Geordie Bangers and Ovington Boats, we make a quick stop at The Engine Room. Aaron's dad Graeme and his manager Mark – also his father-in-law – own the music venue, which they've recently done up. Aaron tells me about the burgeoning little music scene which has sprung up around The Engine Room, and about their vision for The Wheel House coffee shop. The combined ventures, which he sees as a bit of a hub, are attracting people to the area. It stands in contrast to the old Tyne Foods site, derelict for over forty years, where tinned foods would be produced and packaged and which is now a buddleia-strewn eyesore awaiting development. I feel the urge to snap a picture of the decrepit factory, so that, by the time this book is released and the first of the new flats are up for sale, I can say I was there when this site was little more than a husk: all overgrown in butterfly bushes and lazily surrounded by sagging plyboard and chicken wire. Up Brewhouse Bank and adjacent to more light industrial units – a metal basher's, a microbrewery, a furniture and cabinet maker's and a timber yard, we're headed for a quick look at the King Street Social, then off to Aaron's house, the place where he can 'map three generations of his family out in these streets'. We briefly pop inside, where I'm introduced to Leigh, then it's back out to the Tyneside terraces.

Assuming the role of a local tour guide, Aaron shows me the Tynemouth blue plaques, part of a First World War commemoration project honouring the fallen. We cross past St Augustin's Church and walk down Princes Street to see one of the plaques commemorating his great-great grandfather, Wilkinson Cappleman, who died when his trawler hit a mine further down the coast at Hartlepool. He was thirty-two. Aaron, via his uncle, recounts a family anecdote told by his great-great grandmother, in which Wilkinson's body, having being sailed back up the coast to Shields, was greeted by church bells ringing out in respect and remembrance. He can't be certain whether the body was sailed or arrived by other means, but the poetic resonance of the water-bound repatriation is irrefutable. We make a quick dog-leg into Northumberland Park, my pun intentional as Aaron wants to show me the pet cemetery. It's in a quiet corner of the park, behind a bowling green, and here we stop so that Aaron can point out the marks in a tree made by a woodpecker. Thoughts turn to lockdown: Aaron tells me that he'd watch this woodpecker and think, 'Well, he's getting on with it, so I might as well'.

Wending our way into town, we go via Northumberland Square, an elegant and recently renovated Georgian block. From there Aaron wants to show me one more thing, the Stag Line building, which is now the base of North Tyneside's civil ceremonies office. The view south is beguiling: the full Robert Olley 'island' painting[6] coming into force as the

Lawe, South Shields's northernmost district, is foregrounded, appearing to suspend the town between the haze of the sea and the big arc of the river, bending round to the huge DFDS ferry berthed at Royal Quays. Aaron and I shake hands. He seems genuinely pleased to have chaperoned me through his patch and I, equally, have been pleased to be guided by him. One final musing: we discuss the once-mooted but never built bridge which could have connected the two Shields. Designs that I've seen in the past – interestingly, in the pub toilets of The Maltings in South Shields – reveal a Golden Gate-like structure, which would have spanned the Tyne and its mouth. We ponder how the fortunes of the towns might have been more closely aligned – less of this Sand-dancers versus Cod Heeds rubbish – as I make a bee-line for one of the two river crossing options available.

It's a short walk down to the ferry and lines from the South Shields poet James Kirkup are on my mind: 'The sea on sanded feet/Enters a town blue with tars'.[7] I take a circuitous route because I want to look at one of the most imposing buildings on Tynemouth's fringe. Here, in 1840, North Shields Master Mariners Asylum for thirty-two aged mariners and their dependants opened. A statue of the 3rd Duke of Northumberland stands prominent in the garden. It's like a stately home for seafarers. Behind it on the front façade there's a stone inscription with an anchor topped by a sailing boat. It's a message which alludes to North Tyneside's motto, *Messis Ab Altis* – harvest from the deep – in which a collier and a sailor stand proud aside the town's emblem. Walking down the bank past Aaron's coffee shop, and along the fish quay where the wooden dolly statue puffs her chest by The Prince of Wales pub, I think about these words and how resonant they are to the soul of Northumbria, where auld shipmates' tales mix with saintly fables and the space between the start of the sky and the end of the sea is indiscernible. The smell of the river clings to my clothes and I breathe in its briny tang.

Tirtha: Tyne

I'm on the blue pontoon waiting for the *Pride of the Tyne*. Frothing bubbles boil the river as the ferry lands, dunshing cushioning tyres on the jetty. The ramp releases, its gantries opening like butterfly wings as the steel platform makes its 100-degree swing. The metallic thunk as it grounds is satisfying. Out come the canny folk of Shields. After thirty or forty pedestrians and cyclists have disembarked, I board, paying my obol. Tapping the reader with my Pop Card, I take a hard, plastic seat. Inspecting a plan of the vessel, I'm informed that *Pride* was built by Swan Hunter of Wallsend in 1993 – that bastion of industrial might: the place from where famous ships like RMS *Mauretania* and *Esso Northumbria* were cast into the breakwater.

In seven minutes I'll be on the other side, back hyem in South Shields. Four hundred and twenty seconds to offer a prayer to the river gods. Which should I pick, and what should I say? Further up the river at Newcastle, altars to Roman gods were dredged from the Tyne when the foundations were being built for the Swing Bridge in the late nineteenth century. The red and white structure, a modest rotating construction with a mini lighthouse at its centre, is shadowed by its big, younger brother, the Tyne Bridge. This span of the river joins Newcastle to Gateshead at the site of the original *Pons Aelius* crossing. The altars, bearing the symbols of a dolphin entwined with a trident and an anchor, are thought to have marked a shrine at the mid-point of the Romans' stone crossing, where the gods Neptune and Oceanus met in harmony.

Amid a housing estate in Benwell in the west end of Newcastle, the remains of a temple to Antenociticus can be found. Antenociticus was a local deity, later subsumed into the Romans' pantheon as they conscripted my Geordie forebears into their frontier cavalry, stationing them along Hadrian's Wall. This syncretic approach to belief, a sort of melding of official and folk deities, seems to me fitting for Tyneside's mongrel identity, where converging patterns of migration and commercial influence are a hallmark of the area's marine geography and religious and military passageways and watercourses.

My paternal great-grandfather, Joseph Redmayne Campbell, comes to mind. The son of Hawkshead-born John Campbell, Joe was a chief engineer whose Yemeni shipmate, Abdul, helped service the boiler aboard their vessel. Abdul, who left Aden for Shields, stayed aboard for eight years as the crew sailed to South America and then the Indian subcontinent and back like one of those tetherballs circumnavigating the globe. Following this, Joe and Abdul spent six years working for Stephenson Clarke, the oldest shipping company in the world. They were on a 'coaster' transporting coal to power stations along the east coast, from Methil in Fife to Medway in Kent. The so-called race riots of 1930 in Mill Dam were seen as a flashpoint for tensions between demobilised white sailors and the foreign seamen who had begun arriving as cheap labour from the late nineteenth century and who kept the merchant fleet running as Britons were recruited into the Royal Navy.[1] Joe and Abdul were sailing together after the Second World War, and I like to think that as marras they represent the wider comradeship and conscientiousness of my hometown, which in all of my lifetime has seen peaceful cohabitation between differing races and faiths.

As the ferry begins bearing down on the Sand-dancers' side, I muse with Nick, Joe, Abdul and Antenociticus: figureheads at the bow of the boat; sprites of the Tyne. Obviously, I begin whistling 'dance to your daddy, sing to your mammy' under my breath, knowing I'm minutes away from docking Shields-side at the land of my forebears.

In Buddhism, Hinduism and Jainism, a *Tirtha* is a crossing point – a holy place of pilgrimage. There are three kinds: *Jangam Tirtha* (to a place moveable); *Sthawar Tirtha* (to a place immovable); and *Manas Tirtha* (to a place of mind, truth, soul). As the ramp once again begins to descend and I prepare to go ashore, I think about this first leg following the sea on sanded feet. From Bamburgh to North Shields I've been chaperoned most of the way, meeting with impassioned locals to learn about their patch. Before making my way down this coastal part of the Camino, I thought I had a good handle on Northumberland, but I realise now I've only broken through the first seam. On this second leg, as I delve into Cookson country and Bede's World (which had started as the Bede Monastery Museum), where the terrain is much more familiar, I'll have to juggle between the primary and secondary *Tirthas*: trying to unseat baked-in perceptions of the place I've long held dear. The ferry gate opens and I step out onto hallowed turf.

Part II
Stringing Bedes

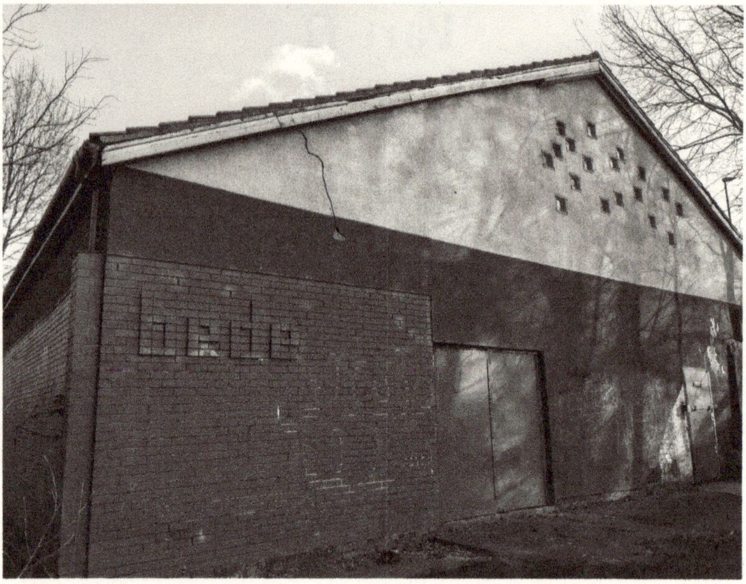
bede

Chapter 6

Following the Don

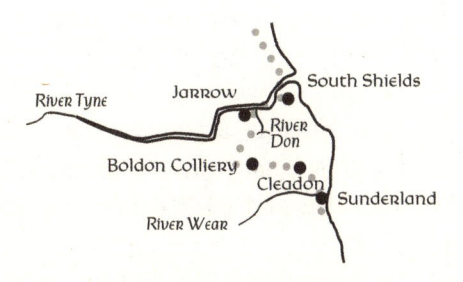

Crocuses are beginning to illuminate the dirt as I wend through the grounds of St Paul's Church in Jarrow. There's a background whirring from the port as ships entering the river with tea leaves and coal (yes, coal is now brought to the Tyne!) are unloaded, while Nissan Quashqis are driven aboard to be transported to continental Europe. Geet big hulking cranes cast shadows over the monastery, which has been here since the late seventh century. A heron takes off over the mud flats at Jarra Slack, a redolent image recalling Bede's spuggy.

In Bede's parable of King Edwin's conversion of the Northumbrians to Christianity, a counsellor tells the king that 'this life of man appears but for a moment; what follows or indeed what went before, we know not at all'.[1] The pagans' godless lack of direction is said to be like a sparrow flying 'swiftly through the hall. It enters in at one door and quickly flies out through the other.' When the poet Anne Stevenson was here forty years ago, she 'painted' into her poem the same 'passing sparrow [...] flying from winter/into winter'.[2]

I watch the heron's drawn-out ascent over the Don estuary and contemplate how everything seems at once static and moving, before the north door to the church opens and I'm greeted by the Reverend Lesley Jones.

What does it mean to make a pilgrimage through your homeland – the place you call hyem? I'll be thinking about this a lot for the next couple of days, as my walk will bring me within a couple of hundred yards of my present house. More than that, I'll pass directly alongside my mam and dad's current home as well as their previous abode, the place I lived in from being fourteen and which they only recently sold. Having come across from a series of Northumbrian walks *owa the watta*, it's reassuring to be on home turf. Since disembarking the ferry at Shields and plotting my course through the Tyne and Wear edgelands in the footsteps of the Venerable Bede, I've wondered how to broach the overlap of the personal and the historical. My sense is that I can only lean into it, embracing how rare it is on a long-distance journey to see the landscape as a mesh of public and private experience.

'Welcome', says Lesley, who introduces me to Fred Hemmer, director of music and organist. I give them the gen on what I'm up to, explaining that my spirit guide has come along. When I take Nick out, Lesley immediately beams: 'Oh, what a rich symbol of light and renewal. How lovely; you must see our lamp.' I'm taken to the south-west of the building, where, up on a windowsill, sits a Davy lamp. Fred begins giving me the background to the bust it is positioned beside: that of Reverend John Hodgson, Rector of Jarrow and Heworth between 1808 and 1823. Following the Felling Colliery disaster of 1812, in which ninety-two men and boys perished, Hodgson worked tirelessly to set up a relief fund, and helped establish the Society for the Prevention of

Accidents in Coal Mines. Incredulous, I interrupt Fred, who's proudly telling me all of this, to say that I'm staggered never to have seen their lamp. I imagine Nick pulsing with the charge of a kindred spirit.

Hodgson was an influential figure – he helped to set up Newcastle's famous Literary & Philosophical Society, from where much of this very book was written – and obviously well connected. The pioneering engineer Humphry Davy came to Hodgson with the prototype for his new safety lamp. Understandably, those men and boys who had grown accustomed to a caged linnet or budgie being their best way of telling whether firedamp was present were sceptical. Hodgson, mindful that his flock, many of whom had lost relatives in the Felling explosion, would fairly be disbelieving of this new tool, agreed to escort a group of miners beneath ground to prove its reliability. In 1822 he opened St Mary's Church at Heworth, where the memorial he raised to victims in the churchyard is thought to be the first in the world to name working-class people. St Paul's is visited by international pilgrims seeking Bede's Knowledge – deliberately there with an upper-case 'K', the kind we might associate with a classical education – so it's reassuring to know that a symbol of the proletariat also shares this space: the scholastic and the socialistic in the same chamber.

I'm shown into the oldest extant part of the church, the chancel to the east. In an aumbry in the chapel, I touch the place from which Bede would have received Holy Communion. A little circular window above contains the oldest example of stained glass in the world. Following archaeological excavations led by Rosemary Cramp from the 1950s, a huge discovery of Anglo-Saxon artefacts was made, including remnants of the original glass decorations from the church's founding in 685. A wily priest reassembled these pieces into the circular panel and it was reinstated into the wall around sixty years ago. This process of collaging, of making new from the old, finds obvious resonance in this lamp I've been lugging about. As a parting gift, I'm given a replica window sticker showing the same window, about the size of a tea plate. I consider all the ways in which history is copied out, repeated, traced and reimagined. On our slow walk out of the door I think about how glasswork and text can re-render these towering figures from the far past, putting them in dialogue with the here and now.

Lesley, who started this job during the first wave of Covid-19 in 2020, tells me that ministering to the parish of Simonside and Jarrow, with its three other idiosyncratic churches, is a tough but rewarding remit. She speaks of individuals within the congregation who are over £300,000 in debt and mentions the family arts and crafts mornings which are bringing youngsters into the space, often for the first time. Once described as the town that was murdered, in 1936 Jarrow became famous for its crusade, a 282-mile protest march to London involving 200 jobless men, led by their firebrand Labour MP Ellen Wilkinson, demanding a solution to their destitution. Today, the town is part of a pilot programme for Universal Basic Income (UBI), in which fifteen Jarrovians will receive £1,600 a month for two years. The scheme, which is seen as inverting the current welfare system, aims to give people long-term stability, increasing public health. It's interesting to me that Jarrow has been picked as one of the trial towns: a place which went from the cradle of the Northumbrian enlightenment to the grave of industrial decline is being offered a radical afterlife. As I set off to follow the course of the River Don from near where it spits out into big brother Tyne, I decide that my vocation as a writer and a poet is a large part of what might be needed in a community like this. Alongside social and economic fixes, writers can offer new narratives, opening up imaginative horizons. The Jarrow-born playwright Alan Plater put it best: 'Our stories should be dream-driven, not market driven, and they should be stories that in one form or another we first heard in a back yard, once upon a time'.[3]

Before leaving, I'm invited to spend some time in contemplation. I head to the consecration stone, staggered by its age and appearance as a material connection back to the time of Bede. And there he is — or rather, there is Fenwick Lawson's 1973 carving of him – quill in hand, contemplative, sanguine. The feathered pen in his right hand is a dart about to be launched: I'll trace its trajectory through the rest of this walk, then aim to carry its sentiments forward through my life. I'll vow, as Bede did, to commit to learning, teaching and writing, and I'll carry my family with me. So went some of my inner monologue before I was asked by the Reverend if she could pray for me. I'm not entirely sure I agreed, but I definitely didn't refuse, and then the benediction came. It's impossible to recall the exact words, and I suppose that recounting them here runs counter to the point, but I know she gave thanks for the touchstone and the lamp at my side, and blessed me and all the people I'd encounter on my way.

I leave the church and look across the green of Charlie's Park to Jarrow Hall. I have huge affection for this verdant idyl slung between the port and the river. When the pioneering archaeologist Rosemary Cramp started digging here in the 1950s, she was unearthing the soul of Northumbria: her work with trowels and sieves revealing the stratified traces of England's Christian roots. Following the energy crises of the 1970s, and with the government favouring privatisation, by 1986 Jarrow had become the borough with the highest unemployment in the UK. It was against this economic backdrop that, in 1988, the Tyne and Wear Development Corporation granted money for the commencement of an experimental farm and Bede Monastery Museum on a reclaimed oil depot. The industrial epoch which had dominated Tyneside for over 200 years may have atrophied, but efforts to explore early medieval Northumbria were booming.

The museum, which went on to be renamed Bede's World, closed in February 2016 due to financial pressures, and I was photographed in front of its locked gates adopting a stern pose by the *Newcastle Evening Chronicle*, for which I'd written a poem situating the closure within the context of wider Conservative-led funding cuts.[4] Thankfully, the site reopened later that year under the new stewardship of the Groundwork charity. While writing this book I would often have Friday mornings off with my daughter, and we'd drive down to Jarrow following the back road through Boldon, where Nick would have worked, cutting through Primrose to arrive for the museum opening. I'd buy paper bags of animal feed and carry her on my shoulders past the Dexter bulls and goats, hurling seeds into the pigs' pen. We'd look at the replica Northumbrian stone cross serenading the Tyne, and she would dance in the grounds of the Thirlings Hall. Somehow the edifice of a huge crane or the crackling power lines overhead added to the multilayered history of the place, and for a moment you could believe that monks were tending to the herb garden or weaving fabrics.

Today, a convoy of nursery-school kids in hi-viz bibs are clambering aboard the wooden Viking ship. I wonder whether any of their parents have been selected for the UBI trial, the paths it might open in their lives. On Jarrow bridge, a stone construction dating to the early eighteenth century, I read about local mine-owner Simon Temple. Having opened Jarrow Colliery in 1803, Temple quickly set about establishing a school, fever house, seminary for young girls and a hospital. While it's very easy and dangerous to romanticise wealthy industrialists' benevolence, especially given the number of young men and boys who died slogging beneath ground, it's difficult to imagine Amazon opening similar civic amenities around one of its new fulfilment centres. I think that people such as Temple must have drawn some influence from the monastic past, from Bede's close-knit fraternity and the principles espoused by early Northumbrian Christendom. While popular culture sometimes pokes fun at Bede (in the BBC comedy-drama *The Detectorists*, for example, Lance says that he was 'full of shit'), his significance cannot be overstated. It's probably farfetched to say that a life lived in communion is taking root again, but the absence of a bigger cause does feel notable. Might we, emerging from the alienating effects of neoliberalism, put some faith in the values espoused by the monks of Jarrow?

The Don. The pun is perfect. Here this little river, there this mighty figure. Don Bede. Born on lands between the rivers Wear and Tyne (tradition favours nearby Monkton, now a Jarrow suburb, while other accounts claim him as a Mackem born closer to modern-day Sunderland), Bede entered the Church at St Peter's aged seven and was then moved to the new sister monastery at Jarrow when he was twelve. From there he went on to become the polymath's polymath, writing on subjects including astronomy, language, poetry, tide times and, of course, scripture. Canonised as a saint in 1899 and recognised in a range of Christian traditions, Bede can be thought of as a sort of Anglo-Saxon Wikipedia. A sage or oracle who worked to establish the date of Easter, and whose writings on the history of these islands as Christianity began to spread, Bede was the first person to assemble a unified account of who we, the English, were and are. This led to the popular moniker 'the Father of English History'. His *Eccesiastical History of the English People* is still in print.

The medievalist Michelle Brown says that Bede's 'reputation is so great because of his remarkably joined-up thinking and his ability to see the bigger picture, his studies embracing diverse areas in pursuit of a "theory of everything" in which the arts, sciences and faith were integrated'.[5] Inhabiting a time when STEM (science, technology, engineering and maths) dominates agendas in education and business, it's reassuring to think back to The Don and his eclecticism. Bede composed verse in Latin and wrote guides on metrical composition. Brown writes of how the 'Wearmouth-Jarrow refectories likely rang to the sound of him joining the singing round the table, including heroic poetry in English'.[6] For anyone familiar with the North East's rich oral history and its continuing folk music scene – a lineage which includes the Elliots of Birtley, broadside ballads and folk songs like 'Cushy Butterfield' – the vision of Bede singing and reciting poetry in a banqueting hall is an easy one to conjure.

This folkloric ancestry has been brought into the twenty-first century by the Newcastle Kingsmen, or the 'Rappers'. I think of the first time I saw them performing, at the Bridge Hotel in Newcastle. One minute I was quietly supping a pint, the next half a dozen men in tights and polished clogs burst in and began dancing a jig to a backing fiddle and English concertina. Spinning arm in arm and tumbling over their swords, their repertoire conjures pit village dances from County Durham and Northumberland. The Newcastle Kingsmen, originally called the King's College Morris Men, started in 1949 as a student rag society at what was then Durham University's Newcastle campus. Having learned the Winlaton rapper dance, and encouraged by their professor, Bill Cassie, who had documented the tradition in towns such as Amble, the group travelled from pub to pub to learn and perfect sub-regional variations, which were then honed and passed on at each performance. Rapper dances hark back to the 1930s Depression period, when unemployed miners dressed in satin huggers and white shirts – the traditional pitmen's duds of the time – performed the ceremonial dances around bars as a way of earning much-needed cash.[7] A rapper was a special signal lever used in coalmines to signify that a conveyor was ready to use.

I remember being at The Cumberland Arms in Byker in 2011, reading at Ten By Ten, a poetry open-mic night MCd by Gosforth writer Jeff Price. Over pints of Wylam Rocket bitter, a rapper group suddenly entered, transfixing poets and punters for five minutes of mad merriment. Their famous steps and knots routine, with its various breakaways, leads to the group's swords mingling as a star, which is often raised around participants at the end. It's a beguiling spectacle to watch, one whose symbology I think Bede would have admired. I can almost see him tapping his feet in the lounge of The Free Trade Inn now, his vocal chords being greased by a glass of mead.

Bede's national and international clout is beyond doubt, but for my purposes I'm more interested in his local contributions to knowledge. A canoniser of the Northumbrian saints – Bede wrote several prose accounts as well as a verse one of the life of Cuthbert, as well as other figures – he can be seen as a proselytiser for the idea of a Northumbrian credo at a time when belligerent factions were still contesting territorial influence. While many of his contemporaries, including Benedict Biscop, travelled to Gaul and Rome, Bede is thought not to have ventured beyond eighty miles. He may have travelled to Melrose in the Scottish Borders, and we have evidence of him visiting Lindisfarne, but otherwise his life was locally circumscribed. Indulging in a bit of vainglory for a moment, this is where the personal first comes into this part of the tale.

I'm from the same place as Bede. I've spent most of my life living between these two great rivers. When I started plotting out the course this book would take, joining Lindisfarne to Durham, I didn't realise but I'd already made an echo of the extent of Bede's travels. I was literally following him to the site of his tomb. While I grant it's a tenuous connection to make, Bede is known for being the patron saint of education and learning and he wrote poetry. I am employed as a teacher in higher education and I've spent nearly twenty years reading and writing poetry! I do wonder how all of this sat in the groundwater and was subconsciously imbibed by my wandering thought processes. What is certain is that Bede and his entourage would have travelled between their two monasteries on foot and/or by coble, joining the two sites in much the same way that university campuses are linked today. Hence why, in 2004, the Bede's Way footpath was established, allowing pedestrians to recreate the short domestic pilgrimage that the monks of the Wearmouth-Jarrow monasteries would have made. Bede's entourage of monks may have been early adopters of pedestrian travel, but their methods would be adopted and politicised in the early twentieth century by a campaign originally dubbed the Jarrow Pilgrimage, aka the Jarrow Crusade.

The first leg of the route takes me along a tree-lined path to the Tyne Tunnel. A circular mosaic on the floor, in a poor state of repair, has shades of the Lindisfarne Gospels' colour palette and weave. I descend beneath the A185 Jarrow–South Shields turnpike, its concrete balustrades adorned in a rich pattern of graffiti. Discarded tins of spray paint suggest that some of this work may have been done in the last few days, and I speculate as to whether the artists, donning masks and head torches, were aware of the history of illuminated manuscript production which went on upstream over a thousand years earlier. Importing the techniques of continental Europe – from the monasteries of Gaul in present-day France and Italy – the making of codexes was one of the primary purposes of St Paul's Church. The most famous of these, the hefty Codex Amiatinus, was created here as a papal gift. It was taken overseas and then carried across Europe to Rome, where its courier, Ceolfrith, died. It ended up in Florence, where it can be viewed today. Northumbrian hagiography – which would have, no doubt, required Bede's assistants to seek out natural dyes and materials in the reedy wetlands around the River Don or in the pasture and woodland later built over as terraced streets – was justly famed and the Monkwearmouth–Jarrow sites were at the centre of this process of exegesis: a nucleus of cultural production and learning, some of whose patterns and styles I see reflected in the graffiti-covered concrete stanchions of the bypass.

Dipping under the dual carriageway, the Don culverted through a narrow channel, I emerge at the back of Jarrow Cemetery to follow the Don Valley south through South Tyneside for a couple of miles. A semi-rural, suburban expanse, a wildlife corridor in microcosm, it effectively bisects the borough's biggest towns – South Shields and Jarrow – as a natural cut paralleling the A19 takes me south to Primrose. I take a pew looking over the sliver of the Don and half drain my flask of coffee. Behind me, Jarrow School. I consider what the pupils might be learning, and how many of them know about Bede – other than his name being given to the burn that runs behind their house, or the Metro station where they get off, or the industrial estate where a relative works. I know that Key Stage Two pupils (in primary school) have a curriculum opportunity for a local history case study, but how many of the teenagers behind me are encouraged to contemplate the life of their town's most famous son?

Deviating slightly from Bede's Way proper, I detour to the west through Springwell Park. I want to visit a former Cold War bunker. At the corner of the atmospherically named Butcher's Bridge Road, I find it. In 1970, the artist Vince Rea took charge of this disused bunker and converted it into the Bede Gallery. Here, until 1996, Rea and his wife Willa curated a thriving exhibition space, which brought work by the likes of Picasso, Matisse and Hockney to Tyneside. Big proponents of local history, the Reas dedicated a section of the gallery to a collection of images and objects connected to the heritage of the town. Many of Vince Rea's own artworks took cues from local history, including a stunning, large-scale depiction of the gibbeting of William Jobling. Accused of knocking South Shields magistrate Nicholas Fairles from his horse while riding on the beach, Jobling, a Jarrow pitman, was the last man to be sentenced to death by gibbeting. A fall guy who was used as an example to discourage strikes, his tarred and feathered body was left in a man-sized cage suspended over the Tyne. Following his death, his body was recovered by his friends and family.

Rea was also known for his candid photography: a series of his wonderful pictures document ordinary lives in and around Jarrow. That he also made a powerful relief sculpture of the Jarrow Marchers, mounted at the town's Metro station, tells me that there might be something to my theory of Jarrovian groundwater, gannin' all the way back to Bede. A custodian of his people and a chronicler of their lives, Bede's mission echoes through Rea's work, which was deeply attuned to the particularities of place and fiercely keen to show the beauty and dignity in working lives. A pity today that the building, shut up and showing signs of structural damage, is no longer able to showcase the creativity of local people while inspiring them with touring works. I recall the Tute up in Cambois, and the way certain places are able to sustain a mythos while others fall to rack and ruin. I pause in front of the site. Spelled out in lower-case letters made of bricks that are proud of the mortar, a double after-image juts from the gable wall, announcing its *genius loci*: b e d e

The Don Valley around Primrose is a haven amid the sprawl of urban Tyneside. The last time I walked this way, in 2015, was for an arts project, 'Stringing Bedes: A Poetry and Print Pilgrimage'. Facilitated by the University of Sunderland's WALK (Walking, Art, Landskip, Knowledge) research group, and led by natural historian Keith Bowey, I was invited to offer a poetic take on the route and went on to write a sequence of poems in response, including the one, stoked by my ire at the sudden closure of Bede's World, lamenting the museum and its promotion of cultural heritage. All of the public participants were given contemplation cards, with quotes broadly related to the philosophy of walking. I remember receiving a line by the blind British adventurer James Holman, 'I see things better with my feet', and find myself stopping today at pretty much the same point I did nine years ago. In the background the cityscape churns away with sirens and the drone of the A19. But after a moment I tune into my immediate surrounds: a moor hen cheeping on the pond, the call of a rooster at the farmhouse behind, the cooing pigeons at the crees on the bank at the top. I also smell horse shit. As a way of navigating naturally, it's not foolproof, but I begin to try and pick out cadences, colours and textures in a way that medieval monks would have been extremely sensitive to.

After passing the stables accounting for the stench, I come out at the back end of King George's playing fields, a much wider and more open expanse through which the Don gently weaves. Nine years ago for Stringing Bedes I was taken by the incongruous image of parents with their young son dressed in a Spider-Man onesie crossing a little wooden bridge at this point. Keith had us gathered in contemplation of the adjacent crack willow tree, rustling in the breeze, and our moment of mindfulness was broken by the family joyfully coming past. Now, as a father, I view the scene differently. One or two people walk their dogs, but otherwise it's very quiet. I take a moment to listen to the same tree: my current self encountering the former self, wondering where a decade has gone.

Passing The Robin Hood pub – like Brendan Foster commentating on the Great North Run, I refuse to call it Vespa's Bar, despite the fact it hasn't been The Robin Hood for many years – I'm now in Monkton, where Bede was thought to be born. I'll soon reach the Metro track and take a left heading east. This little slip road off Leam Lane is the first place I've encountered vehicles for about an hour, and it's quite a shock to hear a double-decker bus passing. While the landscape of the Don Valley hasn't changed drastically from Bede's day, most people's experiences of getting to or around it certainly have. I continue to follow the course of the river until I get to Hedworth Lane, where the inclined bend takes me to The Greyhound pub and the train line. I watch as a freight train passes along and above me, thinking about the ways in which the economy of this place is so bound up in a complex series of transport networks and just-in-time delivery systems. Walking east parallel to the line, I look down into the deep gorge through which the Don now flows, shaking my head at all the fly-tipped waste, before cautiously skirting round a bloke in his early forties, mountain bike on its side at his feet, tab in one hand and bottle of Hardy's rosé in the other. It's half eleven in the morning.

The route comes up again suddenly by the A19. This time I have to make a hairpin manoeuvre, crossing over it on a pedestrian footbridge to get to the fringes of Boldon Colliery. Some wordsmith has daubed 'SMAKRAT' on a fence at the back of Perth Green community centre, and once again I despair at the amount of rubbish strewn in the bushes. Cans, McDonald's packets, the now-ubiquitous fluorescent cannisters of vapes. Even the carcass of an unwanted hoover. I do wonder what Bede might have made of such wastefulness and excess, what he might have thought of these plastic, metal and cardboard items speedily consumed and then jettisoned into the bushes. When Keith led us this way, he stopped to reach cherries from a tree off Calf Close Lane and pointed out plums growing on the verge of the road. The motorists zooming through who discard their cans of Monster Energy might have travelled further than Bede ever did by the time I conclude my walk today, but will they have really known this place, passing through it at seventy miles per hour?

That all sounds a bit worthy. Perhaps it is. Certainly, I'm riven by double standards, having been dropped off at the start point this morning by car and regularly racking up hundreds of miles a month behind the wheel. But, given that one of the points of conversation this morning with Reverend Jones centred on slowing down and breaking pilgrimages into smaller chunks, so that they might be more realistically achievable to those who aren't fortunate enough to be able to take several weeks off work, it seems a shame that the part of the Camino of the North East closest to my doorstep – the section that in many ways I'm the most proud to represent – is blighted by litter.

Ho-hum: I grumble on to Boldon Colliery, the day's major detour. Normally the route skirts the northern edges of the Cotswolds Estate, proceeding to follow the Don through its eastern valley extent, but today I need to take an old miner back hyem. So, I cut through the 1980s housing estate, looking in all my clobber – muddy boots, waterproof trousers, Montane soft-shell – somewhat incongruous to the streets of well-kept semi-detached houses, and press on to the heart of NE35. Once I'm over Cotswold Lane the former-pit-village vibes come on thick. I'm within a couple of miles of home now, but in acknowledgement of the hypocrisy above, I admit that until today I knew Boldon Colliery only from the car. Travelling to places like Jarrow Hall from home, I've taken to making dog-legs through the village, to admire the architecture of the place where my great-grandfather spent most of his working life.

On foot it's the same story in grand detail. The first thing that strikes me about Boldon Colliery is that there seem to be as many allotments as there are houses. Straight away, I resist donning rose-tinted specs. You could be fooled into thinking you were in an extended version of Beamish Museum, where history as an active ongoing event has been paused, but geet fat leeks and marrows are still prised from the earth and there's a dance every Friday at the Miners' Welfare Hall. Terraced houses from the late nineteenth and early twentieth centuries have long front gardens. A spider's web of chares, ginnels and snickets connects the grid of back lanes to these russet abodes, and a similar network of chares and passages links the many allotments together. North Road, with its now-redundant police station and seemingly open independent Methodist church, is indented beside a Co-Operative Funeralcare and the Red Lantern Chinese takeaway, whose gable wall is painted with a mural of the colliery winding gear and a date of memorial: 1869–1982. On Brockley Terrace I take a photo of Body Forge & Tan, before feeling conspicuous and voyeuristic. Then, walking west along Hedworth Lane passing an old haberdasher's, I stop to admire the Crown Hotel and can't resist another photo, which I'll never do anything with but which reinforces my impression that this is a very workaday place peppered with some quite grand architectural statements.

My main reason for coming, though, is to see the Aged Minerworkers' Homes at the north-western extent of the village. Passing St Nicholas's Church – I try the door but the Benefice of the Boldons aren't in; I whisper to Nick that he isn't being anointed by the Father today – I round the bend to a small but very impressive collection of DAMHA cottages: Durham Aged Mineworkers' Homes Association. The Harton Collieries group (Boldon Colliery was in the Harton Coal Company's orbit) opened these in 1928. Created in 1898, DAMHA raised funds to build houses for retired miners, as well as for newly married couples. The scheme was a forerunner to government-led social housing, and was inspired by the miner and Methodist lay preacher Joseph Hopper, who staunchly believed that loyal miners should not be evicted from their tied colliery homes in the way he had been following retirement. Financed by small levies voluntarily placed on miners' wages and by donations of land and materials from landowners, it soon gathered momentum. During the 1910s, nearly every Lodge area in the county built homes, all let free of charge.[8]

At the entrance to the village, beside the slip-road which takes cars on and off the busy A19, a three-carriage coal wagon welcomes visitors. I have brought Nick back – if not home, then to the place where he and his marras worked. Boldon Colliery today is popularly known for its giant Asda superstore, which opened five years after the mine closed, replacing the once-dominant winding gear and colliery buildings. There's a Cineworld with a Nando's. There are dozens of light industrial units. There's a hotel with a swimming pool, Boldon Leisure. There's a Greene King pub called The Story Book, which, to its credit, has retained an archival image of colliery workers on its roadside sign. It feels like Ashington. You can really sense, especially in those terraced streets with stately names like Gladstone Terrace, that something used to happen here. The earth beneath used to swelter and shake. Men dug around in its capillaries becoming the marrow in the bones of Boldon. Men like Nick, who used this lamp to check for firedamp, and which will never go underground again, but will lead me on the way, out past another block of allotments nodding to an auld gadgie who, I guarantee, worked some of the latter shifts doon there, out past the woman on the scooter with the terrier on a lead tied to the handlebars, out to the fringes of this little place which for years now has loomed large in my mind, out to the overgrown edges of the estate, where a clarty path leads back down to Bede's burn and my way hyem.

I get a bit further along the burn before stopping to finish my coffee. The Don is pronounced here, which is unsurprising given the amount of rainfall recently. Culverted beneath the Metro line, a lot of it here is recently maintained, the structural integrity of the riverscape having to be well kept this close to a train line, I suppose. I cross it once (north) to go up the bank adjacent to Brockley Whins Metro station, which has a dual purpose of serving residents of Boldon Colliery and the South Shields suburb of Biddick Hall, before dipping back down the bank to come to a final crossing point. Here I discover one of the oldest railway structures in the North East. The stone abutments on the disused railway bridge date back to 1830. It was a crucial part of the Stanhope & Tyne Railway, with the nearby Pontop crossing allowing onward access to the coal staithes at South Shields by providing safe passage over the River Don into County Durham. Limestone at Stanhope in Weardale would have been sent to fuel industries along the Wear and Tyne and a passenger service also ran. I survey the site for a moment and decide it's a stupid idea to try to scramble up. Then, in a 'fuck it' moment, I charge up and pound to the top. It gives a great view out over the Don and colliery woods. Looking down the length of the bridge from behind a metal fence, I'm taken by the thought that Nick made his own small contribution to the many hundreds of thousands of tonnes of coal which came from the earth and were loaded on to wagons and sent directly along this line to the big river.

The scramble back down is more perilous but somehow I manage not to fall, though I do wait for a Metro train to pass in case I go arse over tit in front of a coach load of passengers. Crossing the Don for the final time, a burnt-out scrambler bike beneath the bridge tells me what this relic is used for today. I realise there's an interesting crossing point here. With the x axis carrying a ghostly procession of carriages loaded with the mineral wealth of Boldon, and a y axis formed by the Don, the same river Bede would have followed if travelling on foot to the sister monastery at Wearmouth, the origin site is this railway bridge: a point of convergence; a layering of pasts – the religious and the industrial. I take my notepad out, marking the figure of the cross, noting the obvious symbolism, and scrawl a question: where am I? I go back to my muse, Nick, and think about what it means to make a mark. I've marked out a cross. Two possible ways, me in the middle. Both point to pasts – shallow and deep – but both are that: *past*. I've passed Bede and Boldon on my way, yet somehow I carry them with me. By marking these words, I move them forward. I am the mark-maker. Bede, 'illuminating' the 'dark ages'; Nick literally lighting the tunnels. Me, making imprints – my boots in the soil, my bloodied finger smudging my notebook, the ink from my pen becoming the twelve-point type on my screen and ultimately the type on the printed page.

Trudging on through sludge that's thick enough to warrant the wellies I don't have, clarts of mud squelching with every step, I take stock of the position I've found myself in: of being a recorder. Coming up from these pasts – as the poet Anne Michaels says, 'we do not descend, but rise from our histories'[9] – I know I'm privileged. Just as I try to gauge how proud of that I should be, a whining sound brings me to a halt. At first think it's a horse, this being prime farrier country, but then I spot the mutt down in the river. It's stuck on a shopping trolley, visibly shivering. The Don has thinned here, in both width and ferocity, but there's no way I can reach over to save the dog without gannin' in meself. I'd be up to the knees in water, at best, and God knows what kind of other shite might have been tipped in it. There appears to be no way for the dog, which looks young, to get back across. I think of Cuthbert. I'm sure he would have plodged right in and hooked the hound oot. But I don't fancy the final hour's walk back to the house half covered in slurry. Bugger.

The RSPCA hotline is no good, so I do the only thing I can and log a 'distressed and trapped dog' call with the local authority. I'm told that the warden will be notified. I try once more to entice the pooch oot by dangling a health bar in front of its trembling flews, but I doubt even a prime link of pork sausages would do the trick. 'It's alright, little man, I've phoned for help', I say, 'take care', as I put my foot back up to my bootlaces in the mud and pass through a kissing gate. Round through the colliery wood which was planted following the closure of the mine – the Great North Forest project was a big initiative from the late 1980s – I've been away from the dog only ten minutes when Tyne and Wear Fire and Rescue's animal department ring and I begin issuing directions. 'It's about a third of a mile west of Newton Garth Farm', I say.

I imagine adding 'You know, the one recorded in the Boldon Book?'[10]

'Err, is that the one John the pantry-steward holds?'

'Aye, that's it.'

'Eeeh, did y' knaa he pays twenty shillings a year on it?'

'Haddaway an' shite, does he?'

'Aye, but it does have twelve rent payers holding two bovates of land each, so it's a canny return when y' think aboot it.'

'Some acres to turn those hens' eggs, eh?'

'Oh, absolutely, pet, you're not gannin' short of omelettes there!'

Two hours later I'm phoned to say that the hound has been safely retrieved and is warming in a towel at the local stables and will be taken to the kennels in Cleadon by the farmer later. I feel like my Cuthbertian good deed for the day has been achieved, my ethics as uncompromised as my still-dry clothes. I emerge on to New Road by Boldon Comprehensive School, where it's a mile to my house in Cleadon. Crossing the Tilesheds level crossing, I wind on to a few paths in that triangle of flat-lands between Boldon, Cleadon and South Shields. I think of all the times I've jogged along here, all the times we've pushed the kids in buggies or trikes to the pond where the Don discharges. I think of the spirit of Bede at our side. As I pass the green man statue which marks the western boundary of Cleadon, at least in my interactions with the village, I bid Bede farewell for the night – he and his monks carrying on off over the hills as I squelch through the last hundred yards of muddy field to enjoy a sanctuary space rare to the pilgrim: his own bed and home comforts.

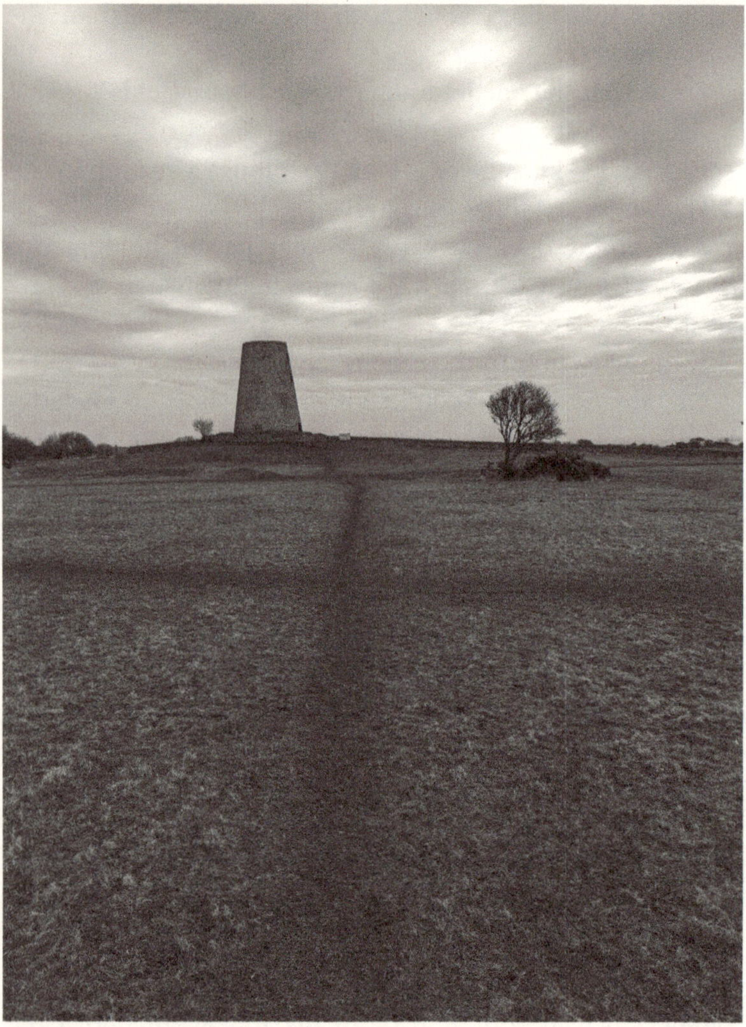

Chapter 7

The Ash Path

I leave the house at quarter past eight. Within minutes I'm back where I finished yesterday, at the Whiteleas allotments at the southern periphery of South Shields. It's a short walk adjacent to the closed school before I join the Ridgeway at the edge of town. After crossing from Temple Park on King George Road, the long boulevard which creates the town's major north–south axis, I stop by an Esso garage. A mini-cab driver inflates his tyres. People put overpriced diesel in vans. Someone comes out with the *Daily Mail* and an elevated heart rate. There's a cut up the side: a tumble-down fence leaning drunk into the hawthorn bushes. On a Bede's Way signpost, someone has stuck a 'Northumbrian blood & soil' sticker – a reminder that a weird kind of far-right movement is contorting the narrative of these northern saints to decidedly xenophobic ends.

After crossing Sunderland Road, I'm on the Ash Path – the bridleway which flanks the ridge-and-furrow fields separating Shields from Cleadon. I don't know how true this is, but I like to think it got its name from the days when coal fires still heated homes. Having collected the remains in their pans, people would come out here and hoy the ashes into the field, literally chucking out at the end of town. *It'll be good for fertilising the snadgies*, I can hear the auld biddies saying. This is where, when I was fourteen, my parents moved us from Harton further into Shields, to be in the most desirable part of town. The neighbours at the back have built a new brick garage. I stop at the end of Sunnilaws, mindful not to linger, but voyeuristically interested in what's become of the house at the end of the cul-de-sac which, until five years ago, was my parents' home. When I was sixteen and had started an AS-level course in art, I began to experiment with oil paints. One of the first views I captured was from the rear bedroom window of that house. I based it on a photograph I'd taken with a Minolta digital camera I'd received as a birthday present a year earlier, at a time when digital photography was beginning its journey towards ubiquity.

I see myself taking the photo: a late spring sunset a few weeks after my birthday, the sky a smudge of firedamp. Most of the image is stratus clouds, their wispy undercarriages lit in the salmon sky. How I used to stare from this window, surveying the prospect: the city in the distance, its glinting towers proffering excitement, suggesting the adventures I might have beyond this town, shackled to the sea and bound by its own sense of dejection. But I thought beyond Newcastle, too: to the places way beyond, where a more interesting life might be had, where people didn't just sit on the back of the bus smoking bongs or drive to retail parks to frivolously spend; where they took seriously the things I was beginning to value – music, art, poetry.

Let's gan. I need to be further along the Ash Path, round a bend where protruding bushes have made a bulge in the side of the field. This bend in the path has formed only recently, and certainly wasn't here a decade ago when I would still

The Ash Path

walk my parents' dogs up the path to Cleadon Hills. Up to the top beside Sunniside Farm, in the shadow of Cleadon Water Tower. This Italianate structure served as a chimney for the South Shields and Sunderland Water Company's cleaning works below. Built in the 1860s, it's the 'pin' to the adjacent 'plug' of the defunct flour mill — vestigial vertical markers from a time when the parish baked its own bread and sanitised its own water.

In a fine early spring breeze, I think of the Eucharist. I think of the bodies which were saved from typhoid, cholera, dysentery. I think of the millstone churning wheat, the breadbasket of Cleadon. I think about the sandwich in my bag: the bread manufactured ... who knows where. I think of the Colombian coffee ground into the flask. I think of Elizabeth Gibbon, the heartbroken miller's daughter who threw herself from the top of the mill after her father discovered her dalliance with a pirate seaman. I think of the echoes that might still be pulsing, the goldfinches bobbing on the breeze. I think of the ashes of two of our dogs scattered up here, one minute bounding through clover, the next returned to the soil.

As Cleadon Hills open out – this is the highest point in the borough and its view are spectacular – I feel like it's the first part of the route where Bede might not have felt totally estranged. Notwithstanding the mill and the water tower, there's a timelessness to the landscape which I think he would have recognised. My feet beat the limestone escarpments which protrude through the incline up to the top. Most of the county can be seen from Cleadon Hills and further, into Durham and Northumberland. Visibility isn't perfect today: on a clear day the Cheviots hold the horizon, while the other way Hartlepool's headland and the Cleveland Hills above give the tail to the Cheviots' top. The other way, I can see the beginning of the Wear Valley, where my lodestar's body lies in state. I can hold nearly all of Bede's vistas in my line of sight. Known not to have travelled further than eighty miles – to Lindisfarne and perhaps to abbeys in the Scottish Borders – Bede's whole domain rolls away down the bank. I gaze down on the whole of hyem. I draw my eye along the line of the river to the tunnel funnel – the chimney stack expelling fumes from the Tyne underpass. Bede's house at St Paul's isn't visible, but I know that it's only a quarter of a mile (or, from here, a thumb's length) east. I veer left, tracing the course of the River Don as I followed it yesterday. The sun begins to come out as the Exmoor ponies, placed here for conservation grazing, nuzzle the wild grasses. The other way, a sliver of sea is lit up silver, with the church spire in Whitburn and Roker Lighthouse beyond beckoning me on.

Locally, part of this way is known as the salt path, but I struggled to find much information on it. Before major roads were put in, a South Shields to Sunderland stagecoach would have followed roughly the course of the A1018 below me, but I don't know, beyond using an individually packed horse, how practicable it would have been to transport salt over this way. The presence of the Marsden White Horse on the other side of the hills captures some folk memory. At Marsden's old quarry overlooking the town, a large white mare can still be found painted onto the cliffs. Reputedly painted in honour of Whitburn nobleman Sir Hedworth Williamson, the image is a memento for his late wife, who, according to the legend, fell with her steed while riding one day and never returned. The horse was one of those quirky background textures to my youth walking at Marsden, and I've seen recent pictures of members of the community coming out to brighten it up and remove certain features such as the mysterious fifth leg. While the 'tribute to rich local landowner' tale seems to be the most commonly accepted one, I like to think that what the horse represented was a way marker. Painted white and high on the hills, riders bearing salt to be traded between the two rivers will have seen this spot as a kind of halfway house: a place to dismount, for the horses to drink and, if for nothing else, to take in those majestic views back down to town, up and away from the feculent river.

Cleadon gets called 'posh', and while it's no Richmond (London or North Yorks, take your pick), its equidistance between two historically very busy and polluted industrial rivers makes its appeal clear. Here, wealthy shipyard owners and glassmakers, colliery chiefs and mercantile classes could have a house out of the smog, in the countryside without being out in the sticks. Its twinned village, Whitburn, which I'm walking to next, also grew from south and north. To the south, its dunes, still prominent in the latter part of the nineteenth century, made it naturally cut off from the larger settlement of Sunderland. Fishing and farming were the order of the day, but there was also a paper mill, opened in 1889 to service the demand for newsprint. With overspill from the growing Whitburn Colliery requiring additional housing stock, the northern limits of the village began to be populated by my fellow Shieldsmen – those grafters who themselves had outgrown the town and the salt trade which gave it its purpose.

By the early seventeenth century, South Shields was one of the biggest salt-panning areas of England, before continental imports gave it a hammering.[1] I think of the monks, centuries earlier, bringing salt over these hills to brine their fish and feed the abbeys. The simple, rustic life it conjures is a beguiling one, and part of me wants to stay up here with the limestone and the linnets, admiring this Tyneside bucolic which might have been partially familiar to Bede, but the salt path is pushing me on. I speak aloud the words you're not supposed to write down for charges of sentimentality: *we're lucky to live here, y'knaa.*

Down into Whitburn, Bede's Way comes out through farm buildings off Wellands Lane. Into the village proper, I pass its wonderful open green and duck pond before hooking onto Sandy Chare. I'm walking down this chare recounting other chares – Broad, Denton, Pudding, Peppercorn – when a car pulls up next to me. My mother and father-in-law, with my daughter, Elma, in the back. They're taking her for a drive along the coast then to the Word library in town. Elma frowns at me through the window, wondering why her dad is beside the road in his stupid cap and walking boots. It's a pleasant interlude and an unusual one, reminding me of the benefits of a pilgrimage which crosses through where you live.

On Front Street the daffodils are in bloom and the village looks at its best. The drinking fountain and cenotaph, both recently restored, are gleaming, the union flag rippling. It's all very picture postcard: a slice of quintessential Englishness that, had I not been writing this, I might have taken for granted. And while the very idea of the English establishment makes me quiver, it's worth remembering that pockets of it are firmly entrenched in Northumbria. Bede to Britain: strawberries and cream on the lawn, washed down with Lindisfarne mead. As if by thought, the urge for a pee comes on. I could open up my parents' house which is just around the corner, but instead I hot-foot it to the church. I forget what time it is and as I push the creaky door open, its sneck sending ripples down the pews, I realise it's still only mid-morning. Holy Communion. I take a seat at the back and wait for twenty minutes, before catching the Reverend and asking kindly to use the facilities. The congregation is small: numbering only eight people, myself included. I briefly

The Ash Path

explain what I'm up to, contemplating saying that Bede sent me as a scout. On a window to the north of the church I see the two Bs – Benedict Biscop and Bede – noting that it is dedicated to the widow and family of Hedworth Williamson (he with the mare). Here a church-sanctioned memorial in vibrant technicolour, there volunteers with buckets of white emulsion and borrowed brushes.

Out of the church and passing the wonderful cricketer's cottage, with its stone wickets on the chimney, into Cornthwaite Park for a brief sojourn. All very odd to be treading the same path from my parents' house with the bairns: passing the play park where they spend so many hours on the slides and the swings, but today trying to keep a medieval monk in mind. Unlike Seahouses or Craster, Whitburn almost seems to have its back turned on its beach. From the north end, at Souter Lighthouse – the world's first electrically powered lighthouse – down to here there's a feeling of ruggedness to the coast; that the inhabitants don't want to fully embrace it. As Whitburn gives out to Seaburn, and as once more I cross an imaginary line that marks the local authority boundary to leave South Tyneside and formally enter the City of Sunderland, I take the opportunity to rejoin the strand.

In front of Whitburn Bents cottages, I pocket a few pebbles. The smell of the sea again: a tang that I hope never leaves me. If Bede and his entourage had taken the 'quick' way here, via water, this is where I imagine they would have landed their coble. Having boarded it at the mouth of the Don and rounded the promontory at Shields, they would have somehow had to have left the Tyne without hitting the Black Middens. Following that, four miles of sailing south would have had them first pass the bay at Marsden, before a further mile and a half brought them out here to Whitburn Steel.

Maybe this wasn't exactly where they stopped, but it seems to me that here or nearby, having put in many hours of hard rowing, the sight of land near their mother monastery must have been a relief. Today, a rider is training an immature horse to gallop on the sand, while many other smaller, four-legged friends are being walked along the beach. I walk as close as I can to the breakwater, thinking of the miles covered so far and the end beginning to focalise.

A fish restaurant on the promenade has recently opened with the name NORTH, and I contemplate the currency that such an appellation now brings. In what ways have we fetishised this 'north', used it to market bouji small plates or trendy coffee houses? What do we actually mean when we deploy 'north' in this way? I'm guessing from a commercial marketing perspective it's supposed to be synonymous with friendliness. You consume here and you'll have a positive experience because we're northern – we'll talk to you. I'm not trying to be cynical – the whole frontage of SR6 has been improved enormously in the time I've lived in the postcode, with a range of new eateries and hotels doubtlessly adding to the tourist experience – but to boldly use that framing, north, is at once intriguing and a bit enigmatic to me.

I have to come off the beach just before Roker Cliff Park, passing the old south pier lighthouse, which was moved here in 1983 to allow for harbour improvements. I take a bench and absorb the views back along the coast. The school at Whitburn is where I did my GCSEs. In drafty Victorian quadrangles and in modular buildings intended to be used for a few years but in service for decades, this is where I first remember reading poetry. The title of the anthology we were issued, *Best Words*, stems from Coleridge's dictum that poetry is 'the best words in the best order'; the volume contained little by living poets, and nothing from the North East of England, but

The Ash Path

it did ignite a spark of beguilement for the love of language. While I imagined the pastoral elegies of John Clare's fenlands playing out on Cleadon Hills, or envisaged Tennyson's eagle circling Marsden Rock, it wasn't until much later in my poetic apprenticeship that I was introduced to poets who had actually come from these places – who had walked these same shores and deemed it fair game to write about them. So, after an hour butchering 'La Belle Dame Sans Merci', we were sent on a cross-country run: a three-mile round excursion along the clifftops, past the rifle range and back in the ball-binding Whitburn wind. I may have overstated the jeopardy, but there was a ruggedness to my comprehensive school experience – where I'd eat cheese sandwiches looking at a flat iron sea or embarrassedly have to ask a marra to fasten my trouser buttons after PE because my fingers had gone numb with cold – that must have lent me some mettle, and with it imprinted a sense of seascape that an education in an inland school just wouldn't have provided.

Bede's Cross on Roker Battery is easy to bypass, but difficult to forget once its intricacy has been appreciated. Until 1904 and the erection of this cross, there was no memorial to Bede in the North East. Inscriptions on its west facade include extracts of Bede's *Life of St Cuthbert* and his *Ecclesiastical History*. Straining my neck, I start mouthing words to the wind:

TO THE HO
LY BISHOP
EADFRITH

> AND THE
> BRETHREN
> WHO SERVE
> CHRIST IN
> THE ISLAND
> OF LINDIS
> FARNE.

Eyes gan doon, neck starting to soothe. Oh, I'm back on Lindisfarne. Class.

> I HAVE NOT
> PRESVMED TO
> WRITE DOWN
> ANYTHING OF
> SVCH A MAN
> AS OVR FATHER
> CUTHBERT WITH
> OVT THE CLOSEST
> ENQVIRY INTO
> THE FACTS NOR
> TO PVBLISH WHAT
> I HAD WRITTEN
> WITHOVT THE
> MOST CAREFVL
> OF SVRE WITNESSES

Eyes up. Brethren seems a loaded word: one I, a broadly liberal person, wouldn't fashionably say I liked, but do. Witnesses, facts, care. Marras.

> TO THE MOST
> GLORIOVS KING
> CEOLVVLF
> BEADA SERVANT
> OF CHRIST

The Ash Path

AND PRIEST
AT YOVR REQVEST
O KING I GLADLY
SENT SOMETIME
AGO MY DRAFT
OF THE CHVRCH
HISTORY OF THE
ENGLISH RACE
THAT YOV MIGHT
READ AND APPROVE
IT. I NOW SEND
IT TO YOV AGAIN
TO BE COPIED
OVT THAT YOV
MAY STUDY IT
MORE FVLLY AT
YOVR LEISVRE.

On the eastern side, we see depictions of key moments from his biography: Baeda comes to Jarrow; Baeda writing the *History*; Baeda's last moments. Around each of these panels, an intricate meshwork of Northumbrian latticing, itself drawing on Celtic knotwork, binds the scenes together using interlocking patterns found in the porch of nearby St Peter's Church, which I'll see soon. It seems to represent a melange of serpents, birds and other critters. Its beauty, like many Anglo-Saxon stone carvings, comes simultaneously from its size and stature, but then from the fine detailing of its surfaces. Whenever I drive past here, I point it out to my kids – *Look, there's Bede's Cross!* – and it's come to represent to me the whole synergy of Bede's endeavour: diligently capturing reliable testimony, penning vast hagiographies and remaining steadfastly committed to the word of God while retaining an earthbound presence to his community – ministering to their needs and working for their advancement. Before the carbon arc was lit at Souter and before this cross testified to his life's works, a man called Bede made manifest his faith by writing it down – and then it was chiselled into this monument, sculpted, so the interpretation board tells me, by G. W. Milburn of York with a design by Clement Hodges. We live in an age sceptical of monuments, often with good reason, but I can't see this one having a noose roped around its mount any time soon and being pulled into the North Sea.

I decide to detour to St Andrew's Church in Roker, which has been called the Cathedral of the Arts and Crafts Movement. A volunteer shows me in. I try to avoid the carpet, which is an original William Morris, but she waves her hand, telling me carpets are meant to be walked on, before she pulls back the curtains on a panel behind the altar to reveal a fabulous tapestry by Edward Burne-Jones, *The Adoration of the Magi*. It's a stunning space, but closer inspection reveals the damage wrought by recent storms. The volunteer tells me about the costs to damp-proof the stonework: scaffolding alone is a four-figure sum. But with a dwindling congregation making fewer donations, the damage continues to accrue. Walls seep, paint flakes. The tapestry is covered up again and I'm led to the door, not before depositing a couple of quid in the slot in exchange for an addition to my postcard collection.

As I walk out of St Andrew's, I think about how different a space it is to the church I set off from yesterday morning. St Paul's in Jarrow, apart from its obviously being smaller, seemed a more austere place. Here, at St Andrew's, the ornamentation and decoration of the building add to its sense of purpose. St Andrew's opened in 1906, when Sunderland was still an industrial centre, and it's easy to imagine its well-to-do congregation drawn from the affluent suburb of Roker filling the pews and being inspired by William Morris's maxim: 'Have nothing in your house that you do not know to be useful, or believe to be beautiful'. It's a beautiful early afternoon as I segue through Roker Park, passing the miniature railway down the slope to where the bandstand is being repaired and a new café is being built. From here I cut through the Roker Dolomite – those cinder-toffee-coloured cliffs – back to sea level.

The promenade at Roker has been redeveloped in recent years, with a range of trendy bars and eateries established and new street furniture and sculptures installed. At Adventure Sunderland, you can take guided paddle-boarding lessons in the mouth of the Wear, or descend the tunnel to walk beneath Roker Lighthouse and emerge at the other end ready to gaze on a pod of dolphins. Finish it off with a third of Vaux craft beer. If this is all sounding a little saccharine, like tourist board text, then the city planners have probably done their job well. And it isn't just consumption of cakes, chips and coffees that dominates down here: the Coast to Coast cycle route concludes at Roker, as does the Walney to Wear cycleway. Both have reframed how the city approaches sport and culture. What might this mean for a nascent Camino of the North East? The Visit County Durham Northern Saints Trails initiative positions one these routes as the 'Way of Learning', which is difficult to refute, but I wonder if what it also now entails is a way of leisure. As groups of cyclists in felt-tip-pen jerseys wheel past me, their panniers loaded, their CamelBaks mounted, I think about the pilgrimages they've just been on, over from Cumbria, making a northern cross of their own.

Where the beach gives out, the riverside begins. Sunderland Marina, redeveloped in 1994, was described at the time by round-the-world sailor Chay Blyth CBE as 'not a yuppy marina, it is a proper harbour for real sailors'.[2] A sign by the club house confirms this, reassuring prospective sailors that they needn't own boats to become members. Unlike other thirty-year-old developments, the associated new flats and apartments that were built on this site have stood the test of time and the place is still well kempt. A few blokes are fishing by the end of the pier as I pass. Even though I've never cast a rod in my life, it's somehow heartening to know that Bede and his emissaries would have done the same thing 1,300 years ago: turning to the water for their dinner.

All along the marina, with small vessels' rigging twanging in the breeze, I'm accompanied by brilliant public art, including a herring gull taking flight in five stages. The works, created by sculptor Colin Wilbourn and writer Chaz Brenchley, were developed with local people, and include a magnificent hammerhead crane, which would have been a common sight on Wearside a few decades back. There are also representations of illuminated Gospel books, reminding us of the area's debt to Bede. Thinking back to Amble, where the Bord Waalk sculpture trail was much more egregious, it seems that artworks here have been sympathetically designed and installed. Soon I'm nearing St Peter's itself, the University of Sunderland's riverside campus and home to the soon-to-be-defunct National Glass Centre. This is the most politically volatile part of this section of the route, where a centuries-old tradition is about to be eradicated from the banks of the River Wear.

When Benedict Biscop hired glassmakers from Gaul to create stained-glass windows for the new monastery at St Peter's, he couldn't have foreseen that, 1,300 years later, defunct architecture would be scuppering the industrial heritage of the craftsmanship his seat of learning instigated. Bede, writing on Benedict Biscop's founding of St Peter's, tells us that:

> When the building was nearing completion he sent his agents across to France to bring over glaziers – craftsmen as yet

unknown in Britain – to glaze the windows in the body of the church and in the chapels and clerestory. The glaziers came over as requested but they did not merely execute their commission: they helped the English to understand and to learn for themselves the art of glass-making, an art which was to prove invaluable in the making of lamps for the church and many other kinds of vessel.[3]

This is the type of networked north I see as making the region a connected community of artisans. From the threatened National Glass Centre I turn to the monastery, throwing my gaze back across the centuries. The monks are at morning prayer. It's winter in Wearmouth and Jarrow, and until recently this procession to mass had been a gloomy affair. Now, their newly created lamps swing by their sides, the hall lit with fluorescence as medieval confetti begins prisming through the new windows.

When the National Glass Centre opened in 1998, thanks to cash from the Tyne and Wear Development Corporation and National Lottery funding, it was seen as the jewel in the crown of Wearside's redevelopment. Now, because of corroding steel, roof leaks and broken glazing, the NGC, which since 2010 has been owned by the University of Sunderland, will be mothballed. Along with the closure of the site, the university's taught courses in glassmaking will be cut, ditto a range of talented glassblowers who can ply their trade only from its specialist facilities. Supporters of the #Save the National Glass Centre decry the University of Sunderland's decision to axe the site, which reminds me of this polemic by the bard of Blyth, Paul Summers:

> this north, this cold acknowledged land
> where rule is cheap & underhand
>
> where heritage is all the rage
> & all our rage now heritage.[4]

As a child of the 1990s, I think a lot about the period. Twelve miles away, in the same year the NGC was built, the *Angel of the North* was installed at the top of the Bowes Incline in a field overlooking Birtley. Tyneside's own icon of post-industrial spirit, designed by Antony Gormley, set the scene for the opening of three other riverside redevelopments: Gateshead's Millennium Bridge in 2001, the Baltic art gallery in 2002 and the Sage concert hall in 2004. As Pyrex casserole dishes and stout bottles were being commemorated on Wearside – indeed, as the skills of glass-making were being ushered into the new millennium – and as central Tyneside, under its new Blairite mission, was reframing itself as a place to see modern art or listen to the Northern Sinfonia, I was doing what all good teenagers do: plotting my exit. Now, when I come down to these places and think of the cultural vandalism taking place, I despair, wanting my Camino to be a rallying point for their preservation.

Approaching St Peter's Church from the east, the first thing a visitor sees is Bede's Bakehouse, the modern refectory appended to a structure which in part goes back to the seventh century. In what ways has Bede imprinted on to the physical and mental geography of this place? I keep a rolling tally of Bede-named things: Bede Metro station, Bede Motor Company, Bede Taxis, Bede Family Hub, Bede Industrial Estate, Bede Burn Road Social Club, Saint Bede's Chambers. There's a Bede's Well between Jarrow and Hebburn, where supposedly monks from St Paul's were sent to collect holy water and dowse the sick and infirm. Right up until the industrial period, the ailing and afflicted were cleansed in water from Saint Bede's Well. The area was gradually reclaimed as dockyards and factories withered. There's a pin on Google Maps: a picture of a muddy circle framed by an ungainly block of paving slabs and ubiquitous cans of lager. When we look to the landscaped areas of post-industrial Tyneside – nearby Hebburn Riverside Park being a pristine example – scarred land which once had manufacturing effluence coursing through its veins is now returning to clusters of forest and manicured parkland. Has it, in some roundabout way, been cured by the imprint of Bede?

I cursorily push on the door to St Peter's, the heavy sneck satisfactorily catching as I shut out the natural light. I'm welcomed by an elderly volunteer, but first I want to deposit my Whitburn beach pebble at the nave. Setting the stone down then diverting into the Bakehouse for a can of pop, I join the volunteers. They're waiting for a coach-load of kids, the chief volunteer distractedly looking to the door. The party are already ten minutes late. I give the trio of helpers the lowdown on why I'm here, enjoying a few minutes of genial conversation about the recently refurbished RNLI watch house along the promenade before the entourage arrives. Thirty-odd primary school kids and their teachers are dutifully shown around the building. I hear snippets of call and response.

'Does anybody know who Bede was?'

'He did that history and stuff didn't he, sir?'

Left to their sheet of activities, pursuing their own course through the church, the bairns make a treasure-hunt of the site. It's getting on to half two so they have only another twenty minutes. Half an hour doesn't seem enough time to take in the significance of this space, but then I feel intimidated by it all, too. Once the kids have filed out back to their coach, I bid the volunteers farewell. Lingering in the west porch door, part of which does date back 1,300 years, I hover in the liminal space. A brine-tinged breeze blows up off the Wear, drawing me out, drawing me once more down to the river. I walk along the last course of the sculpture trail, to come up on the view of the Wearmouth Bridge, spanning the gorge like a bottlenose dolphin frozen in flight.

The River Wear was once the shipbuilding centre of the British Isles. But before the caulking, riveting and plating of boats and vessels which were sent off to service the merchant navy, other things were delivered from the Wear to the world. In the early eighth century, Abbot Ceolfrith, who was Bede's warden, took to a coracle. In it, he had a hefty gift, the Codex Amiatinus, one of three bibles produced at the Wearmouth-Jarrow scriptorium. This bible was intended as a gift for the Pope, to be sent to St Peter's shrine in Rome. Ceolfrith, who had taken stewardship of the Wearmouth monastery after his predecessor, Benedict Biscop, had died, had dramatically increased the volume of the library. This enormous tome, the oldest surviving Latin Vulgate bible in the world, had quite the journey. Having decided to make a final pilgrimage to Rome, its carrier got as far as Gaul on horseback before becoming increasingly ill. Ceolfrith died in Langres in north-eastern France on 29 September 716. A party of monks travelling with him took up the baton, and the Codex Amiatinus was chaperoned over the Alps to arrive safely with the Pope. It is now kept in the Medicea Laurenziana Library in Florence and considered one of the world's most important manuscripts.

When I tell people about Bede and about this part of the world – about the little churches nestled between two great northern rivers, where works of towering intellect and artistic majesty fomented, and where the disparate strands of what we now understand as the English race began to be woven into a discernible thread – I worry that I'm overegging it. But walking the short route between the monasteries these past couple of days, reacquainting myself with the craftsmanship and civilisation which came from this crucible, I begin to have the opposite feeling: maybe I've undersold it. For anyone who's come from this place, it should be a great source of pride to understand that this was once a prodigious centre of cultural production. As a writer, knowing that I stem from the same place as people like Biscop, Ceolfrith and Bede – that I've trod the same hills, walked the same riverbanks, listened to the chattering of the same birds – I feel enormously humbled. The writer's vocation is often a solitary one. When I look out over the Tyne or stand by its smaller tributary, the Don, imagining the scribes working by candlelight in drafty monasteries, I can hear the call of kinship at my side. Put these words in a coracle, sail them over the waves. Whatever's on the other side of that great frequency, however far or near these sentences sail, I'll always appreciate the long trail of ink from Bede's quill.

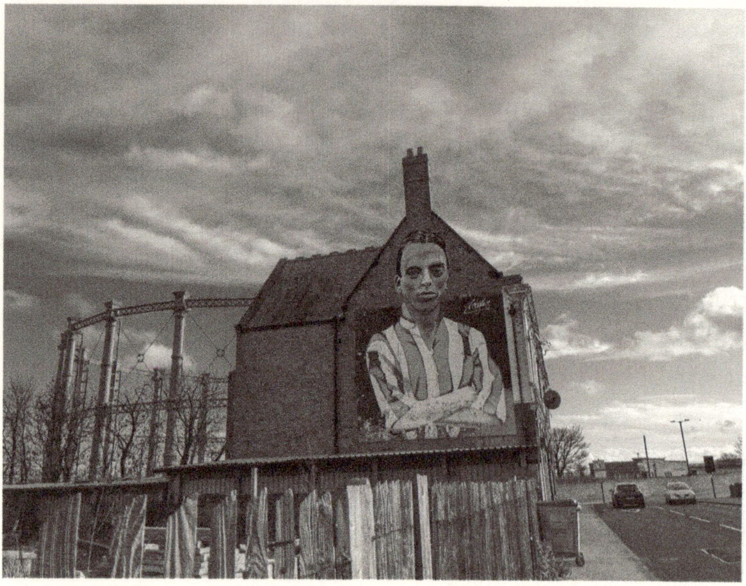

Chapter 8

Ghosts of the East End

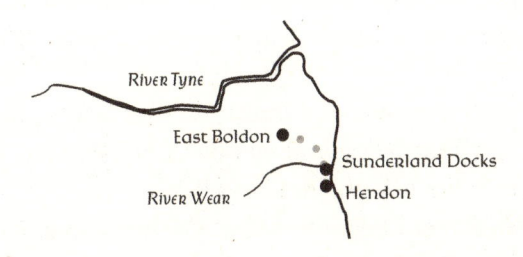

I board a packed Metro train at East Boldon. Delayed morning workers heading from Tyneside towards Sunderland begin to spill out with me at St Peter's, along with a crowd of students heading down the bank to the university campus. This is the first time my Camino has felt like a commute; I quietly revel in the fact that I'm not heading to a seminar room or an office, but to explore the industrial and religious vestiges of the deep city. I cross the five lanes of traffic at the north end of the Wearmouth Bridge and take a brief detour down to a pre-fab wooden wall with plastic fascias advertising a route to the monastery. Some bright spark has dubbed the word 'LAME' in scrawny black spray-paint over the interpretation boards telling of Wearmouth-Jarrow's candidacy as a UNESCO World Heritage Site. In the middle of the bridge, I stop to admire the city's crest and coat of arms set in wrought iron, with the motto *Nil Desperandum Auspice Deo*, roughly translating as: have no fear in the face of God.

On the south side I make my way down Pann's Bank, stopping by a defunct Tyne and Wear Development Corporation sign which advises pedestrians to take care on the rickety steps to the quay. The prospect isn't a particularly inviting one – the steps do look truly treacherous – but I pause to take in more graffiti partially obscuring a board telling us this is WHERE SHIPS WERE BORN. Both the medieval and maritime pasts of Sunderland seem to be loathed by its local vandals. I've got an hour until meeting my sherpa for the day, Andy Martin, so I make a detour into Pop Recs for a flat white. The venue, now into its third space, has become a hub for alternative music and culture in the city: earlier in the summer I saw Futureheads singer Barry Hyde here, showcasing songs from his *Miners' Ballads* LP.

Along Villiers Street I begin to notice the remnants of older religious infrastructure: the Baptist Chapel converted into the Redeemed Christian Church of God, the Bethesda Free Chapel, the Sunderland Catholic Club opposite. Many of the buildings here are in a poor state of repair. Material deprivation seems deeply interwoven into Sunderland's ambiance, and it's hard to shake the feeling, looking at boarded up foundries and buildings with windows and tiles missing, that we're firmly *post* the post-industrial. Outside the Pearlman Building I ring for Andy. The space is shared with a music studio and a fight club. Andy arrives and gives me a whistle-stop tour of the building, whose idiosyncrasies include *mezuzahs*, small scroll-holdings on the door frames – casings in which Hebrew verses from the Torah could be stored. The Pearlmans were a Jewish family and Andy reckons there's still a bunch of items in the attic from when this building served simultaneously as a chandlery and as a religious meeting point.

We walk back down Villiers Street, stopping to note the Beyoncé poster which has recently appeared on the corner of Peter Smith's old antiques store, a building which, Andy tells me, will soon be converted into luxury flats. Even before he's really started on his story, I interrupt him, telling him I know what's coming next. It's a pattern I've observed in other parts of the region as I've walked down this coast: the managed decline of older buildings, which are spruced up with parachuted-in arts schemes to raise the profile, desirability and price of the area.

Andy tells me about the group of 'street artists' responsible, a Brighton-based collective commissioned by Sunderland City Council as part of its 'Future Walls' initiative. It's a scheme which has rankled Sunderland's tight-knit arts community, who see it as a top-down way of bringing a flawed perception of what culture is in from outside of the area. The thinking, I suppose, is that pasting up images of mega-stars who have recently played huge concerts at the Stadium of Light – Tina Turner and Elton John have also been spotted plastered on to old walls – indicates that Sunderland can attract top talent; and that by applying a street-art sheen to dilapidated buildings, the sense of coolness will increase, and with it the desire for property building.

As Andy says, though, 'There has to be a better way of doing it. I'll show you one.' Fifty yards or so along the street, opposite Biscop House (he of the monastery on the north bank), is a building which, frankly, appears to be on its last legs. We cross to inspect the street-level wall. From a way away it just looks like a painted-over block hiding old graffiti, but Andy traces out a few letters. Beneath a vent, a Q and a U. This is the famous SIR NIAL QUINN wall. Talking about official versus vernacular narratives, this specimen seems to epitomise the other way: folk art which truly does belong to the street. In 2006, seven Irish businessmen, led by Niall Quinn – Sunderland's revered striker who netted 61 goals in over 203 appearances for the club between 1996 and 2002 – set up the Drumaville Consortium to take over Sunderland Football Club. The mysterious graffiti, which appeared overnight and contains a misspelling of Quinn's forename (Nial, not Niall, with the 'Sir' double underlined to highlight the man's credence), has since been rubbed out, but Andy remembers its appearance and the fleeting sense of optimism it seemed to capture. Further along Villiers Street, we pause at the 1825 St George's Presbyterian Church. On a ghost sign above the door, we can still just about make out the words TECHNICAL SCHOOL. Now home to artists' spaces, this place is where Andy had his first studio – when one of the floors was used as a methadone clinic – and it used to host the Sunderland Black and Minority Ethnic Network and other non-profit organisations.

Further along Villiers Street, on an open strip of grassland between MOT service stations, is the site of an underground crypt. This, Andy tells me, was once the site of a Nonconformist Bethel chapel, later built over to make a Sunday school. Construction work in the late twentieth century uncovered the hidden vaults, in which the remains of over 400 cholera victims were discovered. As the Sunniside area of Sunderland was renovated, its history was briefly revealed. We leave the area and its macabre past behind.

'This is really the start of my patch', Andy says, 'the old haunts that I used to photograph'. Crossing the A1018 ring road onto High Street East, we're entering what's known as Old Sunderland, the east end of the city, cut off – literally sundered – from the monastery on the other side, the Bishop's Wearmouth. Opposite the former Garths flats – a social housing scheme demolished in the late 1990s – we admire the Eagle Building, which from the late seventeenth century had been a pub, and take in the Quayside Exchange, now a wedding and conference venue but, from 1814, the administrative hub for booming trade on the river.

As we plateau with the river, we reach one of Andy's favourite spots, with its wonderful view back west to the bridges, spanning the gorge where the magnesium limestone flanks the murky waters of the Wear. 'This is where I'd take my granddad after we'd done his shopping at Morrison's in Seaburn. He always asked to be driven back this way, down High Street East past the places he knew as a young man.' I ask what he did, assuming that he was a shipyard worker or in some way involved with heavy industry. 'He was a cabinet maker. People assume because of the kind of photos I take that he built ships or something.' I think back to the people I've met and how their forebears' lives have marked their own: Katherine's parents and grandparents up in Amble; Aaron's in North Shields. While Andy's outputs might be materially different to his grandfather's, they share a reverence born of close attention.

In his latter years, when his grandfather became really ill and infirm and could no longer leave the house, Andy would come down here to the fish quay and to the docks and port, and photograph the changing vistas. Taking these images back to his grandfather would set off a series of reminiscences. Andy captured this testimony in his grandfather's own hand, and has set his own images against his family's memories. With an industrial relic in tow, it's a mission I can fully empathise with. I put this to Andy: 'There's something in this whole thing of younger men like us, from the North East, tracing their fathers' or grandfathers' worlds, isn't there?' He agrees, but caveats that there's a real need to not sink into the trappings of nostalgia.

Making our way up Bull Lane, an eighteenth-century cut patched up with Usworth bricks and flanked by Sunderland's oldest pub, The Clarendon, Andy begins telling me of the 'bogeymen' who haunted this place in his youth – local 'enforcers' like Ernie Bewick, a violent man of the streets. Bewick, who was jailed for manslaughter in 1999, is remembered as 'everyone's uncle', a phony moniker that Andy came to see through only as an older man. This sort of vernacular memory lingers in many of Sunderland's eccentricities, perhaps no better summed up than in the iconic graffiti 'Pensher Woolys Eat Deer', a jibe by the townies of inner Sunderland aimed at their rural outliers to the west. These folk tales are often recirculated and argued over on the Ready To Go Forum: ostensibly an early 2000s message board for supporters of SAFC to discuss the (mis)fortunes of the club, the site has remained a kind of virtual town crier's office.

The port is coming into view now. We walk past one of Frank Styles's murals of Sunderland-built ships, approaching what was once Bartram's Shipyard. About fifteen years ago Andy started 'hanging around' the port, and soon became pally with the local guards, who, sensing that he was up to good, introduced him to a manager, who soon issued him with a port pass. For three years Andy had free rein, walking around the site and its outbuildings – often at night – capturing elements that the ordinary resident would never see. 'My intention was to show people what was here', he tells me, reminiscing over a map of the docks that the guards had added their own embellishments to, highlighting the areas where fishers would try to get in and hinting at the dim places where illicit dealings had happened or been rumoured to have happened, once upon a dark and stormy.

Noting that a person with a camera often gets carte blanche, Andy tells me about his wider perambulations of the city: his tour on foot around Wearside, entering spaces long-since vanished. He went into the Hahnemann Court flats in Southwick before they were demolished and an Aldi put in their place, and he captured the fibre-glass animals and stained water slides of the old Crowtree Leisure Centre before it was shut. Perhaps most atmospherically, he shot Cherry Knowle, a notorious psychiatric hospital that used to stand to the south of the city at Ryhope. Looking at a particularly haunting image of a wheelchair left in the grounds of the hospital, I'm reminded that, in the early 1990s, Cherry Knocker (as it was known in full Sunderland slang) was a byword for 'lunatic asylum': a place you might slip or slide into and never return from, if life got the better of you. 'I felt like I had to do this, to remember what Sunderland was like', Andy adds. 'We're our own worst critics.'

On from The Welcome Tavern – with its wonderful old Vaux signage – we make our way to the site of what Andy calls the 'Hall of Fame', now a vast brownfield site of crumbled bricks perpendicular to the mineral line. 'Fucking Hell. I cannit believe that. The last of it has gone. Literally in the past few months.' In Andy's telling, this was Wearside graffiti makers' playground: a place where the real guerilla artists of Sunderland tried out new markings and luminous burners – a waving mural of illuminated tags harking back to the intricate Gospel decorators who came before them. Through the gaps in a steel fence by the pub, I look down on a rusty old yellow swing bridge. The Gladstone Bridge, Andy tells me. Somehow it seems apt that all of this is now out of bounds behind a geet big fence. We push on to the Town Moor, originally eighty acres given to the freemen of Wearmouth by Hugh de Puisit, Bishop of Durham, in his 1154 charter. In the seventeenth and eighteenth centuries, bull-baiting, horseracing and boxing used to take place here, and rabbits were once skinned for local hat makers. Andy recalls a place with a 'bad rep', where, as a teenager walking back to Grangetown at dusk, he feared 'being jumped'.

The remnants of last weekend's bonfire celebrations still mark the grass, which is littered with exploded pumpkin flesh and various remains of consumer shite. Our way now is a largely open expanse of grassland surrounded by late twentieth-century social housing stock. Several blue plaques record buildings long gone – local coal-fitter John Thornhill's Chapel, built to ease overcrowding at the parish church, demolished in 1972; and Sunderland's Town Moor Railway Station, built as a passenger station in 1836 and later serving the South Dock coal staithes in 1859. Lyrics from local punk band Leatherface come to mind – 'leaving only the water, we still have old wives' tales'[1] – as I imagine all of the ghosts of these soot-covered worshippers coming to mingle at the town moor and pray in their chapels, before buying half a pound of flesh and retreating to their slums by the putrid river.

Coming off the moor, we turn down Church Way, to the back of Trafalgar Square and the Aged Merchant Seamen's Homes. These alms houses, built in 1840, honour the seventy-six sailors from Old Sunderland present at the Battle of Trafalgar in 1805. Along the chare, flanked by silver birch trees adjacent to the old workhouse, we come upon the Donnison School. Set up in 1798 following instructions left in the will of Elizabeth Donnison, wife of the local churchwarden, the school offered free education to thirty-six poor girls. It's not far from the Sunderland Boys' Orphanage, opened in 1861. Tragic tales from Georgian and Victorian Sunderland often involved local 'needy' children, and the work of philanthropists to provide for them is still carefully preserved in this quaint part of the city, whose star, the newly refurbished 1719 Holy Trinity Church, we're about to come upon.

Ghosts of the East End

'I believe in the communion of saints'

Message on a plaque in Holy Trinity Church, in dedication to Thomas Randell (1848–1915), Rector of Sunderland (1892–1910)

We walk into a space which is bright, spacious, clean. Chamber music is being played. The tea is cheap. They have oat milk. Built in 1719 by Sunderland's booming merchant class to service the needs of the rapidly growing populace of the East End, the Holy Trinity building served initially as Sunderland's first magistrates' court and town hall. The town's first library was also situated here. Following a drawn-out power shift which gradually saw Sunderland's sphere of influence move from the east during the late-eighteenth century to a more westerly centre during the nineteenth century, the church fell into disrepair and disuse. With congregation numbers dwindling in the latter part of the twentieth century, and with slum housing being cleared to once again open up Old Sunderland, Holy Trinity closed its doors in 1988, when the Churches Conservation Trust took stewardship of the site. Now, lovingly restored since 2021, it stands as a venue for heritage, arts and culture. Its dilapidated organ, underused and damaged by water ingress, was saved and gifted to the Basillica of Christ the King in Paola, Malta, in February 2021.

While the organ was reborn on an island in the Mediterranean Sea, one of the choirboys, who would have been familiar with its dulcet tones, found a new life even further away, in Rhode Island. The then nineteen-year-old William Elliot set off from the North East in 1903, to enlist in the US Navy, where he went on to have a forty-two-year career, fighting in both World Wars. Elliot, who described himself as 'the leading boy of this choir', had been left parentless and spent six years in Sunderland Orphanage Asylum. A year before leaving the orphanage in 1898, he stashed a heartfelt plea to be kept 'in remembrance of me'. His handwritten note on the back of a service booklet was found down the back of a pew by Master Craftsman Stevie Hardy in 2020, when the church was being restored.[2] In that first year of the pandemic, when much of the world fell out of its normal cadence, the phantasmal past of part of Sunderland's East End began to rise. The careful work of preservation that must go on lest these community's architectural assets fall into oblivion often uncovers immaterial legacies. I trace my hands along the whitewashed walls, wondering what it is I might be seeking communion with.

On a plaque by the vestry, there's a memorial to another of those Sunderland 'names', Jack Crawford, a man whose legacy was at first very much a material one, but whose deeds have become common parlance: *nail your colours to the mast*. Born in Sunderland's East End and likely press-ganged into Royal Navy service, he fought against Revolutionary France. At the 1797 Battle of Camperdown, while he was serving on the HMS *Venerable* under Admiral Duncan, the ship's colours were shot down by the Dutch fleet. With the lowering of a ship's colours normally signalling defeat, Jack Crawford, despite being shot at, climbed the mast to nail the flag back on. Hailed as a local hero at the time and inspiring poets and painters, Crawford sadly returned to the destitution of early nineteenth-century Sunderland, where he died as one of the first victims of the town's cholera outbreak.

We step out of the church, where in the adjacent grounds we can see the Crawford memorial. It strikes me that this part of Sunderland, saturated in the old, is paradoxically actually rediscovering a sense of purpose. The missionary work of the early Northumbrian Christian saints lives on here, in these spaces where the maritime and industrial pasts of the city are in part being erased and in part being salvaged. As we round the Sunderland Boys' Orphanage, a wonderful example of late-Victorian architecture, I muse on how that stratified society – at once producing some of the country's finest glass while pumping toxic waste into the river – relied on the need for altruists working broadly in the spirit of Christian values to shore up those less fortunate. While it's a stretch to say that Andy is an apostle working in the same tradition, I do think in some senses that he's a revivalist, somebody who, with his 1960s Hasselblad medium-format camera, has felt compelled to document that which otherwise will forever be lost to the slipway.

While Andy is still not sure of the exact boundaries of Hendon and the East End, we begin to enter a light-industrial area, which feels completely different. I know this place a little. Here, between scrapyards and part-worn tyre centres, at the back of the old tripe factory, where, I'm told, a young woman once died falling into a vat of the boiling stomach lining of farm animals, I used to drop car parts off to the mechanics of Hendon. Arriving at MOT service stations and back-lane garages where overweight men and their underweight sons would be hammering the brake discs off Citroën Berlingos, I'd park up and timidly drop off the spark plugs or cam-belts or drive shafts they'd ordered. With 1990s and 2000s SoCal punk bands loaded into the CD deck and a flask of coffee in a holder by the handbrake, I'd drive a Fiat Fiorino round SR2 in the only appropriate manner: like a prick.

Until today I didn't realise that Andy and I shared this early employment. While I was making deliveries for my dad's car parts business in South Shields, Andy was based at a similar firm in Sunderland. We reminisce about the back alleys where mixed martial arts rings would be set up and, in one particularly bizarre instance I recall from a delivery to Pelaw in nearby Gateshead, a cockfight was in full swing, a pair of squawking roosters screaming at each other while men waved tenners in the back of an oil-stained warehouse.

Down the back lanes we gan, where fly-tipped domestic waste is more common a sight than trees, and where the tops of paprika-coloured brick walls resemble heart monitor graphs, their peaks counted out in broken beer bottles. I don't know if this is a particularly North East deterrent, but it is one I associate with all the back lanes of my youth: where enterprising homeowners fed up with being burgled had hauled all their Double Maxim or Brown Ale bottles into a haversack, stamped on them, then spread a glistening layer of cement on top of their wall before inserting the shards into it to set, issuing a mighty *fuck off* to the local thieves. We pass an obligatory burger van and a number of now sealed-off entrance arches beneath the railway, where Andy's grandfather would have been able to easily pass to the beach, and where, even ten years ago, there was less of a barricade between the city and its southerly strand.

As previously explored on the other side of the Wear, Sunderland's twin resorts of Roker and Seaburn tend to exclude the fact of one of its other beaches at Hendon. This is understandable. To reach it we pass down a narrow lane with a blind corner at its end. There is no discernible footpath. However, once out and in front of it, it's the most unassuming beach I've encountered – and I've walked many miles of them. The beach connecting Cambois and North Blyth may have felt left behind by its proximity to the Northumbrian star coastal attractions to its immediate north, but Hendon

Beach just feels left alone. A few hardy souls are fishing and one or two people are out walking their dogs, but it is, undeniably, bleak and unwelcoming. That said, it isn't dislikeable. In fact, its very ordinariness – the fact that it patently isn't going for the kiss-me-quick thing, that it just exists as the factual collision point of the land and the sea – is actually quite refreshing.

We mount the steps to the headland, pass a discarded dildo box and look out over where we've just come. Andy points out the concrete groyne, originally wooden posts erected to prevent longshore sand drifts. This one has been damaged in recent storms and is leaning, ready to fall into the sea. Like the Bartram's Shipyard, which, unusually, launched vessels straight into the North Sea, soon this coastal defence will go into the history books.

Before we make a one-eighty to head back to his studio, Andy tells me about a lady called Winnie Davies, Queen of the East End Carnival, when jazz bands and floats would fill the streets with laughter and colour. He also remembers quieter moments, as told to him by his grandfather, of groups of men playing 'walley', a coin-based gamblers' game, and accordion players who would offer a quiet serenade from the clifftops to the unending waves below. It's a romantic contrast to the reams of cranes down at the docks and the gasworks, factories and chemical plants that kept industrial Sunderland pummelling along. Now some of their latter-day traces are preserved in Andy's photographs, themselves testament to Sunderland's period of flux.

We set off walking through a dog excrement-covered track of broken-down walls and waste paper, as I optimistically try to gauge where the city is going. Setting aside the material deprivation in this part of the city, I focus on the bright lights blinking on to its horizon: the Crown Works film studios currently being developed along the river at Pallion the brightest star in the city's growing cultural firmament, which also includes the Music City initiative. I ask Andy his thoughts on its future. 'I don't know. Sunderland's a more ethnically diverse place now, and that can only be a good thing. There's a tension with some of the things the council are doing with those arts initiatives.' Not for the first time he proclaims: 'There has to be a better way of doing things'.

We come out of the thicket of weeds and concrete at the side of the gasometer, the last one in Hendon, which Andy scaled a few years ago to get some shots. By The Blue House pub, with its standout Raich Carter mural announcing this as the site of Sunderland's original footballing home, we cross into Hendon's circuit-board of housing, cut up Corporation Road, then hook a left and pass the brilliantly named Canon Cockin Street to Villette Road, where we stop at the Swiss-Italian bakery Müller's. From here we wind through the terraced streets back north, where everything is routine and familiar, where the buildings all look the same and seem to be homogenous in their history. That is, until Andy begins pointing out curiosities, like the 'Approved Coal Merchant' sign still clinging on to a skip-hire site on the corner of Salisbury Street. We pass behind the Sunderland Bangladesh International Centre, Andy explaining how the area's demographic is changing to accommodate new faiths, foods and, importantly, feelings about itself.

As we walk below the massive tower blocks dominating the skyline, I think that this may be one new way through the old north: an embracing of migration in our multifaith society and all the vibrancy it can bring. Where the former Christian centre of the East End has been repurposed as a heritage space, Bangladeshi families are now using the city centre's more modern church buildings to come out in force on Sundays. It seems to me that, as custodians making use of these spaces, the Bangladeshi worshippers are really enlarging the religious project set down here in the early medieval period.

Back at Andy's studio, the kettle goes on and we chat before he begins to set things up for my shoot. He's doing me tintype headshots using the wet collodion method. I'm interested in how he got into photography in the first place. We start with where he grew up, 'Betwixt and between Barnes and Millfield', where he attended a 'small, idyllic school full of eccentrics which encouraged children's passions'. Later, after moving to Grangetown for secondary school, 'which I hated', he went on to study photography at college. This before an ill-judged decision, soon abandoned, to take it as a degree subject.

Andy began to develop his passion, realising that his main subject could be right on his doorstep. From there it developed into a bit of an obsession, and he would make multiple late-night trips into the parts of town nobody had thought to document, often returning many times to photograph the same scene in a different season or under alternative atmospheric conditions. He became a gatherer of 'second-hand pasts', and while that comes with a degree of freedom, it comes with the responsibility of knowing you're curating that past in a certain way.

Turning things around, Andy wants to know more about my lamp. I retrieve Nick from the bag and set him down next to his camera – the one that all of his original 'This Is Sunderland' photos were taken on – and which was the reason I got to know him in the first place. On a 'This Isn't Sunderland' part of that website which documented the project from its origins in 2007, I came across a moody shot of the Herd Groyne Lighthouse in South Shields. The picture was used as the cover image for my first pamphlet of poems, *Definitions of Distance*, which came out in 2012.

Andy inspects Nick and notes the Pyrex stamp on the glass. Pyrex was the first glassware to be marketed to housewives in the early twentieth century and was renowned for being high quality and durable. Manufactured by Jobling's Wear glassworks from 1922, the glass in my lamp will have almost certainly been made there.

As I have often done on these walks and in my encounters with people along the way, I begin to waffle. The thing about waffle is, it's great conversational holding material – a way of getting thoughts out raw and aloud – but trying to set it down in print somehow blunts its lustre. What am I doing with this thing? Maybe it's something to do with making links in the dark: finding my allies, the people who are the new pioneers and innovators. The people who won't settle for simply trying to resuscitate the embers; but those who have designs on starting new fires, sending out new flares, raising fresh palms to the walls of the caves.

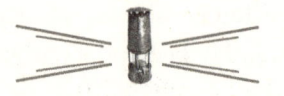

In the ruby glow of the darkroom I'm waiting for my face to develop. We've just done the first shot. Andy has had me pose on a wooden chair in front of a mounted De Vere Monorail camera ('Made in England', in case you were wondering) from the 1950s. But its lens, a Dallmeyer Petzval, designed by the Slovakian mathematician and physicist Jozef Maximilián Petzval, is from 1864. This is the same photographic method that captured young Americans returning from the horrors of the Civil War. The process, invented by Englishman Frederick Scott Archer in 1851, is a long one, harking back to the tactility of photography as a physical medium. The preparation stage involves coating a thin sheet of glass, or in this case aluminium, with a collodion solution before it's placed into a bath of silver nitrate. Once sensitised by the silver – it takes another five minutes of patience – the plate is then loaded into the camera and the exposure made. After the photo has been taken – we did a further five – it is developed in a ferrous sulphate-based mixture, then fixed, washed and varnished with gum sandarac.[3]

The example at the end of this chapter is my favourite of the results. If I look a little pretentious in that scarf, let me tell you that a professional photographer suggested I put it on! After the first image of me without it, wearing only a black shirt, made the light contrast too flat, those spotted tones drew out my better side. Several days later I went to collect the images, and drove back again round the East End turnpike up to Andy's studio. I was – am – amazed by the results, which are truly unique, haunting even. When I showed them to my grandparents, my nana said that it made me look like her dad – Nick – and a less personal quip was made by a colleague, who suggested that the image almost made me appear to step back into the atmospheric conditions she would associate with a mid-twentieth-century miner. I can say with honesty that that was not the conscious intention. However, it is accurate to say that Andy's wet collodion tintype portraits do have a startling effect: one is taken from the moment of exposure somehow into a realm permanently suspended *in memoria*.

As each photograph is being developed, Andy tells me about his journey through photography, going from purchasing his trusty Hasselblad on eBay to his experimentations in the world of wet collodion. Watching him at work – preparing the solutions, mounting the lighting rig, even noting the handwritten 'old reliable' note on one of his bottles of chemicals – it strikes me that here is another craftsman. Aye, he uses old tools, but he does so to reposition the here and now. And that also makes him an artist: giving us a slant angle on what might have been eluding our vision, despite it being right beneath our noses.

I leave the studio and make my way back through town. The middle of Sunderland, with its Victorian centre skewed to the west of its older origins, seems much brighter and bolder than the terrain I've just traversed. Opposite the Winter Gardens, I make for the new railway station façade, then plunge into the basement where the inevitably delayed Metro eventually turns up. Trundling over the railway bridge towards St Peter's where I alighted this morning, I have a fleeting glimpse of the River Wear beneath.

Gone is Benedict Biscop and his fat bible; gone is Bede and his big brain; gone are the shipyards and the boilermakers; gone, in many ways, are the Mackems. But there are still real makers here, makkin' things like photos. I think of all the tools and dyes and solutions and chemicals and presses and tongs and mallets and caulking guns and rivets and dry docks and countless other industrial appendages that I don't have the inventory for. And I think about people like Andy's grandfather, his ghost still floating around the docks, the way the camera is so adept at capturing the human spirit. In its blend of art and science, the photograph seems to me the perfect medium for a city like Sunderland, which has always been working out new ways to do things, while also being capable of sending itself up, not taking itself too seriously, knowing that ultimately whether it's the making of a ship, the writing of a song, or the exposure of a photograph, we do these things first and foremost for our fellow folk.

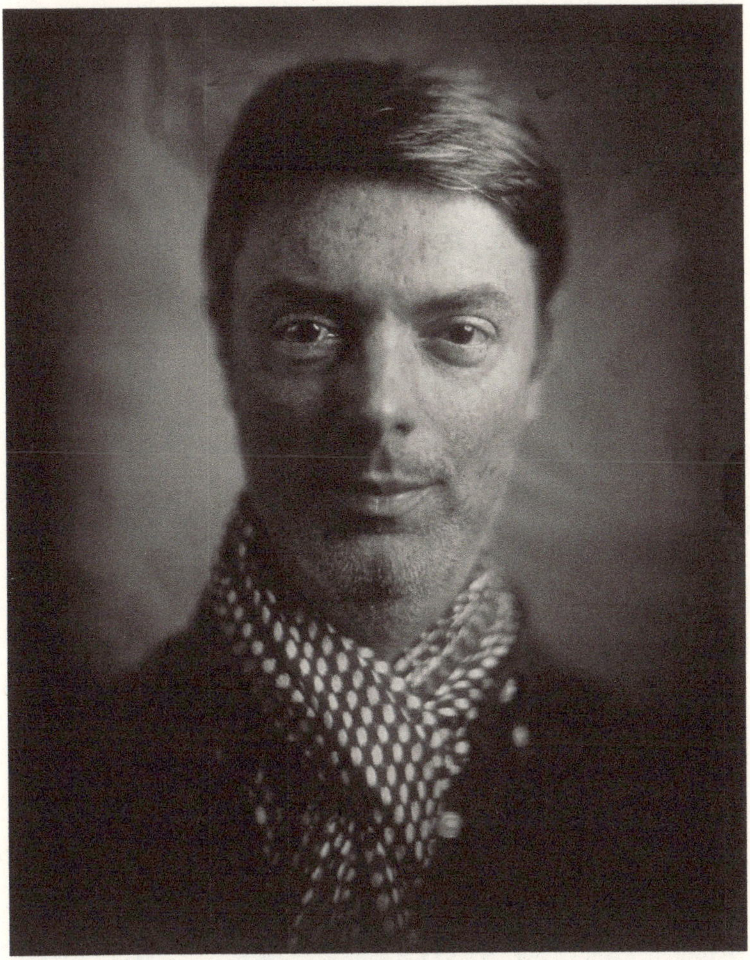

VAUX

THE
COPT HILL

Chapter 9

What kingdom without common feasting?

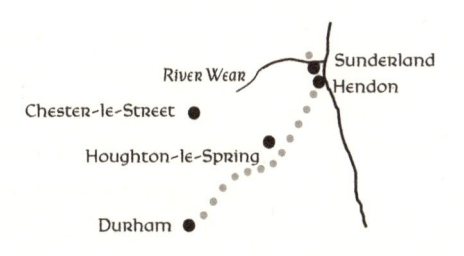

We're sat in a horseshoe on plastic garden furniture at the back of Easthope, a post-war semi in the southern suburbs of Sunderland. Foxgloves and lobelia are in bloom. The sun is well into the sky, this being the Saturday following the summer solstice. Two tables are set up: on one there's a selection of refreshments – McVitie's Family Circle biscuits, cartons of fruit juice, plastic beakers – and on another a stack of poetry books next to a framed photo of their author, Bill Martin. I set down Nick and my tropical juice. The author's son, Graham, is fiddling with a CD player, which looks every inch its age. Even though it's probably only from the early 2000s, its status as an artifact seems almost as certain as my lamp. There are a few minutes of frustrated stabbing at buttons and checking of cords before we finally make it to track 14. Graham hits 'play' on a recording of his dad reading 'Durham Beatitude', the poem paying tribute to the 1951 Easington Colliery disaster. We all sit in dignified silence – the odd wood pigeon the only sound – and from the stereo come the mellifluous tones of Bill with his soft Wearside lilt, his socialist rhetoric elevating the poem above mere pathos.

We've been gathering like this once a year to remember Bill and his poetry since 2016. Or, at least, I have. Older members of the party started doing so in the mid-1980s. The poet Peter Armstrong, bard of Blaydon, who has travelled today from Stocksfield in the Tyne Valley, remembers joining the second or third of these gatherings when they'd originally start by the banks of the Wear a few miles to the north, at the old (but still intact) railway line that took coal to the river. Barring 2019 (childbirth) and 2020 (a global pandemic) I've come back each time to walk this route – fifteen miles, more or less – to Durham Cathedral. It seems fitting that it will comprise the final leg of my Camino of the North East. My sixth time of doing it, I think back to the first. As we all know, the referendum on the UK's membership of the European Union in 2016 was a huge rupture. Just as the city we're now sat in is sundered by its river – one side within the monastic walls, the other cast out beyond its ecclesiastic boundary – 2016 was marked by division. But we're here today to celebrate coming-together, as Graham reminds us in his opening welcome speech, to remember what, as a society, we're starting to forget: the simple act of joining together in common purpose.

I make a short statement about my part in the walk – which will become clear as we go – explaining that it's significant that I carry my great-grandfather's lamp with me today. Pulling a pebble from my shorts pocket, I also mention the importance of laying a natural offering at Cuthbert's shrine, closing the distance between his coastal brethren at Lindisfarne and his sanctuary on the hill. It feels strange to have got this far, to be at once concluding the larger symbolic route I've been following from Holy Island while being so

What kingdom without common feasting?

familiar with its lattermost stage. What follows, then, is not simply an account of the walk in one year – 2023 – but something of an amalgam: a record of my half-dozen times of doing it, and how it connects to some of the broader cultural, social and spiritual notions I've been mulling along the way so far. We apply factor 30 and gather in the front garden for a photo at the beginning, taken by Graham's next-door neighbour, who proudly sports a t-shirt parodying the famous Marvel films logo: Mackem.

As we start walking towards Tunstall Hills, my North Walian compatriots Mike and Emma ask what the word means. I tell them about the city's shipbuilding history, that *we mak 'em, yay tak 'em*. The Wrexham couple – brought up on a linguistic smorgasbord of Cymraeg and Marches Scouse – laugh, saying it's a bit like their own weird words and phrases: you just get used to them. The Scots have a similar word, *makar*, for their national poet laureate. Kathleen Jamie, the incumbent appointed in 2021, has said of her role: 'I'm beginning to think that, in poetry reading and writing, people sense virtues which have become increasingly rare in public life. I mean truth, sincerity, and integrity, and the dignity of language.'[1]

In Bill's poetry, the craft of language – the very making of the poem – was chiselled and hewn from the carbon-rich earth on which his community depended. When I first started researching Bill's poetry in 2016, I was shown into his study in the attic conversion of Easthope. Hanging on a wall was a nineteenth-century pick, the tool used by his grandfather, whose own father, Ralph, the notes to *Tidings of Our Bairnsea* tell us, was:

> A shipwright and independent preacher
> When told by police
> That he might be 'locked up'

For preaching on Sunderland Town Hall steps
Said he would 'sing and praise God'
Till they were glad to let him out[2]

A sort of poem in its own right, Bill's 'About the author' in that collection also contains the following wonderful biographical sketches. Reading them now, it's not difficult to see why I gravitated towards his work.

Northumbrian
Born 1925 Silksworth Co. Durham

'My father and his father were miners
Their dust is in my spit'

Carried beneath banners
Still there

[...]

Came with those long dead
Down the wagonway[3]

On the colophon to that publication – Bill's first, which I remember picking up for 50p from a sell-off at the Lit & Phil in Newcastle – we're told that it was published for the Wearmouth 1300 Festival 'to celebrate the founding of ST. PETER'S CHURCH at WEARMOUTH in the year 674 and Bede's birth in 673'. The note goes on to add, and I find this absolutely poignant, 'Remembering also with affection the "shapers" who worked in the early Christian Communities of NORTHUMBRIA'.

Movers and shakers. Poets as shapers. We'll stop along this way a few times today to read from Bill's long poem 'Malkuth', his verse impression of walking this same way with his marra Gordon D. Brown, to whom, in latter years, the pilgrimage also became a kind of memorial service. Brown threw himself into the Wear in 2000, opposite the racecourse from where rhapsodic political speeches made each year at the Miners' Gala electrified the currents of the water with a potent concoction of grief and solidarity.

2022. My marra Liam, 'Smithy', joins us, up from London but back to his roots in Redhouse on the north side of the city. We walk from the trig point on Tunstall Hills over a rough field where Smithy remembers refereeing football matches as a fifteen-year-old but having to bow out because of increasingly barbed insults from the sidelines. Bill knew Tunstall Hills as the Maiden Paps, paps being a Mackem slang word for breasts. A pagan fertility symbol representing the figure of a goddess in the landscape, Bill saw this landscape as at once intimate and animated.

Smithy and I went to an all-boys sixth form down the hill, half a mile beyond Easthope in the leafy district of Ashbrooke, where teenagers still cracked on at 'paps' and 'chebs' (penises). In 2004, six years before Bill died, the only poetry I knew came from the lyrics to Futureheads and Arctic Monkeys songs. Barry Hyde and Alex Turner would blast out of a hi-fi set up on a workbench at the back of a grotty pre-fab, itself at the arse end of St Aidan's Catholic Academy, where I'd come a few hours a week to dabble in A-level art. Though I didn't actively think in such terms at the time, painting brought me out of myself and the stultifying place I felt hemmed into. While the lads wailed along to Alex Turner's South Yorkshire beat poetry, I clamped Bose headphones over my lugs and selected Bit-torrented mp3s of punk bands from Santa Monica and the California coast, dreaming of anywhere but the dreary North East shoreline, suffused in what one of its sons, Frankie Stubbs, decried as its 'dead industrial atmosphere'.[4]

We leave the vista of the city behind – morning sea glitter bouncing up from Hendon docks to the Stadium of Light, site of the last coalmine to close in the Durham coalfield – and I tip my hat to Cleadon Water Tower on the horizon. Further up the coast you can just make out the Simonside Hills, near to where this Camino started. We make our way down to Silksworth, passing the cottages the DAMHA put in for the residents of the mining village and where Bill recalls playing games like 'Jack shine the Magi' and 'Mountykitty', the streets lit by gaslight with no or very few cars about. It's an idyllic image, certainly, but Bill is sure to offset it with the brutal realities of eviction strikes: the 'peppered candymen' who came as paramilitaries, effectively, to turf out striking miners – including his grandfather Alexander, who was killed in an 1893 eviction. As the cost-of-living crisis bites in this hot summer and home repossessions begin to go up with rising mortgage costs, reading Bill's lines reminds us that the struggle for basic necessities of food and shelter have marked this part of the world for a long time.

Now here's something new. Kind of. A giant pit wheel behind the miners' cottages. Last year they were putting in the founds. Now, here it is, with a fresh lick of paint, moved from Albany a few miles away in Washington, back to the community it originally served between 1868 and 1971. It seems incongruous in so many ways that 'new' memorials to a decades-dead way of life keep springing up. How many times have I seen such pit wheels sandwiched into round-abouts on the approaches to small towns, on the jumpers of primary schools, on football club crests? What will the bairns twenty, thirty, one hundred years from now wish to erect in places like Silksworth, when they're running as local councillors and remembering the glory days of the 2010s and 2020s, I wonder.

Past the Silksworth sports complex – its dry ski slope built on the pit-heap of the former colliery – where Graham remembers from his primary school days the embers still glowing on the slag pile at the adjacent Ryhope Colliery, a miniature Mount Vesuvius – we push on to our first toilet break, a joke shared each year in the gents' toilets about the Soviet-era hand drier. My sister and I learned to ski here, at the Polar Bear Club, coming on a minibus from nearby Whitburn. That might mark out our typically middle-class leisure pursuits, but bear in mind that this is the only significant snow-sports facility either side of Leeds or Edinburgh and you have some sense of the local authority's thinking in what it would do to reincarnate the spoils of industry.

Crossing over to Gilley Law – six Antipodean-named residential towers looking decidedly Stalinist, in contrast to the housing surrounding them – we're on the Walney to Wear cycle route now, following the old gravity railway track on the Hetton colliery railway, a route which celebrated its two hundredth anniversary in 2022. Here, wagons would be hauled along the tracks using the gravity pull system. Bill would have known this place, as a bairn, when the network of wagonways was still in active use, and while his poems celebrate their peak, there is a sense now that his work was on an apex, and that the industry he chronicled was already on its way into the annals of history. I want to look beyond this, though, much documented and mythologised as it is.

Along past Doxford Park – designated an Enterprise Zone in 1990, the period after coal and ships – we're parallel to the A19 now, that main arterial road into and out of Sunderland, connecting prosperous York to south-east Northumberland. Crossing the bridge over four lanes of traffic at 70 mph (I'm frequently the motorist making that journey), it's hard not to think of Sunderland as a place marked by departure: the withering of its coal, glass and shipbuilding industries. At least our great football team, having been relegated to League One in 2018, is once again on the rise, having returned to the Championship. After these high-water marks, what comes next?

The writer Dougald Hine suggests that in order to facilitate a 'living culture', we should 'compost our traditions'.[5] In the time-worn image of the pit wheel, saturated in cliché and past the point of meaning for, I'd argue, half of this 277,000-strong populace, I see echoes of the scallop shell, the symbol of the Camino de Santiago, which shows the disparate starting points people come from to converge at the shrine of Saint James. In the pulley wheel, with its spokes fanning out from an axle at its centre, I see now the opposite movement: the way people shifted out from the former industrial hub in all different directions. Change is good: as a Millennial northerner, I accept that we've moved on, but the lines of flight in both images draw my eye back to a centre, and I think about how to repurpose the pit wheel as a mandala diagram, a search for wholeness in the absence of a clear vision of fullness. It certainly would have appealed to Bill, whose time spent as a radio technician with the RAF in Karachi during the Second World War brought him into close contact with the Eastern religious and spiritual traditions for whom the mandala is a kind of inward-bound soul-searching.

Mending the radios of British troops stationed high up in the mountains of what was then India, Bill would use periods of leave to make pilgrimages of his own. Travelling to holy sites like Mount Abu, he would encounter the saints of Guru

Shikhar. This, Bill tells us, is where he 'found Socialism',[6] a striking claim for a man brought up in the Great Northern Coalfield, as we would expect his leftward political leanings to have been fomented by that crucible. But no, encountering the three-headed god Dattatreya at a temple 1,700 metres above sea level, nearly 4,000 miles from home, Bill experienced an epiphany: here, he realised, he could fuse the teachings of his comrades from back home with the notion of spiritual oneness intoned by Hindu, Jain and Buddhist beliefs. Bill's thinking manifested in his neologism 'Marradharma', a poetic credo brought back with him to County Durham. He travelled, as Graham told us this morning, in the cargo hold of a Lancaster bomber, having contracted typhoid while in service. It would go on to charge all of the work he produced from the 1970s onwards, much of it first trodden on the same paths we're walking today.

After we cross the A19, the landscape changes quickly. We leave the city behind and enter a proto-countryside. Large, well-kept farmhouses and livery yards replace the terraces and semi-detacheds. There's a feeling of space. Thistles are everywhere. Sagging cow parsley with squashed cans of Monster Energy at their roots. We have an awkward half mile, traipsing along a connecting B-road, a few daft lads in BMWs speeding towards us recklessly, but before long we're crossing over the road and heading up the hill to Warden Law.

This was supposedly the last stopping place for Cuthbert's body before Durham. Having returned from Ripon, where they'd spent a few months to escape further Danish threats, his entourage headed north. A return to Chester-le-Street was planned, but these hummocky hills had other ideas. A wheel dislodged from the cart and his carriers were unable to proceed. I sympathise with their plight: it's not easy going, much less so when you're carting a bier of holy relics. Bishop

Aldhun, head of the followers, supposedly had a vision of Saint Cuthbert, who demanded to be moved to 'Dunholme'. Flummoxed, the followers were guided by a cow girl, who consulted another shepherdess looking for a lost dun (brown) cow. At this point, Cuthbert's miraculous powers restarted and the bier was able to move on towards Durham.

A more prosaic explanation for this miracle involves a wedding dowry. Aldhun, who had married into the family of Uchtred, Earl of Northumbria, came to be a strategic son-in-law for the Northumbrian nobility, who needed an excuse to build a safe stronghold towards the southern limit of their sphere of influence.[7] Bill succinctly describes the episode thus: 'Cuthbert's brief dream/And high resting place/Here before Durham'.[8] This is the Cuthbert I'm really fascinated by: not the incorruptible bodily relic, nor the Cuthbert of historical testimony, but the Cuthbert of the ether – the saintly essence existing by degrees in embellished and handed-down tales – the *legend-has-it Cuthbert*, performed and reanimated each time this pilgrimage takes its awkward dog-leg along a lonely limestone ridge.

Passing horse-riders nod pleasant hellos, but otherwise there are few people about. Other poets have been this way before. One of them, Linda France, wrote a sequence of poems in the 1990s commemorating the Hetton Lyons Sheds, where George Stephenson's Puffing Billy engine would have hauled the coals Bill's ancestors dug up. A few weeks after the walk, I emailed Linda, who remembered the Marratide pilgrimages, and she sent over a photo of a leaflet with her poem 'On the Line'. Produced as part of a larger public art project marking the Stephenson Trail, it makes me think about the role poets have in interpreting history. Wylam-born George Stephenson is more closely associated with the Stockton and Darlington Line, which is famously known as the world's first railway, but the Hetton Line is where he first made his mark, operating successful locomotives here to service the burgeoning coal industry from 1822. Linda's poem, with its 'red flag & three whistles',[9] recalls local people's memories of the coal-wagon way as it passed through the open streets of Hetton-le-Hole. Socially engaged arts practice like this – popular and greatly needed in the former coalfield areas of East Durham – frequently involves artists (often given the bureaucratic label 'practitioners') collaborating with local communities to authentically record an event or to commemorate a significant occurrence from the layperson's point of view. But what is it that makes the artist, in this case the poet, uniquely placed to validate these pasts? We put trust in them to do justice in ways that I don't think the 'official' record can.

When I started doing these Marratide walks in 2016 – and then, later, when I began thinking about the broader geography and cultures they encompassed as I formulated this Camino through the North East – I started thinking in terms of a poets' pilgrimage. Traversing the grounds of these places, it's worth thinking about how they've been overwritten by the elegiac impulse: how a poet's peregrinations might inscribe into these tracks and byways the kinds of folk memory that is first experienced bodily and then transmitted into the spoken and written word. I think back to meeting Katrina Porteous in Part I: her lyrical testimony of the Beadnell fisherfolk is cut from the same cloth – this idea that what the census data fails to capture, the lyric poem can reclaim.

Which makes me think about the problematic omission of coal-mining from my own secondary-school and sixth-form education. At school, nobody taught us about the coal industry, nor about George Stephenson's pioneering works of engineering, and we certainly didn't learn anything about the 1984–1985 miners' strike. Then again, attending a comprehensive school in South Tyneside from 1999 to 2004, when the Labour heir apparent David Miliband was our local MP, it seems clear why a Blairite vision of a North East secondary school curriculum would want to avoid our recent, embattled history. For me, poetry was my way into these subjects: something I began researching independently, but not until I was into my mid-twenties and I'd started reading references to them in the works of the North East poets I would go on to study at doctoral level. Writing in response to Shelley's 'A Defence of Poetry', in which Shelley made the famous claim that poets are the 'unacknowledged legislators of the world', Jonathan Davidson suggests that 'while there are "public rights of way" [involved in the dissemination of contemporary poetry], there are many routes barred and large tracts of poetry are removed from what might otherwise be common land'.[10]

While I was learning about Field Marshal Horatio Herbert Kitchener's efforts in the Boer War, or failing to understand quadratic equations, there existed in and around my local vicinity, sometimes less than ten miles from my home, poets who were busy documenting the industrial changes and fallout which had marked the previous centuries. As Nick's body spent its sixth decade decomposing in Harton Cemetery, his lamp left to blend into the backdrop of the workaday chorus of suburban life in South Shields, and as the last years of the New Labour government played out in parallel to my transitions from GCSE to A-level to undergraduate study, it never occurred to me that this most democratic of artforms could be turned to the advantage of the people in my immediate orbit.

On through Warden Law to eventually come out at The Copt Hill Inn on the outskirts of Houghton-le-Spring. Last year, the pub was boarded up and sealed off with a wire fence.

What kingdom without common feasting?

But entrepreneurial – and serendipitously named – Poetic Licence gin company in Roker has taken it on and spent a lot of money on turning it into a kind of bouji twenty-first-century coaching inn. The Sunderland AFC legend Bobby Kerr, who famously captained my club to its FA Cup win against Leeds United in 1973, was the licensee of The Copt from the late 1990s until the early 2000s, pulling pints and drawing in punters from across Wearside as a local sporting celebrity capable of building up an alternative pension. According to Marratide lore, The Copt is the first traditional stopping point. This has been captured by Peter Armstong's wonderful pictures from the mid-1990s, around the same time Kerr would have been pulling pints of Vaux's Sampson bitter and Scorpion lager. In one of the photos we see Bill Martin standing proudly beneath The Copt's elegant old sign, the hills of north Durham spread out behind him.

In 2021, when the pub appeared on its last legs but we were nevertheless able to buy something to drink and use their *netty*, this old sign had been taken down and left unceremoniously stored at the rear beer garden. I had it in mind last year to trespass and try to steal it, but common sense kicked in as I didn't fancy some Rottweiler being unleashed on me, nor did I really want to haul a geet big pub sign a further eight miles to Durham. But the image it depicts, painted by Gavin Mayhew, is a beguiling one – a piece of pub history now presumably lost to development. When I emailed Mayhew – whose sobriquet 'the pub sign painter' is accurate if banal, given he did over 1,000 of them – he tells me that he cannot recall the exact details of the one he did for The Copt, but that the figure walking down the path I'd identified was him. The artist's signature was to include himself in all of his designs.

With scran eaten and suncream reapplied, we cross the road to investigate the copse of trees from which the pub takes its name. Known as the Seven Sisters, they're a distinct landscape feature, sitting above what's thought to be a neolithic round barrow. In 2016, we scattered the third sprinkling of Bill's ashes here, reading lines from 'Malkuth' as kids down the hill supped cans of pop by their mountain bikes. Today we're all just as impressed by the copse, which, in contrast to the brand-new development of identikit houses below, seems positively ancient and mysterious. It's not difficult, and you hope it happens still, to imagine kids coming up here to hug the Treebeard trunks, or else to imagine an Alan Garner-inspired Mackem version of his Cheshire Blackden, the high sandstone crags of Alderley Edge being replaced by the Durham Magnesian outcrops and all the serpents they might contain. *Wisht, lads, had ya gobs, an all tell yuz aall an aafull story. Wisht, lads, had ya gobs an al tell yuz aboot the worm.*

From here it's down into Hetton Bogs, much more pleasant to walk through than to speak aloud. We see one of Bill's much-loved purple orchids amid verdant woods, which are a welcome relief from the twenty-odd-degree sun. Through the willow and sycamore, a kingdom of water voles and dragonflies, we tramp on, talking about all the things that have happened since last year's beating of the bounds. At the north-western exit/entrance point, a fence post contains a diamond-shaped marker for the Coalfield Way. It's very faded but on it a heron overlays a pit wheel. Nick Malyan, a bit of an authority on these matters, says he's never heard of such a way, which I take as reassurance for my own embryonic Camino: name it and they might come.

We're expelled from the trees at the back of East Rainton, where we join a long-running track through a bit of a hollow adjacent to fields into the County Durham fringes. A couple of miles further on, at High Moorsley, Nick points out 'the finest DMA cottages ever built', high up on a promontory overlooking the rural lands. Here a few of us divert off the track, through a clearing flanked by fragrant dog rose, so that we can get a closer look at a field of wild poppies which it would only be right to deem pulchritudinous.

Onwards to Pittington and another shut-down pub, The Blacksmith's Arms. In the lead-up to this, in 2019 (when I was otherwise engaged with a three-week-old), Graham stumbled coming down a stile, faceplanting into the verge. Later told he'd had a TIA (transient ischaemic attack, a ministroke), he soldiered on to Durham, where at Redhills the premiere of *The Big Meeting* was being screened. The film's director, Dan, is with us today, and he remembers a brilliant showing for his film, which in 2018 I had a small hand in, being filmed on top of Tunstall Hills and in the garden of Easthope talking about the significance of Bill's poetry. Graham went on to have another, larger stroke, and understandably needed to take some time out from the walks, but he's back on his feet now, carrying the flame his father lit.

Up the hill above here, Peter tells us, at St Laurence's Church in High Pittington, there are rare twelfth-century wall paintings showing scenes from the life of Saint Cuthbert. But it's a bloody big hill, and we're on the clock for Durham Cathedral, so we cross the road. Carrying on south-west, we enter a field of big cows at the back of Ramside Hall, and tread firmly so as not to alarm them. I think again of Doris Zinkeisen's *Durham, Pilgrims* railway poster, as the heifers eyeball us, Peter lightly swaying his stick as we walk on past yet another golf course to the abandoned railway bridge between Sherburn and Belmont.

Once the original part of the East Coast Mainline between Edinburgh and London, the old Leameside Line was the main source of mineral freight and coal exports from County

Durham; it closed to passenger traffic under the Beeching cuts of 1964. Nick, who grew up nearby, remembers rival gangs of kids from opposing schools in Belmont and Sherburn meeting by this abandoned bridge to lob bits of railway ballast at each other. A way further back up the line, Graham recalls walking with his dad at the height of the miners' strike and seeing colliers digging into the embankments for any coal spoil they might find to heat their homes. In a region like the North East, I suppose because of such politically heated tensions and their subsequent fallout, the line between humanistic solidarity and tribal aggression is often difficult to make out.

We reach an underpass taking us beneath the A1, and suddenly we're in a different world: the Dragonville industrial estate, with its ubiquitous out-of-town every-place monotony. At the end of Renny's Lane, which a quarter of a mile ago was a fertile byway but is now a pallid thoroughfare for cars filling up at Home & Bargains,[11] we contemplate a swift one at Gilesgate Moor Hotel. A few years ago, we had a canny pint of lager in here while some old boys played dominoes. Today we leave it be, putting the shopping frenzy behind to cut onto Bent House Lane, where we'll shortly get our first glimpse of the cathedral. When it comes, rising above a wheat field studded with cardinal poppies, it's glorious. The aspect we're seeing, less commonly viewed like this, from the east, shows off the Rose Window perfectly. It was Bill's preferred view of the cathedral, an opinion that's hard to argue with. We read again from Malkuth – 'So we are there [...] South-east edge of the city'[12] – remembering that, where a woman with her passing spaniel is now sniffing at the floor, some fibres of Bill's remains are forever on the mud.

With its proximity to the city proper, the walk down to Old Durham Gardens is where you begin to sense the university town. South-east accents on the passing youngsters,

What kingdom without common feasting?

well kempt in their Ralph Lauren rugby shirts, begin to mix with the vernacular. At Pelaw Wood a few years ago, when a landslip caused us to divert through the woods, I remember being told to 'just follee the track, marra', when asking how to get around the blockage. No folly today: we glide along the final riverside stretch, first coming out at the back of the Mediterranean-looking gardens, and then passing crumbling and weed-covered brick railway stanchions for what would have been the bridge over to Durham Elvet Station, where Bill and his dad would alight from a train to go to the Gala.

We press on round the Wear's sickle bend, passing a huge marquee set up by the rowing club with families and couples in summer suits and dresses quaffing Prosecco. Casual rowers and the university's teams glide along, as the number of pedestrians suddenly thickens when we hit the throng of Saturday afternoon drinkers. Up the steep bank behind Klute – regarded as Europe's worst nightclub and once staffed by Barnard Castle's biggest fan, Dominic Cummings – we take a hairpin left at the Magdalene steps. The cathedral is now plainly in sight, just a few more minutes away, but we realise we're out of time. It shut ten minutes ago.

We retreat to The Victoria Inn on Hallgarth Street to come up with a plan. Mike and Emma take the opportunity to drop their bags at the hotel and get a shower, while the rest of us order pints and packets of crisps. Evensong begins at five, so it's not impossible we could sneak in then. Chris and Gillian, along with Peter and Dan, myself and Nick and all the ghosts of Marratides past, raise a toast to Bill, and to other dearly departed comrades, including Gordon. Last year we were treated to an explanation of heraldry by the recently elected Stockton North MP Chris McDonald, and the pub itself has become the official ending point for the pilgrimage. But, even though we've done it in the past, today we haven't passed the sanctuary ring knocker and entered the cathedral. So it's time to down glasses. Mike and Emma are back, and joined by Nick, the four of us set off to pay our respects.

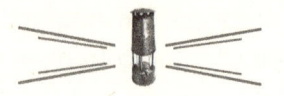

2017. The year we spread Bill's ashes. Our penultimate stop, the shrine of Saint Cuthbert, where, unbeknownst to the dean, specks of the Durham bard now fill the cracks in the tomb marked CUTHBERTUS. Graham, understandably physically tired by the fifteen-mile walk at this stage, is also emotionally drained. Taking to his honkers, and reaching to the ram's horn he's carried all this way, he dashes once over the flagstones, then crouches down, almost fully on his hands and knees, to use both palms, rubbing his father's ashes into the final resting place of his cherished saint.

Having followed Cuthbert's creed along the coast, I think back to how intense it was seeing him venerated in this way. I've spent so long reading about the disciples who ferried his bier down to Durham, and been absorbed in images of the ill and infirm brought back to health and vitality by coming into contact with his miraculous body. To see a flesh-and-blood person offering their father's remains to Cuthbert for eternal protection added a profound three-dimensional angle to the textual memorial by the shrine, which reads:

BORNE BY HIS
FAITHFUL FRIENDS
FROM HIS LOVED HOME
OF LINDISFARNE
HERE, AFTER LONG WANDERINGS,
RESTS THE BODY
OF ST. CUTHBERT

What kingdom without common feasting?

IN WHOSE HONOUR
WILLIAM OF ST. CARILEPH
BUILT THIS CATHEDRAL CHURCH
AND AT HIS SIDE LIES BURIED
THE HEAD OF
ST. OSWALD
KING OF NORTHUMBRIA
AND MARTYR, SLAIN IN BATTLE
BY THE HEATHEN
WHOM HE SO LONG DEFIED.

Exiting by the cloisters and wending down to Prebends Bridge, I find myself tasked with the final release. With my torso pressed hard into the stonework of the bridge, I lean as far as my arm will stretch into space, then tilt. The last of Bill soars to the waiting River Wear below, ready eventually to follow its tidal course passing his home city by the sea, leaving the harbour to glide back into infinity. In imagining the eternal return of the water cycle, I like to think that some miniscule particles of his, having been caught on the current and leaving Roker Pier, have since washed up on the shores of Lindisfarne.

I blink and six years pass in a heartbeat. In 2023, we make it into the cathedral at five past six, having sweet-talked the guard who had just locked up, by hamming up our credentials as pilgrims. We're granted five minutes, just enough time to lay pebbles and have a photo taken of me and Nick looking down the nave and showing the miner's lamp at the spiritual heart of the North East. It's true this isn't quite the ceremonious arrival we might have expected, but in a sense its modesty befits the occasion.

I've only once, in six years of doing this memorial walk, managed to get to Cuthbert's shrine. Between 1242 and 1280, the Chapel of Nine Altars was added to accommodate the growing number of pilgrims arriving to visit him. A line on the floor of the feretory shows the original extent of the Norman nave. In the intervening 700-odd years, interest in Cuthbert doesn't seem to have waned: on several occasions now we've been scuppered by tourists or the setting-up of choral evensong and had to lay our pebbles in the Galilee Chapel at the cathedral's west end instead. As a native South Tynesider, of course, it made sense for me to honour my brethren Bede.

Today we can't even do that. So, we make do with being in the space for five minutes of contemplation, which is actually perfect. It's been a long walk – sixteen miles today and many more racked up on the journey before it – so it's good to be able to just sit for a few minutes taking stock. I realise, of course, that I am biased, but this must be the best building in the world. It's certainly come to feel like the most important. I have carried one of my poetic heroes here and helped inscribe his ashes into its masonry. Today, I've spearheaded a small band of pilgrims a little way across a long road. It's a road that goes back at least 1,300 years, and who knows how far into the future. It might only be eighty miles, but this Camino of the North East, from the coast to the cathedral, has been my way of honouring this place I come from. I've often had doubts about calling myself an ambassador – feeling embarrassed to think that I could be a custodian for something nebulous like an English region – but in making these journeys this summer, I've come to heed the call of the Camino, all the voices of its past wayfarers somehow connecting us across the cavernous gulf of time and space. As Bill had it, 'it's a way of arms linking/a dance of life'.[13]

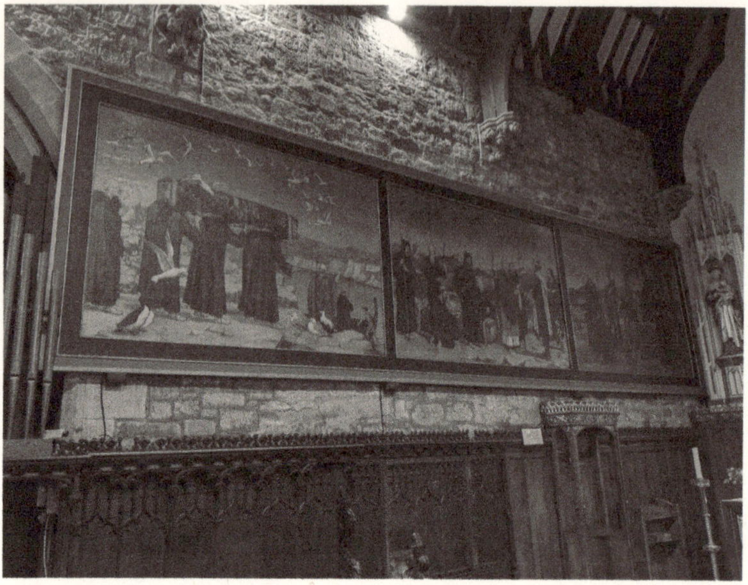

Chapter 10

Light moved on

> as the snow fell and the snow fell
> in Chester-le-Street that winter and the light moved on
> elsewhere.
>
> Andrew Waterhouse, 'Making the Book'[1]

A bleeper sounds, a whistle blows, the guard lowers his baton. My train leaves Newcastle Central Station's arches behind to sail over the great span of the Tyne. I'll be in Chester-le-Street in eight minutes. This small stop between Durham and Newcastle is often forgotten in the story of Northumbria. For over a century, it was a holding place for Cuthbert and his relics before they moved to their permanent home in Durham. In supporting the Viking kingdom of York to crown the Danish king Guthred, the monks of Chester-le-Street were granted the site of the ancient Roman fort and began to build a timber church. Bishop Eardulf's shrine to Cuthbert began attracting pilgrims, and the Saxon kings of Wessex, Athelstan and Edmund, are known to have visited, with gifts of gold and precious books. None of these books are left in the town, so I'm left wondering, in the wake of this cultural high-water mark, when territorial alignments were forged and kingly pacts were made in the presence of a miracle-worker's remains, what Cuthbertian sediment might be found. I alight from the train a bit disoriented. My reading on the journey by the late Andrew Waterhouse confirms my suspicions: this is a place overlooked.

Chunky cumulonimbus clouds part above platform two, allowing Waterhousian light to bathe the spire of St Mary's & St Cuthbert's, the place I'm heading. My soon-to-be-nationalised TransPennine train's doors hiss shut and it's off south. Moments later, as I'm reading a heritage interpretation panel by the station concourse, a northbound LNER hurtles past. Having sped up the coast, the train will soon be adjacent to Lindisfarne, its eastern-facing carriages giving passengers a moment's glimpse of the castle rising magically from the sea. From there, it will round the Firth of Forth, having covered half of the ancient kingdom of Northumbria in a little over an hour. It's a sharp contrast to the drawn-out journey I've made down here from Holy Island, and even more starkly set against the months of tramping it will have taken Cuthbert's entourage to travel here. The lonesome platform reminds me that few people now start or end their journeys here, but that doesn't mean the place is static.

Despite shuttling through many hundreds of times over the years, I'm pretty sure this is the first time I've set foot in Chester-le-Street. I've arranged to meet with Carl Kears, Senior Lecturer in Medieval Literature at King's College London, and someone very well acquainted with this town, having grown up in Chester-le-Street, after spending his very early life in Washington. Carl has long been researching the role of the early medieval past, and Old English, in contemporary culture and place, and in our correspondence over the previous year he has stressed how he has been increasingly drawn back here through his research. We begin to talk through the ways in which people experience Chester-le-Street in the present.

A thought for the day, one that Carl and I have been puzzling over since meeting last autumn and realising our shared roots and interests in the North East of England, centres on the history of craft in this region. Carl acknowledges that the Old English word 'cræft' is multivalent. He points me to the *Bosworth-Toller Anglo-Saxon Dictionary*, which tells us that the word can mean 'art', 'skill', 'trade' or 'work', as well as 'power', 'might' and 'strength'. What does it mean for a scholar of Old English and a contemporary poet, meeting in a provincial town in England's North East, to go in search of craft workers and craft works?

One such work that Carl pointed out to me, which I'd been intending to visit on foot for some time, is artist Ant Macari's Lindisfarne Gospels-inspired mural. The twenty-foot-high fresco, showing a black, cream and white ribbon of eddying patterns akin to the knotworks adorning the famous book, was painted along the length of Go North East's former bus depot on the A167 entry into the town. Commissioned in 2013 for the Gospels' visit to Durham, the fresco, which originally had beaming dots of red outlining the swirls, is now at risk due to the site being sold for development. I first saw Macari's impressive mural when I was driving around Chester-le-Street on my way to Pity Me. Readers hoping for a rock'n'roll conclusion to that particular anecdote may feel let down: I was going to a garden centre to buy some bedding plants for the flat I'd recently moved into. It's too far off the path for us to visit today, so I later set down the Google Street View icon along the verge to take in its full glory. The mural's shelf-life will be determined by the outcome of a property developer's will and, given its proximity to the Riverside cricket ground, where in 2013 spectators watched England's triumphant Ashes win over Australia, this is likely to be before too long. It's a reminder of Chester-le-Street as a space for remnants and temporary refuge: a place where things seem to be held for a while before being summoned elsewhere.

Macari's painting reminds me of another wall-mounted image, alluding to the Golden Age of Northumbria: Clayton and Gelson's 1963 mosaic mural on the side of the County Hall in Durham, showing scenes from the county's history, including a brilliantly pixelated Lambton Worm and Cuthbert looking like a character in a sixteen-bit video game. The site of County Hall at Aykley Heads was the former headquarters of Durham County Council, and at the time of writing in early 2024 was about to be decommissioned. As with Macari's mural, I turned to the internet for up-to-date photos, with several correspondents on X sharing images and expressing their fondness for the site. The archaeologist David Petts told me he believes it should be listed, while Sally Dixon, Assistant Director at Beamish Museum, shared images from around the building during her attendance at a D-Day celebration event at County Hall, including a wonderful piece by Julian Cooper, the *Durham County Council Centenary* painting of 1989. If these artworks – like the Vaux pub sign for The Copt Hill Inn discussed in the last chapter – do end up being destroyed, something more than their material legacy will be lost. Some vital testimony will also be gone with them: imaginative renderings which captured how a community felt about itself at one specific spot at one specific moment in history.

Back to the present, and the walk doon toon. Visitors to the town arriving by the East Coast Main Line are greeted by a cousin of craft when they first see McCarrick Homes' signage. 'WANTED:', shouts a board above the station's taxi turning-circle, 'BRICKLAYERS, JOINERS & LABOURERS'. Imagining a parallel universe in which the scriptorium at Saint Cuthbert's church had continued beyond the last millennium, I envisage a version of this sign:

WANTED:
BARDS,
BALLADEERS &
WORD-SMITHS
Tel. 0191 ...

Echoing the poet Peter Armstrong, whom I walked with in the last chapter and who hears 'the refrain of the dead//who rise to meet us in the outlying towns',[2] I've come seeking traces, searching for imprints. Coming from similarly outlying settlements – Carl from Barmston, then Chester-le-Street and now North London; myself from Cleadon and Whitburn via South Shields – we're interested in the road beneath the road. In his backpack, Carl carries a horseshoe once belonging to his granddad, its U-shape mirroring the Wear's contours around Chester Moor and Picktree. Carl reflects on all the places his granddad would take him around the North East when he shoed horses. It was a skill in demand 'because', Carl tells me, 'there weren't too many who could do it well, and probably none who would do it for free'.

We walk past Turkish barber shops and Methodist chapels, Cestria Tyre & Exhaust and Window to the Womb. We walk past the headquarters of the Durham Aged Miners' Homes and we walk past The Wicket Gate, the local Wetherspoons. As a pedestrian, the real Chester-le-Street reveals itself to be something different from my imagination. In the shadow of the Osborne Workmen's Club, its Newcastle Breweries blue star lit up like a relic in the firmament, an auld boy sparking a tab spies us. This is a fighting town: it's inscribed into its DNA. Time to move. We make for Front Street and St Cuthbert's Walk Shopping Centre, a small precinct which I've heard is decorated with folk images of the saint. Above a walkway between a Boots and a Greggs, surrounded by side panels set in shimmering maroon and turquoise geometric patterns, hangs Cuthbert. Installed as a replica stained-glass window, and I presume printed on to a Perspex screen, the saint dangles above the shoppers. The image shows a triptych of classic Cuthbertian tales: the otters warming his feet, the eider duck cradled at his breast, and the ravens which, having initially been warned off by Cuthbert for taking straw from a nearby dwelling, showed their contrition by bringing back to Inner Farne a lump of pig's lard. Cuthbert was said to invite monks to grease their shoes with it.

We leave the precinct and discuss Cuthbert's after-image. The triptych of the ethereal saint might be offensive to true believers – I'm not sure how godly it really is to stick a whacking great image of a saint in a shopping mall – but then it has to be better than a giant selfie mirror or hyperactive advertising screens. As if to prove the point of Cuthbert's afterlife, one of the first retail units outside is a charity shop run by St Cuthbert's Hospice, which provides care for people with life-limiting illnesses. There's an argument to be made that this type of Christian commodification is gaudy and unsanctified, but I think that obscures a bigger and more important point: about how we memorialise and remember; the ways we come to know. Yes, it's a bit tacky that Cuthbert has been deployed to oversee the shoppers of Chester-le-Street scoffing sausage rolls, but I think it speaks to something characteristic of this part of the world that we do take our foundation stories seriously. What could have been marketing space to be sold to the highest bidder has been kept and given over to an artist to interpret, brightening the space not for commercial revenue but for communal pride. That's an interesting moral decision. We might even call it Cuthbertian.

In the REfUSE café on Front Street, over Americanos and geet big slices of cake, Carl sets down a battered old horseshoe on the table. It is a fitting object for us to think about Chester-le-Street and its history, Carl suggests, because this is the place the Romans called *Concangis* – 'place of horse people'. Beside Nick, my own potent icon, the two make an anachronistic pairing, in this bustling community interest company set up to intercept food waste by turning it into healthy meals to be served back to the grandparents and toddlers of the local area. Just as the presence of Cuthbert lives on in his namesake at the hospice, the hospitality and sense of duty to the environment espoused by Cuthbert in life lives on here at REfUSE, where the ethos is about 'showing the value in things, places or people that are unjustly wasted or overlooked'.[3] It seems a fitting mission statement for a café in a town which itself is in the shadows. As we hack our way into the cakes and take a caffeine buzz, Carl again acknowledges that the research and writing he pursues now have their roots here, and in the North East more widely. This becomes clearer as he talks about his late granddad, a vital-sounding athlete, farrier and balladeer, and the man whose 'old Geordie' accent and language planted the roots for Carl to be drawn to the sound of Old English.

'He'd drive all over on Sunday mornings – from Washington to Blaydon, from Shields to Haltwhistle – to shoe these horses, and I remember watching on.' This notion of watching on – of the apprentice learning a skill or trade over the shoulder of his tutor – is a common discussion point for Carl and I, children of the post-industrial period. We think about the paths and tracks that have led here: Cuthbert's community in 883; the Jarrow Marchers in 1936; us today, now – and we wonder about the word 'track'. What does it mean to track something? Carl has drawn me to another Old English word that is relevant here: 'last' or 'lastas', meaning track or line, or, even, a footprint someone leaves behind for us to follow. My mind gans back to first-footing. We might think about this word, Carl adds, in connection to the Old English word 'mærc': a 'border, boundary, mark on the land, stain, curse, mirk or murk [marsh/land;march/land], bloodmark, etc.'[4] So, we've come here to make a mark – or to remark and follow older lines – and each of us has with us our talisman and psalm book, so off to church we gan.

We cut along High Chare on to Church Chare, marking the turns inscribed in the Old English etymology of the word 'chare'. St Mary's & St Cuthbert's is right in front of us now. We're met in the grounds by one of the wardens. She's dead-heading flowers from one of the well-kept baskets. We're welcomed inside the place where, in 883, Cuthbert's body was brought. While the saint is on our minds, the stone effigies of the Lumley family draw our eyes first. George Lord Lumley looks like he has a trendy sleeve tattoo. But his arm is actually fossilised. Held in dark grey Frosterley Marble – cut and polished limestone made ornamental – rests the squashed impression of an extinct solitary coral, *Dibunophyllum bipartitum*. Submerged 325 million years ago, caught up in a Carboniferous tropical sea that would have once covered this part of northern England, it was quarried high up in Weardale, twenty miles south-west.[5] Lying prone beneath stained glass, wilting gypsophila on his belly, his chipped sword lain along his chest, the knight and former Sheriff of Northumberland lies with thirteen other 'Lumley Warriors' – stone tomb effigies brought to the church in the sixteenth century, collected by John Lord Lumley as his supposed ancestors. The Lumley family were prominent Northumbrian landowners, soldiers and administrators. Their family manor house, converted into Lumley Castle in 1389, stands above Durham's Riverside cricket ground high up above the Wear, and is today a hotel and wedding venue.

Splayed out along his forearms, the fossils look like they might creep away at any moment, carrying their host on a briny tide to some distant ocean-bound burial. Latching on to the Saxon stonework, deconstructing by degrees, they might dismantle this church, stripping it back to its timber-framed origins, when it was first built as a shrine to Saint Cuthbert. Katrina Porteous's poem 'Durham Cathedral'[6] imaginatively recodes the masonry of the region's iconic basilica – six miles south of where we're standing now – back to the words and stories which pre-date its creation. Riffing off 'the old words' which 'loom,/High, mysterious,/Lit up from within', Porteous sees 'Its towers/toppled' before she reaches back through 'a blacker seam' to the Old English origins of her Northumbrian encomium: *Hyeven, Hinny, Hyem*'. It's a powerful reminder that everything – stone, story, seabed – is always slowly shifting. From this place – this original Durham Cathedral, as the volunteer guide insists we call it – it's possible to read the geology of Chester-le-Street back through its multi-million-year-layered past, to its literal bedrock. A triptych hanging in the nave begins with Cuthbert's coffin being hauled off Lindisfarne, a flock of gulls forming a ceremonial send-off. He's then seen by the banks of the Wear, and then with his monks, who are felling trees to begin his edifice.

In around the 950s to the 960s, a priest called Aldred the Scribe translated the Latin of the Lindisfarne Gospels into a vernacular Northumbrian form of Old English. Working from the Chester-le-Street scriptorium, he added a colophon which gave information on the history of the Gospels book. Aldred's work in the margins – he glossed word-for-word literal translations in the lines above the original Latin script – made him a critical part of the Gospels' story: a key figure in their transmission, he was responsible for making the first translation of the Gospels into the English language. Arriving at Chester-le-Street today, it's possible to think of the town itself as similarly 'glossed'. A staging post on the Great North Road between London and Edinburgh, today submerged beneath Front Street, the town is often overlooked by visitors making their way to Newcastle, the glitzy big city ten miles to the north, or it's forgotten by the pilgrims who travel straight to Durham and its medieval cobbled stone streets, a stage set for the many thousands of international tourists who want to be photographed beneath the gothic splendour of the castle and cathedral, high up above the river. Even the A1 Motorway – paralleling the original through-course of the Roman highway – makes a dog-leg around the town, suggesting that to come here, one needs a very particular reason.

One such reason might be to get up close and personal with the Lindisfarne Gospels (redux). The volunteers show us their replica book in a glass box at the side of the church, beneath a curtained drape. Costing £10,000 and made by a company in Sweden – 'Nar, Switzerland!' shouts the other gadgie – what we can do today, donning the requisite cotton gloves, is turn the pages of a copy of the great codex. While it might be a facsimile, there's something about the low-key nature of this experience which chimes with me far more than the official, stringently curated exhibition I last saw, when the Gospels were displayed at the Laing Gallery in Newcastle in 2022. As we use a magnifying glass and torch to interpret the detailed lace knotwork patterns on the carpet pages – intricate patterns of bird and animal ornaments, spirals and interlocked curves forming the shape of the cross – I feel a proximity to the material that I've not encountered before. As Carl reads out an Old English gloss from the Mark incipit, and as the guides recount the tale of their maker, Bishop Eadfrith, cheekily having a 'cat' reaching down the page to try and chase a bird, the full materiality of the work comes to life. As we stand to leave, leaflets and brochures being thrust into our hands, a few quid in coins offered in exchange, the volunteer says something that sticks with me: 'Don't forget about us here at Chester-le-Street, Durham's original cathedral for a hundred and ten years!'

The volunteer's enthusiasm – a term which, as Elizabeth Oldfield informs me, comes 'from the Greek *en theos*, filled with God'[7] – reminds me of a slogan popularised across the North East in the early 2000s: *Passionate People, Passionate Places*. Launched in 2005 by One North East, the regional development agency which rose with the New Labour government, the campaign was seen as a way of altering popular consciousness of the area – to unshackle from staid, twentieth-century clichés so that the tourism and trading potential of the region could be maximised. Implying that the North East was a great place to live, work, invest and study, a glitzy campaign video asked: 'When does a place become part of you?'[8] Opening with a beautiful dusk panorama of the Sycamore Gap on Hadrian's Wall (the sycamore itself has since been illicitly felled), the narrator, speaking, interestingly, not in a North East accent, continues over piano keys: 'when its history echoes down to you through the ages'. The sound of gulls' calls takes us from Bamburgh Castle to the sanctuary knocker at Durham Cathedral, the voiceover adding 'when it offers sanctuary from a restless world' as the camera pans down the nave.

I've thought a lot about that slogan while writing this book. It ran for only six years and, despite being briefly resuscitated in 2020, now seems a vestige of an easier time. As an abstract noun, 'passion' is a red-flag word: the type I'd ordinarily highlight in a student's work, recommending that they find a more concrete substitute. *Show us* this passion, I might intone. And yet somehow it is the perfect appellation for us Northumbrians, an example of a PR agency getting it bang on. I think of many – not all – of the people I know in the North East as being passionate about where they live in a way that I haven't experienced to quite the same intensity in other areas of the country. Absolutely, there is a risk of grandstanding in saying any of this, but we are fiercely ardent about our territory and its local distinctiveness. My fervent views and unashamed opinions have often been remarked on by my mid-Walian in-laws – sometimes, I admit, because of the self-parodying Jake who morphs into a *Viz* caricature after a bottle of Merlot on Christmas Day – but I've rarely heard such passion being discussed in negative terms. Whether I'm on-brand espousing a North East cause or proclaiming my heritage, or just generally expressing zealous beliefs, I feel that the historical precedence for this attitude is complicatedly woven into the fibres of Northumbria as a place which has had to stand firm and defend as often as it has had to advance forward and campaign.

As we walk back along Church Chare, the car park opposite now covering the Roman settlement from which the town first sprang, I think about all the people I've met along the way who I'd have no quibble over describing as passionate. The famous Holman Hunt image *The Light of the World*, which was etched into stained glass on the north wall of St Mary's & St Cuthbert's, comes to mind. Not everything remains illuminated – the light, as Waterhouse reminds us, is always journeying elsewhere – but the impressions it makes in the dark can still serve and be our guide. It would be wrong to claim that everyone in the region sees themselves as a torch-bearer, but maybe what Chester-le-Street has proven is that it is a large part of our personality. Heading for Front Street again, we jump on to the 21 'Angel' bus back to Tyneside, lamp and horseshoe alongside us. The bus presses on through Barley Mow and the Angel of the North soon comes into view, welcoming us with its copper-coloured wingspan. *Hiya, hinny! Alreet, mate!*

We're at the district limits now, lines of Peter's once more coming to mind: 'Tonight we walk the hinterland, the common places/where the hills might burn, our eyes settle/on a particular wilderness'.[9] Fields begin to thin as northern Durham's pastures give way to Ravensworth's tower blocks and Low Fell's Victorian grandeur. We've passed over another of those imaginary lines, this one marking the border of the Metropolitan Borough of Gateshead. Carl and I alight at The Microbus, a small trinket of craft beer at the southern end of the High Level Bridge. We debrief on our sojourn through the 'Street, where we've come into close contact with the residues of the Northumbrian soul. This is a storied land and I'm beginning to see that there's no definitive way of telling that story. Like the tall tales of our grandfathers – Carl describes his as an old Geordie from the Jarrow–Boldon fringes, a man whose deep-toned accent somehow spoke to ideas of the upstanding gentleman – there's always a variant, a spin-off, embroidery. While popular telling has it that Cuthbert's community fled raiding Norsemen, their trajectory to Durham was more likely a strategic following of patronage. 'Cuthbert's community under Bishop Eardwulf [...] was closer to a shrewd corporation moving between politically advantageous locations.'[10] Twelfth-century accounts by Symeon of Durham, who, 'as cantor of the cathedral was responsible both for supervising the singing and for looking after the community's books', also 'elaborated the traditions'.[11] Coming to Chester-le-Street today, talking with Carl and being chaperoned through the church by the volunteers, I feel like, to go to the etymological root of 'tradition', ideas, concepts and wisdom have been handed over to me. The shuttle is in my hands, or rather in my larynx.

This doesn't occlude, but rather supports, my impression that the Northumbrian numen has always been reinforced by storytelling. It's woven into our fabric. The land grants and protections of benevolent kings may have been what actually kept the *Haliwerfolc* going, but, to quote the New York mayor Mario Cuomo, 'you campaign in poetry, you govern in prose'. Few tourists venture to Chester-le-Street, but to understand the orbit of Northumbria – from influential kingdom and intellectual powerhouse to romantic tourist getaway today – it's important to understand the position it held in sustaining the Cuthbert hagiography. More than that, it's a place which shows us the ways in which we shouldn't be afraid to be passionate, to proclaim our part in the story.

Aye, it is possible to be dissatisfied with Chester-le-Street's simulacra: the way it literally re-presents what has gone before. Its duplications of the Lindisfarne Gospels, held in facsimile or as details on a crumbling bus depot wall, might well disappoint purists. But, in a sense, I think these absences speak to a deeper afterglow in the North East, and they help us understand the need for the lights of old to be refracted into the new. Academics such as Carl, who's taking deeply felt impressions of his familial connections to the town and combining them with new scholarly interpretations, point to exciting ways to update these traditions — a process of handing over in which genealogy, language, landscape and lore make a complex and compelling textual weave. Walking through Chester-le-Street with Carl has been a revelatory

Light moved on

experience, and as with numerous other places I've stopped off at on my North East Camino, I feel like I've only really begun making inroads. It is undeniably the case that Durham now eclipses Chester-le-Street, but as I wrote in my poem for the Lindisfarne Gospels' return, a halo has been left around the town. Light is never fully extinguished; it just moves elsewhere.

DURHAM MINERS' ASSOCIATION
BOLDON LODGE
MINERS' HALL 1901
Cones

Chapter 11

The big meeting

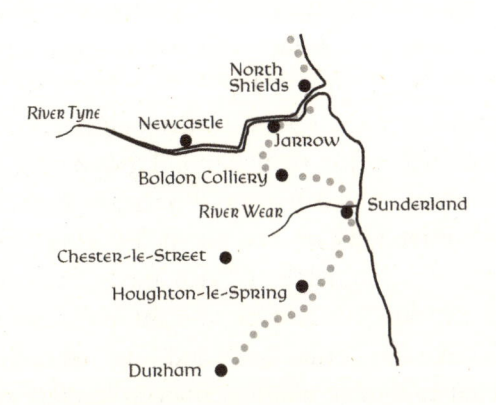

And I shall cry again, and not know why again.
The silken banners summon up the tears,
The men who march beneath them touch the soul.
I have not known the pitmen's hopes and fears,
I learnt them from the books I read at school.
But I shall cry again, and not know why again.

    Alex Glasgow, 'And I Shall Cry Again'[1]

It's seven thirty in the morning in Boldon Community Association. At fold-out tables, people are sipping paper cups of weak tea. From the kitchen come tinfoil-wrapped bacon and sausage sarnies. There's a large, plastic bowl of tomato sauce. I drop two quid in the donation box, take a punt on a pork breakfast, and ask a bloke in a retro Vaux Sunderland away kit (the early-1990s white one with its turquoise checker-plate shoulder patterns) if he knows where I can find Bill Shield. 'He's oot the back sorting stuff for the bus, I think, marra.'

Two spoons of instant coffee go in my cup and I fill it from the giant vat of boiling water. In an adjacent room, a dozen or so young people in black suits with yellow trims and ties are scoffing butties. This is the brass band and they're fuelling up for a long day of marching. There's a semi-official-looking lady in the corner with a folder and wristbands. I pay her eight quid for the bus and ask her Bill's whereabouts. Her reply is interrupted by a man bursting through the doors with another man's throat in his right hand. 'Divven't be fucking taking the piss out of me again, ever, d' y' hear us, eh?'

An awkward quiet falls on the room for a few minutes before the throttler relinquishes his grip and is firmly told to get out. We all chuckle. It's twenty to eight and passions are already high. Vaux man comes back and says I should speak to Micky. I'm led to a table where a man in his late eighties wearing a bomber jacket and flat cap sits with his grandson, wearing an identical cap. I tell Vaux man and Micky why I'm here, that two days ago Bill said I'd be welcome to come along, that I'm writing a book about – I gesture – all of this, and that I've brought along the lamp that my great-granddad used in the same pit. Micky looks intrigued. I pull out Nick and hand him over. Micky's eyes come alive. Just then, Bill comes in, Vaux man collaring him to say that Jake's here.

A friendly hand is proffered.

'Micky's the one to taak tee', Bill says, 'he has aall the stories.'

'Cheers, Bill. Thanks again for having me along. I've paid Brenda.'

'Nee bother, son.'

I float around finishing my excellent sandwich and terrible coffee, feeling a bit like a gate-crasher. But soon it's five to eight and the bus driver wants everyone on board. I take a seat on the coach in front of Micky and his grandson,

The big meeting

Max. The driver makes it plain that the return coach leaves Durham at four o'clock prompt, 'and if you're not there I'll assume you're not coming back. Mind, I hope youse aall are because I want a good whip around – I'm gannin' oot the neet!' Everyone laughs and the engine starts up. Tinnies are cracked open and the coach pulls onto New Road.

Somewhere on the A690, on the outskirts of Durham, I turn to talk to Micky. He tells me my lamp is a deputy or overman's lamp, and was used for testing gas. Unlike the standard flame lamps given to most workers, which would run out of fuel at a set time and need to be relit above ground, this one is a 'relighter' and could be lit again beneath ground using a strip. He points to where you'd use a striker to smack the comb. His description is lyrical and impassioned, but I can't say I understand it. Not for the first time, it has become obvious to me how far away my labour – and the language which surrounds it – is from the working men who went down these mines. Micky's description of my lamp is at odds with what I was previously told online, but if he's right, it means that Nick has been promoted to deputy. Gan on, son! Micky tells me about a near miss his brother once had: a wagon smashed into his legs, but two of his marras hauled him oot by the oxters and he didn't have to have his legs amputated. I ask Max if he's been taught any of this at school. He hasn't, but he tells me how his granddad has been speaking to local school children, giving them first-hand accounts of the work of their forebears.

We alight from the coach at Walkergate, ready to start this biggest of meetings. The Market Square is the historic point of convergence for the Gala, but it would be misleading to think of it as its only starting point. It's true that the various lodges tend to congregate here first before funnelling into Saddler Street and down onto Elvet Bridge, but each lodge's journey really begins in the community from which they came, as the Boldon group's did this morning. The Durham Coalfield was typically thought of as encompassing an area from Shildon in the south to Shields in the north, but there are banners and union representatives here today from across the wider North East region and in fact from right across the United Kingdom and Europe.

In the shadows of the statue of Lord Londonderry we begin to haul the banner up its poles. Londonderry's death in 1854 was not mourned by the Durham miners. Despite his work to establish a port at Seaham, increasing the coal trade to London from east Durham, the Anglo-Irish nobleman, soldier and politician is still loathed in these parts for his views on child exploitation. Prior to the 1842 Mines and Collieries Act, which prevented women and girls outright and boys under ten from working underground, Londonderry – with his vested interests as the owner-operator of coalmines on lands belonging to his wife, Lady Frances Anne Vane – had argued that boys as young as eight should still be working beneath ground, their diminutive frames being more suited to the purpose than those of taller men. As the father of two small children, it's sickening to think that, had I been raising them 200 years ago, some toff would be arguing that my son, in a mere four years' time, would be fit to spend all night miles underground, working as a trapper opening doors and being beaten for the privilege if he dared nod off.

The banner is hauled, the brass band is in place. This is a stop–start affair which can take hours, but today marches along pretty readily. The overture begins and we're off, up along Sadler Street, squeezing between Greggs and HSBC on Durham's thin cobbled streets. It's only a quarter to nine but already the place is thronged. We stop on Elvet Bridge and I remember to take Nick out of my rucksack. I apply a lick of factor thirty and swig from my orange squash. It's hot already and the banner hoisters are sweating. This is physical activity, but we're buoyed on by the band at the front, now about twenty-strong in total, knocking out John Denver, Bruno Mars and Neil Diamond.

Brass bands were once at the heart of the Durham Coalfield and it's testament to their enduring appeal that there's still an enormously popular Brass Festival in the city each summer. This year, sixty-three Durham Coalfield banners were accompanied by fifty-four brass bands and over a hundred additional banners representing a range of trades unions, guilds and good causes, many of them also ushered in by brass music, pipes and drumming bands. This connected theatrical effect – exuberant and intricately designed silk banners imprinted with lines of poetry and portraits of union leaders or/and figures from biblical liturgy combined with horned instrumentation and snare drums – makes for a smorgasbord of colour and sound.

We stop for ten minutes outside The Swan and Three Cygnets, the Sam Smith's pub on the Corner of New Elvet by the River Wear, waiting our turn to march into the pit, the roadside gap beneath the County Hotel. Here, dignitaries, councillors and politicians typically wait to be entertained by each band, who have a few minutes in the spotlight playing their signature tunes to the gathered crowd of left-wing luminaries watching from the balcony. Beyond this point the road is fenced off and you really do begin to feel like you're in a parade. At the barrier, draped in a banner with the text 'Total Eclipse of The Sun', a woman catches sight of Nick and beckons me over. I lift him up and give her the brief history. She asks for a quick hold. There's something elemental about this lamp: its ability to inject energy into people which makes it go beyond the nostalgic.

I think about this gathering, and what it means for the idea of pilgrimage that I've been exploring throughout this book, this way into and through the heart and soul of the place I'm from. When I began at Lindisfarne I was walking by myself. The emptiness of the Northumberland coast had huge charm and appeal – there were many hours of solace and seeing very few others – but gradually as I got towards the Tyne and Wear conurbations, those urbanised and suburban landscapes clustering around Newcastle and Sunderland, the feeling of spaciousness began to dwindle as more people could be seen on the popular beaches of Longsands and Seaburn. Walking from Sunderland to Durham in memory of Bill Martin, our party numbered a dozen. Now, at the other end of the scale, I walk among thousands of people – a grand collective North East Camino which has its roots in the first miners' gala of 1871.

I've never been a marcher, never been one to walk in unison for any political cause and certainly not in time to music, so there's something novel about this for me. This kind of procession takes the idea of the solitary pilgrimage journey and shakes it up. I think it has a lot to do with the magic of collectivity and a feeling that we now suffer from a dearth of opportunity to be able to do things in unison. It's that old adage: strength in numbers. As the Durham miners made their way onto the streets, literally beating the bounds of the citadel with its status, wealth and privilege, they exclaimed each year that they were still here, that their efforts were what kept the show on the road. Their political demonstration of solidarity, coupled with the artistic showcase of their communities, said to the powers that be: we are what feeds your furnaces. And, of course, in the strength of those union leaders they found symbolic charge, the cause being held up on their behalf so that betterment for one meant betterment for all.

The big meeting

It's a speedy march onwards, passing The Dun Cow pub, which namechecks the Cuthbert legend and the cowherd who guided the saints in over a millennium ago, and eventually down on to the Racecourse, confusingly named as it's actually a cricket ground. As we approach the narrow bank down to the field, one of the banner-carriers, Kev, begins to loudly thank everyone for walking in with us. He beats his chest, telling everyone his family are so proud. When we've finally parked up on the grass and got the banner pitched along a fence, I shake his hand and tell him why I'm here. Pulling one of my poetry books from my bag, I give it to him and say I'll be reading later in the cathedral service. My poem 'Davy' recalls my great-grandfather, who worked in Boldon pit for most of his life. Kev is emotionally charged and, without doubt, a bit pissed up, but he takes the book and says he'll read it. 'Normally I'm a real lazy bastard; I'd prefer to watch a show or something, but I'll read this, Jake. What a great thing you're doing.'

I'm naturally pretty modest about things like this and want to avoid embarrassment, so of course I politely reaffirm how glad I am to have been asked to walk in with everyone today; that it means a lot to me personally to be able to do this. Kev shakes my hand again and starts reading my poem, before extemporising on *his* poetry: the punk rock of the Angelic Upstarts. We talk about our respective grandparents for a second, and I ask Kev what he usually does. 'I'm a diamond driller, Jake – you don't know what that is, do you?'

I can't lie. 'Nah.'

'I send robots into building sites to demolish things. But I trained at Sellafield. It was like bloody Chernobyl.'

Our occupations couldn't be much further apart, but today we've met on a par. Coalfield culture is our common currency, a respect for our ancestors something that unites us. In other circumstances, a diamond driller and a writer would be unlikely to chat to each other, but that's the great levelling beauty of an event like the gala. Without warning, he begins reciting the lyrics to the Angelic Upstarts' song 'Heath's Lament':

> Gan yem, Joey, dain't cross the line
> Gan yem, Joey, or you'll be ney friend of mine
> I've knaan y' aall of twenty year and never a bad word said
> But once y' walk across the line me friendship with ye's dead.[2]

A performance poem by the band's singer-songwriter 'Mensi' – Thomas Menforth – who died of Covid-19 in 2021, 'Heath's Lament' recalls Mensi's time at Westoe Colliery (the pit where Nick ended his working days), where he'd followed his dad's occupation until he was nineteen, during the strike-ridden premiership of Edward Heath in the early 1970s. Mensi grew up on the Brockley Whins estate – one of South Shields' post-war overspills – and the Upstarts' signature brand of breakneck 'oi!' gang vocals, power chords and socially charged lyrics typified the second wave of British punk, which paid homage to the grit and determination of life on the tatty fringes of working-class towns, with their boozers, football terraces and, in the case of this poem, tendency to splinter old friendships into the faithful and the scabs.

I shake Kev's hand one final time, leave him on the grass reading my poem and make a note to download the Angelic Upstarts' album. South Tyneside has a rich punk-rock history. As I mentioned earlier, my teenage angst came out in listening to the records of Southern Californian punk bands like NOFX and Social Distortion – whose emergence in the 1990s could be traced back to 1970s bands like Black Flag and the Dead Kennedys. Occasionally, between seeing bands like NOFX and the label-mates they'd bring on tour to showcase their Fat Wreck Chords label, we'd watch some of Tyneside's older punks play in rooms above pubs. The highlights were the Clash-influenced band called 1979 in the function suite of The County in Shields, and Jarrow's Crashed Out at The Cumberland in Heworth, when a mate's then-band, Liberation Now!, came on as the support act. It was a circuitous route for me from the bands I'd pay a few quid to watch in basement bars while sipping at a pint of bitter to the poetry I now read and share, but at the gala it all begins to crystalise into a similar grouping: that is, fiercely passionate lyrics which give voice to community and remain loyally rooted in place, fraternity and fairness. Looking back, it should be no surprise that Tyneside was such a hot-bed for punk bands: as Heath's leadership of the Tory party gave way to Thatcher's, and mineworkers and their families withered on the vine, punk was a vital expression of defiance.

Just after ten I'm offered a Bräu, a stubby green bottle of Spanish lager from a wheely picnic basket. Folk musicians Bill Elliott and Kevin Youldon take to the stage, playing songs from the seam like 'The Black Leg Miner'. The bloke doling out the beers is the grandson of Sam Bartram, a Boldon miner turned goalkeeper who went on to make 579 appearances for Charlton Athletic, a club record. I give out another copy of my poetry book to Bartram Junior, then head for a reccy of the site. My first aim is to try to document some of the magnificent banners which have made their way onto the Racecourse and which, even at eleven in the morning, are still filing in from the city. I tour the periphery of the grounds, pulling out lines of poetry, firing off images on WhatsApp to two marras: my pal Smithy in Harrow (who joined us last year for the Marratide pilgrimage) and Carl, my companion through Chester-le-Street, on the other side of London.

It would be impossible to do full justice to the tactile beauty of these objects: for one thing, their number and scale make it difficult to form a group appraisal. Each banner is an indigenous expression in fabric and paint of the community it represents. As such, each has its own story and history. The Thornley Lodge banner has two pithy lines, 'time passes/ memories linger', whereas the Lambton Lodge one, depicting Christ coming to the aid of a drowning sailor (another image redolent of Cuthbert), catches my eye for the sheer volume of its azure textures. I am looking for, but fail to find, the Chopwell banner, which I know contains lines from the American poet Walt Whitman. Bearing a triptych featuring Lenin, Marx and Keir Hardie, the banner exclaims Whitman's famous celebration of the Westward Rush, from his book *Leaves of Grass*:

> We take up the task eternal
> The burden and the lesson
> Pioneers! Oh! Pioneers![3]

Many of the banners obviously draw upon Christian scenes and biblical sources to chart their community's sense of self. On a more abstract level, their patterns, colours and designs are reminiscent of illuminated manuscripts: the Lindisfarne Gospels' baroque carpet pages echoing from the medieval past through the nineteenth and twentieth centuries to this display before me today. The Pelton Fell Lodge banner, for example, refurbished in 2017, shows a move from oppression to sunshine and liberty, a ring of merry schoolchildren dancing circles in glowing light beneath an angelic figure garlanding a mining family in 'progress', 'education', 'science' and 'art'. At the bottom of the display are lines from the Victorian poet and writer of Methodist hymns, John Addington Symonds:

> These things shall be: A loftier race than e'er the world hath known shall rise ... with a great flame of freedom in their souls and a light of knowledge in their eyes.

Not all banners draw on centuries-old iconographies. The wonderfully straightforward Coppull & Chorley Miners Wives banner from Lancashire testifies to women's support for their picketing husbands during the 1984–1985 strike, a pushback to the divide-and-rule tactics used to strike-break, and which was part of a wider movement of women's efforts to feed the community and lead progressive change more generally for women's issues. Along from this, I spot the Durham Women's Group banner, which shows the collective, founded in 2017, taking an anti-racist stance and, among other things, platforms WASPI – Women Against State Pension Inequality.

I wonder, in my own field, how a writers' guild might formulate and hoist a banner and what such a thing would entail. As I attended the gala, news was building of the strike by the Writers' Guild of America, in response to the use of AI technologies for screenwriting. In 2015, the artist Grayson Perry, filming a Channel 4 documentary on the changing nature of masculinity, marched through Durham behind the Trimdon Grange banner. This led to him creating a banner of his own, 'Death of a Working Class Hero', subsequently blessed at the 2016 service. Perry's exuberant creation shows a miner sparring off against a boxer, beneath which the funeral for said anonymous hero is taking place against the potent iconographies of North Eastern working life: pit wheels, ships, whippets and cranes. Featuring a crossed miner's pick and set of dumbbells, and with the slogan 'A time to fight, a time to talk, a time to change', Perry's banner was a powerful way of reading into how ideas of 'toxic masculinity' might be defused by less fraught and binary representations of male identity – especially in a region still hung up on such monikers.

I look for banners representing South Shields – last year, a trio from Harton, Westoe and St Hilda marched through the streets – but I can't see them. I do, however, find Graham Martin, appropriately by the Silksworth banner. We pick up where we left off a fortnight ago, when I had to sweet-talk the guard into letting me into the cathedral. Little did I know at the time I'd be back so soon, invited in to read at the official service.

After another sprut round the field and some bait on a picnic mat Graham and Kath have brought along, I watch poets Rowan McCabe and Lizzie Lovejoy take to the stage. Rowan is an old acquaintance and stalwart of Tyneside's poetry scene since about 2010. When we were both fledgling graduates with not much else to do, Rowan and I met in the upstairs room of the Bridge Hotel in Newcastle, reading at the university's poems-and-pints night. While I went further into academic and small-press poetry publishing, Rowan became a jobbing versifier, the world's first 'door-to-door poet'. Responding (ironically) to the self-starter mentality made famous by Norman Tebbit's 'get on your bike' speech at the 1981 Conservative Party Conference, Rowan, sporting suit jacket and leather briefcase, began knocking on strangers' doors in the Newcastle suburb of Heaton, talking to them about their life, then coming back a week later with a poem in praise of it.

Lizzie Lovejoy is a Darlington-born writer and illustrator whose artworks capturing the spirit of the north are befitting of the stage at the gala. Both Rowan and Lizzie, working in mentoring capacities with youth groups in Sacriston, bring to the stage a number of kids whose own poetry testifies to life in the North East. While a strong sense of tradition and heritage underscores the bairns' performances, it's fitting that this also seems to be the lens through which these young people are looking to the futures of their culture.

The big meeting

While the political speeches are getting underway the Fishburn band provides the traditional overture to the proselytising with its rendition of 'Gresford', the Miners' hymn. Having avoided the worst of the heavens' downpour by taking shelter in the Redhills tent, I start making my way to the cathedral. With Graham and Kath in tow, I head back up the hill, past the law courts and Dunelm House, the 1966-built Brutalist home of Durham Students' Union, crossing again, as I had only two weeks ago, the Kingsgate footbridge to the back of the cathedral. I see its Rose Window lit up from within, embodying Katrina Porteous's 'hyeven, hinny, hyem'. In the cathedral itself there's still an hour to go until the banners begin processing through. I'm given a dress rehearsal of proceedings by the Acting Dean and Precentor, the Reverend Canon Michael Hampel, before sitting in the second from front row (the front is reserved for the Mayoress of Durham) and preparing to nervously eat a packet of LU petit ganache biscuits. I could murder another of Sam Bartram Junior's stubbies.

The banners begin to make their way along the nave. Escorted by their own bands, the effect is spine-tingling. As the big thumping bass drum gets near me, I swear I can count in its rhythm the same pulse beating away inside my throat.

This year there are three banners to be blessed: those of Coxhoe Colliery, Hetton Lyons and the Durham Aged Mineworkers' Homes Association. The last is particularly suitable for me, looking back, as at the top of my grandparents' street in South Shields, the place from where this lamp has travelled with me today, on Marsden Road, there is a perfect example of these homes. In fact, so typical of both the architectural style and social mission of the DAMHA are they, Beamish Museum has just reproduced its design, building replicas as part of its new 1950s village.

These are the things I think about to try to take my mind off the weight of the occasion. Last night, while I was worrying over how best to dress to meet the competing demands of a weather forecast which promised temperatures in the low twenties and seventy per cent humidity with the gravity of reading a poem in front of 1,200 people at England's favourite building,[4] I decided that navy chino shorts and a black shirt would be the best thing to wear. Having been given a 150-year Durham Miners' Association badge by Nick Malyan (I misplaced my original, pinned as it once was to a favourite denim jacket long since lost to the boozy recesses of some nightclub), I twiddle it on to my breast pocket, swigg my remaining squash, and wait. Absolutely bricking it.

I had wrangled over whether to take Nick up to the pulpit, but in the run-through decided against it. Not only was there no space for props at the lectern, I thought that if I dropped him that might be game over. I do, however, carry up with me a pebble from Holy Island. For some minutes before, I fidget with it in my pocket, then take a deep breath and follow the verger up. I don't want to analyse one of my own poems – it's included after this chapter for you to make up your own mind – but I was heartened when I suggested to Andy Dowson, organiser of the gala, that I should read this one and he agreed. The poem pays homage to my great-grandfather and uses poetic licence to place myself in his shoes, but I think it also speaks to what the trades union movement today is trying to fight for on so many fronts: breathing without thinking of breathing (to paraphrase my own lines) might be said to encapsulate that struggle for fairness and equity, but in honesty I can't say the poem was written as a political project.

In any case, I walk up, consciously pause a few seconds to take in the scale of the event, breathe deeply, and deliver the poem as I have several times in the past in front of a public audience, all twenty-four lines. Then I leave the pulpit and wait until 'Jerusalem' starts up before I'm taken in reverse back across the nave to sit down. Every cliché is in my throat, every feeling in my heart. I can't really say without totally blathering in stereotype how significant an occasion this was. This day which started with the warm embrace of strangers, and which concluded with the privilege of being able to use the only thing I seem to be half good at, to honour my forebears. I can only resort to the Geordie exclamation: wey-aye!

After the service, I want to take some time at the miners' memorial. I leave my Holy Island pebble by the garland of flowers beneath the burning lamp. This feels like another important *tirtha* point: a place where coast meets country; where the clerical collar meets the miner's neckerchief. When I left Lindisfarne, I wondered what I might rediscover along this way. Walking to Durham, entering into communion with its roster of saints, has helped me to feel what the sociologist Émile Durkheim called 'collective effervescence',[5] those shared rituals which drive our search for meaning and underpin our morals. All of the marras are here: Cuthbert and Bede book-ending the church, the ashes of Bill in the chapel of Nine Altars, and the massive congregation today pulsing with the working-class heart of people just like my great-granddad Nick. I think back to Reverend Lesley Jones in Jarrow; how awkward I felt when she asked to pray for me. I don't claim to have been made into a Christian convert on this route, but I have come to harbour a growing sense of kinship. I realise that pinnacle moments like this are rare, and so, in what to many might look like prayer, but which I just call thanks, I whisper my gratitude for being able to take a little walk to the Big Meeting.

Just as poetry was my way into this endeavour, I have come full circle and closed the loop of this narrative. When I graduated in 2010 and was miserably signing on the dole, Nick Malyan and his friend Carlo Viglianisi were pioneering the Empty Shop concept, using empty retail spaces and breathing new life into them by hosting exhibitions, performances and talks. When they opened their second site, above a former Greggs bakery at the end of Framwellgate Bridge, I got in touch to run a few editions of Cellar Door, the poetry night I'd started as an undergraduate in the bars of Chester and which I'd migrated with me back to the North East.

In two later iterations around 2016, I invited poets from the North East and Northern Ireland, along with musicians from the area, to read at Empty Shop. Joanne Clement and I put on 'Haliwerfolc: Poetry and Songs from the Seam', a small-scale and ultimately short-lived event series which nevertheless tied to the famous Colpitts poetry readings going back decades in the city. Walking out of the cathedral with Nick Malyan tonight, making our way down to the County Hotel for the mandatory debriefing pints, it strikes me that this is probably something that's been bubbling through my consciousness for well over a decade: how to use poetry as a way of understanding the heritage and culture of the place I'm from.

At the swelteringly hot and extortionately priced bar in the County, supping pints of pale ale, I talk to Nicola Craddock, Communications and Engagement Manager at Redhills, and her partner Mark, a last-minute volunteer roped in to take photos of proceedings. Nicola, from Bishop Auckland, and Mark, from Middlesbrough, tell me about the importance they feel of having a strong youth presence throughout the day, with which I concur. With their motto 'The past we inherit, the future we build' drawing upon the Durham

The big meeting

Miners' Association's longstanding socialist values, it seems an appropriate theme to dwell on: this idea of seeding the future. A couple of other prominent union figures – along with passing Scouse and Irish barflies – join us as I take Nick the lamp once more to the beer-soaked table and give an informal recital of my poem.

I have a train to catch and kids to see at home: my own future to walk back into. This lamp has been my loyal guide every step of the way. Just as it assisted my own great-grandfather in his work, it has now become my trusty talisman. As the two Nicks – one inanimate, the other Mr Malyan, Director of Redhills – sit beside me, I reflect on heritage, culture, language – all of these things my work has been stewing on for so long and which I'm still not sure how to talk about. But I know it has something to do with keeping the torch burning: not following the past back to its dead-end and becoming mired in sentimentality, but building outwards from there, following the grooves of all who've gone before, taking courage and heart from the tracks they've set down, grasping at the torch they've offered to you, then striking out once again.

Tirtha: Wear

Tatty copies of *Socialist Worker* line the cobbles on Elvet Bridge. I'm backtracking, reversing the course I made into the city this morning. The after-party at the County Hotel is in full swing but I need to get a train back to Tyneside. The bands have gone. Dance music pulses from doorways, where men with translucent earpieces and yellow garlands guard the doors. Saddler Street is filling with Ubers driven in from Newcastle, dispensing lads in white jeans and suit jackets. Buzzcuts. No ties. Young lasses smelling of exotic fruit wearing expensive dresses, arm-in-arm with tattooed pit-yakkers who didn't make it to the gala. Soon they'll all mingle in Durham's champagne bars. I hot-foot it through the market square, flicking the Vs to the Marquess of Londonderry. Down Silver Street and across the Wear again, turning to see Cuthbert's *hoos* silhouetted by dusk. At the end of Framwellgate Bridge, a busker sings 'Which Side Are You On?' I see the ghost of myself hosting poetry nights with Nick Malyan and Carlo Viglianisi at Empty Shop. I think about what this city has meant to me, and how I always feel like I'm making my way up the hill to leave it once more.

Below me, below these balustrades, out of the way of the marchers and the memorialists, the weekend warriors and the coppers, the door-staff and the people selling shots of Jäger from trays in dingy clubs, out of the way of the priests and the pit workers' representatives, the union delegates and the councillors, the people who've bussed in or taken cheap flights, out of the way of all of us, at the city's undercarriage, the river slushes along as a skein. It will trundle over the weir then make its way north-east, curving round Finchale Abbey, where St Godric returned from his sailing journeys to be embraced by the monks of Durham, where it will carry on past Chester-le-Street and Washington, beneath the Victoria Viaduct then Cox Green, Penshaw, where it will rouse the spirit of the serpent coiled round the hill, burping oot sheep bones and bad boys' rot. It will flow on through Hylton past the concrete barge and go under all the bridges of Sunderland. In it will be some trace elements of Bill Martin's body and all the songlines and stories of the northern saints who went with him. It will eventually tumble out into the North Sea and reach the beaches of Hendon and Roker, Marsden and Shields beyond. And I'll pick it back up there, when it reaches the estuary, ash meeting salt, and find that I've crossed over again, back to the bigger pool which berthed it, taking Cuthbert back to the ocean, taking me back to the sea, its sanded feet, the horizon a fine-drawn graphite line.

Davy

I took Great-Granda Nick's Davy lamp
down to the tool shed, set it on the chest freezer,
glugged paraffin into the base,
sparked the flue and waited for ignition.

Hoping to enter his life and times,
to return and hold them as models,
I'd imagined the bowels beneath Boldon
and Westoe: firedamp sky of worlds

more rich despite their autarky.
I have heard that the absence of flames
make the shivering castaway pine more
cruelly: send him hallucinating

snakes of naptha and kerosene.
All along he knew the slag-heaps and wagon
chares, the weight of the earth above
and the distances still to go.

Ornamental now, Davy's become a puzzle
and Nicholas is muzzled.
Get out of this sink estate, Nick:
buff your boots, recite the Lord's prayer,

Davy

slick back your hair and hold your chest high.
You're out of the shaft now, air is crisp.
Put the lamp on the mantle and inhale.
Breathe without thinking of breathing.

Jake Morris-Cambell[1]

Cherished
memories of
my darling beloved husband
NICHOLAS MOORE
died 15TH Feb. 1959
aged 49 years.
also MARY ELLEN
Re-united with her
beloved husband
on 19TH Nov. 1982
aged 69 years.
Happy and smiling
always content
loved and respected

Coda

South Shields

When I was five or six years old, my grandparents put a conservatory on the back of their house. Digging the foundations, my granddad unearthed several bottles – chunky carafes for whisky and slender turquoise gin flasks. These were the remnants from the Victorian tip which their home, and the adjacent graveyard, were built upon. I took it as read that the cemetery at the back of their house had always been there. Looking back now, I see the movement of the living and dead as a great wave – people and their waste bulging out from the banks of the Tyne further into the arable lands of Harton parish. As the graveyard at Westoe on the edge of the town started filling and the population of Shields spread further south, a new cemetery was required. In 1891, the twin chapels at Harton Cemetery were consecrated. Salters' Trod, a track which took merchant traders up from the coal-fired pans at the river through Westoe and Harton and on to Cleadon and Sunderland, would pass near to this spot. In 1959, Nicholas Moore, my nana's father, joined the rows of headstones. Around here, there's a reason we're called the salt of the earth.

I'm here today to pay my respects. Nicholas Moore lies with his wife, Mary Ellen, and their first great-grandchildren, Kristofer and twins Jamie and Robbie, whose names couldn't fit on the headstone but were set on a wooden heart in front. Theirs is a grave much like the thousands of others surrounding it. While there are a few grand monuments – among them one to Robert Readhead, son of Alderman John Readhead of the famed shipbuilding firm – the overwhelming majority of the headstones point to ordinary people who lived simple lives before dying in the town. Finished coal-black with small rose detailing and flanked by flowers, the grave is about as low key as they come. This is why it feels important to visit it. At St Paul's Church in Jarrow I remember reading about the monument to the Felling mining disaster, that it could be the first memorial to name working-class people. How many of the men like that, and their wives and children, have gone into this cold earth without fame or fanfare? How many attract worshippers to prostrate at their tombs or have works of literature written in their honour?

While the bairns flit about on their bubble gum-coloured scooters, I take a moment to pause and reflect in front of the Moore family plot. A few weeks ago, I was in the grand gothic surrounds of Durham Cathedral laying a pebble for Cuthbert. Borne by his faithful friends and visited annually by hundreds of thousands of global pilgrims, Cuddy is in good company. But who will remember Nick and his family? Certainly, there are one or two generations of descendants who will keep coming back to this cemetery to lay flowers for the wider family, but after that – who can say? When I'm in the grave, any grandchildren of mine are unlikely to have recourse to return to Shields to pay homage to some distant relative born a century and half earlier. The poet's job isn't strictly to record, but I think we can perform a sort of cantor role. Reaching beyond our own egos and the particulars of the time we inhabit, we poets can document sacred traditions, strengthen the lineages of our communities and bear witness to bonds held in common with our ancestors — even and especially when history and politics would have them wiped from the record.

'Cheers, marra', I whisper under my breath, thanking Nick and our family for being my spirit guide during this journey. I lay a pebble on the headstone then walk the short way back to my grandparents' house, where the Ringtons tea is stewing and the Brio trains are set out for the bairns. I tell my nana that we've been to her parents' plot, and I thank her again for gifting me the lamp. I hope that, as a pedestrian tribute, the tale I've told here has shone some light on the many villagers it takes to raise a child, along with the sundry overlapping mythologies and handed-down family sagas it requires for that child to process how they belong. I don't know how my ancestors would feel about one of their own becoming a lyric poet, writing about an odyssey from Lindisfarne to Durham. I can only hope that, in balancing the 'high' cultural endeavour of doing so by contrasting to the 'low' stakes of their lives, I've shown what I believe to be the fundamentally egalitarian spirit of the Northumbrian people. Of course, those highs and lows are deliberately scare-quoted to reveal the façade: we're all skin and bones when we gan into the grave or the crematorium, whether we're put there with golden trinkets or only the grease of our toil.

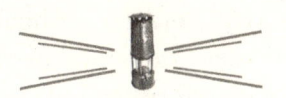

I walk down the wooden steps to Marsden Bay with Kate, Gruff and Elma once more before we move. It's late July and the Welsh Marches are calling us west. When I started this series of walks, this multidimensional journey through the mesh of geography, history, myth, politics, religion and family memories, I'd been burned out and afraid. I arrived on Holy Island intending to collapse the distance between the medieval past of northern saints and the lyricism of the people I was brought up amongst. I didn't realise how profound an inward journey I'd also be making. In committing to a meandering track through a fabled Northumbria, I gained greater clarity on my inner life and what had been motivating me — as well as what had been missing. I first felt inhibited, that the trope of standing on the shoulders of giants was a block on my creativity, and then I just felt alone. But meeting with like-minded folk along the road, discovering the new heart to Northumbria's ancient soul, rekindled my spark. Where I once walked log-legged beneath a fog of anxiety, the coast has cleared, and I now stride confidently forward: buoyed by those who first plotted the course. You could say it's given me faith.

Pilgrimage wisdom dictates that the most challenging aspect of the journey is reacclimatising to normality, heeding the spiritual lessons learned and assimilating them into life going forward. While my physical travels have been relatively modest, it does still feel like part of my brain is in Durham with the echoing footsteps of the Dun Cow entourage. I also feel like a major part of me has never left – will never leave – this shore, where the limestone cliffs boom with the call of kittiwakes and herring gulls and where the horizon holds up the whole day. Souter Lighthouse's red and white hooped tower dominates the south of the bay, no longer beckoning the fleet into the rivers, but nevertheless standing sentinel for all those out beyond the bar. Since being able to walk, I remember being brought to this beach, where tales of smugglers blasting holes into the rocks captivated my young mind. This was the playbook I was gifted, and which forever seared an impression of the town on to my heart. Mushy as it sounds, it's formed my morals and values, and I'll proudly pass it on to my bairns.

Not long after moving here, Kate and I pocketed some pebbles from this beach. It's time they went back. We give the kids the smaller ones then take turns to lob them at the waves, trying to skim the surface. Mine scans half a dozen times then sinks, reminding me of the brief flight of Bede's sparrow: that wonderful metaphor for our earthbound sojourn. The stones will be smoothed by the saline as Shields shrinks by degrees of erosion. We make a small cairn of four more pebbles, ready for the great water cycle. The tide is coming in now, the sun bowing behind the cliffs at our back. Hand in hand, we crunch through the shingle, the coast always ready to receive us.

Glossary of Northumbrian dialect terms

aboot	about
alreet	alright
bairn	child
blaa	blow
chare	a narrow medieval street
clarty	dirty
cree	a kind of shed where pigeon fanciers keep their birds
deed	dead
divven't	don't
doon	down
dunsh	collide or knock into
gadgie	male, typically of elder years
gan	go
gannin	going
gansey	a woollen jumper worn by fisherfolk
geet	signifying large quantities of; great
gegs	glasses
ha'd	hold
haddaway	expression of disbelief – 'get lost!'
heed	head
honkers	knees; to bend down on
hoolie	a strong gale
hoos	house

Glossary of Northumbrian dialect terms

hyem	home
knaa	know
marra	friend or comrade
netty	toilet
oxters	armpits
paggered	very tired
scran	food
snadgies	turnips
sneck	a latch on a door or window
spuggy	sparrow
toon	town
wor	our

Acknowledgements

This book is a product of the conversations and ponderings I've been fortunate enough to share with many fine souls. If I've missed any of them out, I can only apologise.

At Newcastle University, I owe huge thanks to James Annesley and Jenny Richards, who endured my mulling over embryonic ideas.

At Liverpool John Moores University, the following people helped me see more clearly what I was doing. I'm grateful to: Sarah Maclennan, Helen Tookey, Dan Melling, Kate Walchester, Joe Moran, Jude Piesse and Jamie Whitehead. There's one in the pumps at the Roscoe Head for each of you. Thanks also to the Research Institute for Literature and Cultural History (RILCH) at LJMU for support in clearing poetry permissions and for funding the permission to quote from W. S. Graham.

Special thanks to Nick Malyan at Sunderland Culture, who has shared many insights into coalfield culture and the quirks of North East identity. A true marra.

Many other people patiently listened to me trying to formulate the early sketches of this and provided much-needed clarity. My thanks to: Rob Colls, Sarah Rigby, Nancy Campbell, Liz Dean, Torquil MacLeod, Jonnie McAloon, David Petts, Sally Dixon, Julie Sanders, Mike Rossington and Clare Lees.

To my walking companions and confidantes, fellow *Haliwerfolc*, I owe especial thanks. You helped me figure it

Acknowledgements

oot on foot. Raising a glass to: Matt Ball, Katrina Porteous, Katherine Renton, Esther Huss, Alex Oates, Narbi Price, Kris Johnson, John Challis, Aaron Duff, Andy Martin, Carl Kears, Peter Armstrong, Graham Martin and all the Marratide crew.

I'm grateful to Bill Shield and all at the Boldon banner group for allowing me to accompany me with them to the Gala. It was an honour.

I'm so pleased this book found a home with Manchester University Press. First and foremost, I must praise the vision of my editor, Kim Walker, who believed in the project from the outset. Kim stoically listened to me prattling on over long Zoom calls, then suggested pithy revisions. Alun Richards performed editorial wizardry, keeping my dangling modifiers and bizarre tense changes in check. Sales and marketing maestros Becca Parkinson and Mariana Mouzinho helped it reach the people it needed to reach. Thanks also to Christian Lea, Katie Evans, Lisa Barker and David Appleyard at MUP. Many thanks to Ralph Footring for copy-editing the manuscript and getting it into better order than I could have managed solo.

Most importantly, I'm eternally grateful to the love and support of my family. My wife, Kate, has endured several years of my ramblings and wanderings, always in top spirits. I dragged the bairns, Gruffydd and Elma Dilys, to parts of this coastal Camino when they would have much sooner been at soft play. To the three of you, I owe my world. To the wider Morris-Campbell-Flannery clan: cheers! *Semper Paratus*.

Needless to say, any errors, inaccuracies or omissions are entirely my own.

Gan canny.

Notes

Epigraphs

1. W. S. Graham, *The Nightfishing* (London: Faber, 1955), p. 106.
2. William Martin, 'Marratide', in *Cracknrigg* (Langley Park: Taxus Press, 1983).

Prologue: First foot

1. Eleanor Jackson, *The Lindisfarne Gospels: Art, History and Inspiration* (London: British Library, 2022), p. 9.
2. Bambrugh Bones website, 'The afterlife adventures of King Oswald's corpse', https://bamburghbones.org/of-ravens-and-relics-the-afterlife-adventures-of-king-oswalds-corpse (accessed 27 November 2024).

Introduction: Lights of the North

1. Roger Garfitt, 'Walking off the fear', in *Selected Poems* (Manchester: Carcanet, 2000), p. 73.
2. Robert Colls, 'Born again Geordies', in Robert Colls and Bill Lancaster (eds), *Geordies: Roots of Regionalism* (Newcastle upon Tyne: Northumbria University Press, 2005), pp. 1–34, quotes at pp. 3 and 4.
3. Jonathan Miles-Watson, 'Transformed ecologies and transformational saints: exploring new pilgrimage routes in North-East England', *Australian Journal of Anthropology*, volume 33, issue 3, December 2022, pp. 412–427.
4. Ibid.
5. Colls, 'Born again Geordies', p. 24.
6. James Kirkup, 'Maritime', in *Refusal to Conform* (Oxford University Press, 1963).

Chapter 1. The compass takes its weigh

1. Bede, *The Ecclesiastical History of the English People* (Oxford University Press, 2008), book 3, ch. 3, p. 113.

Notes

2 Matthew Hollis, 'Causeway', in Neil Astley (ed.), *Land of Three Rivers: The Poetry of North-East England* (Hexham: Bloodaxe, 2018), p. 164.
3 Degna Stone, 'At Snook Tower', in *Proof of Life on Earth* (Rugby: Nine Arches Press, 2022).
4 Ed Simon, *Relic* (London: Bloomsbury, 2024), p. 28.
5 Bede, *The Ecclesiastical History*, book 3, ch. 5, p. 116.
6 Sean O'Brien, 'Fantasia on a Theme of James Wright', in *The Drowned Book* (London: Picador, 2007), p. 49.
7 Andrew Lacey, 'Humphry Davy and the "safety lamp controversy"', *The Guardian*, https://www.theguardian.com/science/the-h-word/2015/jul/22/humphry-davy-lamp-controversy-history-science (accessed 27 November 2024).
8 A. C. King and A. J. Pollard, 'Border and coalfield: "Northumbria" in the later Middle Ages', in Robert Colls (ed.), *Northumbria: History and Identity 547–2000* (Chichester: Phillimore, 2007), p. 81.

Chapter 2. Coastline of castles

1 The pamphlet of poems published for the project is *A Hut A Byens* (Newcastle upon Tyne: Newcastle Centre for the Literary Arts, 2022).
2 North East Combined Authority, 'Kim McGuinness chairs first cabinet meeting as North East mayor', https://www.northeast-ca.gov.uk/news/kim-mcguinness-chairs-first-cabinet-meeting-as-north-east-mayor (accessed 29 May 2024).
3 Dan Jackson, *The Northumbrians* (London: Hurst, 2019), p. vii.
4 Ad Gefrin, 'Northumbria's golden age', https://adgefrin.co.uk/communities/about/northumbrias-golden-age (accessed 29 May 2024).
5 Jake Morris-Campbell, 'Teeth Dreams', in *A Hut A Byens* (Newcastle upon Tyne: Newcastle Centre for the Literary Arts, 2022).
6 Bede, *The Ecclesiastical History of the English People* (Oxford: Oxford University Press, 2008), book 3, ch. 16, p. 135.
7 British Library, Medieval manuscripts blog, 'A menagerie of miracles: the illustrated life of Saint Cuthbert', https://blogs.bl.uk/digitised manuscripts/2013/01/a-menagerie-of-miracles-the-illustrated-life-of-st-cuthbert.html (accessed 29 May 2024).
8 William Martin, 'Exile', in *Lammas Alanna* (Hexham: Bloodaxe Books, 2000), p. 46.
9 Hector Gannet, 'The Haven of Saint Aidan's', on *Big Harcar*, released by GUGA Records, 2020.
10 Adrian G. Osler and Katrina Porteous, '"Bednelfysch and Iseland fish": continuity in the pre-industrial sea fishing of north Northumberland, 1300–1950', *Mariner's Mirror*, volume 96, issue 1 (2010), https://www.tandfonline.com/doi/abs/10.1080/00253359.2010.10657126 (accessed 29 May 2024).
11 Katrina Porteous, '#rhizodont', in *Rhizodont* (Hexham: Bloodaxe Books, 2024).

Chapter 3. Salt pans and sand dunes

1. The Newsroom, 'Myth of the column built to honour Duke', *Northumberland Gazette*, 12 May 2018, https://www.northumberland gazette.co.uk/news/myth-of-the-column-built-to-honour-duke-293832 (accessed 29 July 2024).
2. Visit Northumberland home page, https://www.visitnorthumberland.com (accessed 3 August 2023).
3. Ian Smith, 'Duke of Northumberland included in Sunday Times Rich list', Northumberland Gazette, 17 May 2024, https://www.northumberlandgazette.co.uk/news/people/duke-of-northumberland-included-in-sunday-times-rich-list-4632604 (accessed 7 January 2025); and House of Commons Library Research Briefing, 'Average earnings by age and region', https://commonslibrary.parliament.uk/research-briefings/cbp-8456 (accessed 7 January 2025).
4. Paul Batchelor, 'To a Halver', *The Acts of Oblivion* (Manchester: Carcanet, 2021), p. 29.
5. Ibid.
6. Chronicle Live, '30,000 children in the North East were "persistently absent" from school last year says online learning campaign', https://www.chroniclelive.co.uk/news/north-east-news/30000-children-north-east-absent-26562320 (accessed 6 August 2024).
7. The Newsroom, 'An alarming incident on Wesley's trail', *Northumberland Gazette*, 10 June 2017, https://www.northumberland gazette.co.uk/news/an-alarming-incident-on-wesleys-trail-417011 (accessed 1 August 2024). See also C. Hardie and S. Rushton, *The Tides of Time: Archaeology on the Northumberland Coast* (Morpeth: Northumberland County Council, 2000).
8. Sykes Holiday Cottages, 'The best places to buy a holiday home in the UK', 9 May 2024, https://www.sykescottages.co.uk/letyourcottage/advice/article/the-best-places-to-buy-a-holiday-home-in-the-uk (accessed 7 January 2025)
9. Bede, *The Ecclesiastical History of the English People* (Oxford University Press, 2008), book 4, ch. 24 p. 216.
10. Charles Eyre, *The History of St. Cuthbert* (London: James Burns, 1849), accessed via Google Books, 12 January 2024, https://books.google.co.uk/books?id=2pFQAAAAcAAJ).
11. Jake Morris-Campbell, 'The Lindisfarne Gospels, somewhere on the A1(M)', first broadcast on *Free Thinking*, BBC Radio 3, 14 September 2022.
12. Chronicle Live, 'MP backing gospels call', https://www.chroniclelive.co.uk/news/north-east-news/mp-backing-gospels-call-1520232 (accessed 29 July 2024).
13. Hansard, 'The Lindisfarne Gospels' House of Lords debate, 2 April 1998, https://hansard.parliament.uk/Lords/1998-04-02/debates/ed5539e3-01b1-4d6b-8212-32025072d952/TheLindisfarneGospels (accessed 30 November 2024).

Chapter 4. The Spine Road

1. Paul Summer, 'art lesson', in *union* (Ripon: Smokestack Books, 2011), p. 20.
2. Ashington Council, 'Ashington history', https://www.ashingtontowncouncil.gov.uk/ashington-history.php (accessed 7 January 2025).
3. Paul Batchelor, 'To a Halver', in *The Acts of Oblivion* (Manchester: Carcanet, 2021), p. 28.
4. Narbi Price, 'The Ashington Paintings', https://www.narbiprice.co.uk/the-ashington-paintings (accessed 4 November 2023).
5. Ibid.
6. Dougald Hine, *At Work in the Ruins* (London: Chelsea Green, 2023), p. 166.
7. Pippa Little, 'Seacoaling *(Lynemouth)*', in *Overwintering* (Manchester: Carcanet, 2012).
8. Data supplied by Alex Oates cross-referring to Arts Council England (ACE) Project Grant figures and German state data. See also https://mwk.baden-wuerttemberg.de/en/arts-and-culture (accessed 10 November 2023).
9. BBC News, 'Council paves way for data centre on Britishvolt site', https://www.bbc.co.uk/news/articles/c51n2pgm4kxo (accessed 30 November 2024).
10. BBC News, '£10bn investment in AI data centre confirmed', https://www.bbc.co.uk/news/articles/c3e957k9d1yo (accessed 30 November 2024).
11. Politico, 'UK's Keir Starmer: Don't be scared of AI', https://www.politico.eu/article/britain-must-run-towards-ai-opportunities-says-keir-starmer (accessed 30 November 2024).
12. Steve Robson, '"We're losing talent": authors call on government to fund writing centre in North', *i* newspaper, 19 October 2024, https://inews.co.uk/news/losing-talent-authors-call-government-writing-centre-north-3330103?srsltid=AfmBOooQmNzQ5LtOqY-O1cfrq2HVFKnmNwUXiKXeqCSIoUWpvKxlvBt9 (accessed 30 November 2024).

Chapter 5. Harvest from the deep

1. John Challis, 'The Best Is Still Below', in *Hallsong* (Newcastle upon Tyne: New Writing North, 2022).
2. Shakespeare, *Macbeth*, act V, scene 7, 2468.
3. James Kirkup, 'The harbour: Tynemouth', in Neil Astley (ed.), *Land of Three Rivers* (Hexham: Bloodaxe Books, 2017), p. 351.
4. Bede, *Life of Cuthbert* (Oxford: Oxford University Press, 2008), p. 49.
5. Alistair Elliot, 'Talking to Bede', in *My Country: Collected Poems* (Manchester: Carcanet, 1989), p. 65.
6. See the web page 'Robert Olley – North East artist and sculptor', at https://www.robertolley.co.uk/products/lawe-top-the-island (accessed 6 November 2024).

7 James Kirkup, 'Maritime', in *Refusal to Conform* (Oxford: Oxford University Press, 1963).

Tirtha: Tyne

1 For a wider contextual summary see https://www.bbc.co.uk/tyne/roots/2003/10/arabontyne.shtml (accessed 6 August 2024).

Chapter 6. Following the Don

1 Bede, *Ecclesiastical History of the English People* (Oxford: Oxford University Press, 1969), p. 95.
2 Anne Stevenson, 'Jarrow', in *Poems: 1955–2005* (Tarset: Bloodaxe Books, 2005).
3 Alan Plater, 'The drama of the North East', in Robert Colls and Bill Lancaster (eds), *Geordies: Roots of Regionalism* (Newcastle upon Tyne: Northumbria University Press, 2005), p. 84.
4 Chronicle Live, 'Closure of Bede's World museum inspires South Tyneside poet to put pen to paper', https://www.chroniclelive.co.uk/news/north-east-news/closure-bedes-world-museum-inspires-10926933 (accessed 6 August 2024).
5 Michelle P. Brown, *Bede and the Theory of Everything* (London: Reaktion Books, 2023), pp. 7–8.
6 Ibid., p. 120.
7 Bill Cassie, 'The Amble sword dance', https://www.rapper.org.uk/notations/amble.pdf (accessed 27 April 2024).
8 Nicola Craddock, 'Celebrating Aged Miners Homes 125th year anniversary', Redhills website, 10 August 2023, https://redhillsdurham.org/celebrating-aged-miners-homes-125th-year-anniversary (accessed 7 January 2025).
9 Anne Michaels, 'Lake of Two Rivers', in *Poems* (New York: Alfred A. Knopf, 2001), p. 11.
10 This imagined conversation draws on real information recorded in *The Boldon Book*, a kind of Domesday Book for County Durham and parts of Northumberland. The real information recorded here comes from the entry for Newton near Boldon. David Austin (ed.), *Domesday Book Supplementary Volume: The Boldon Book* (Chichester: Phillimore, 1982), p. 15.

Chapter 7. The Ash Path

1 Sitelines – Gateway to the Tyne and Wear's Historic Environment Record, 'South Shields, salt pans', https://www.twsitelines.info/SMR/4489 (accessed 29 July 2024).
2 Chris Cordner, 'Five memories from the 1994, the year Sunderland Marina opened', *Sunderland Echo*, 11 January 2024, https://www.

sunderlandecho.com/retro/sunderland-1994-marina-retro-4467760. (accessed 9 April 2024).
3   Bede, *The Lives of the Abbots of Wearmouth and Jarrow*, trans. D. H. Farmer, in *The Age of Bede* (London: Penguin, 1998), p. 191.
4   Paul Summers, 'acknowledged land', in *union* (Ripon: Smokestack Books, 2011), p. 172.

Chapter 8. Ghosts of the East End

1   Leatherface, 'Shipyards', from *The Last*, released on Domino Records, 1994.
2   For more on the William Elliot story, see BBC News, 'Sunderland orphanage choirboy mystery solved after church note', https://www.bbc.co.uk/news/uk-england-tyne-61259094 (accessed 6 August 2024).
3   More details on Andy's process are given on his website, https://silversunbeam.co.uk/the-process (accessed 7 January 2025).

Chapter 9. What kingdom without common feasting?

1   Kathleen Jamie, 'What being Scotland's Makar means to me', *The National*, 22 August 2021, https://www.thenational.scot/culture/19529517.kathleen-jamie-scotlands-makar-means (accessed 7 November 2024).
2   William Martin, *Tidings of Our Bairnsea* (printed for the Wearmouth 1300 Festival, 1973).
3   William Martin, 'About the author', in ibid.
4   Leatherface, *Mush*, released on Roughneck Records (1991).
5   Dougald Hine, *At Work in the Ruins* (London: Chelsea Green, 2023), p. 166.
6   Martin, 'About the author'.
7   Durham World Heritage Site, 'Cuthbert's move to Durham: two stories', https://www.durhamworldheritagesite.com/learn/history/st-cuthbert/body/durham (accessed 7 January 2025).
8   William Martin, 'Malkuth', section 16, in *Hinny Beata* (Stamford: Taxus Press, 1987).
9   Based on personal correspondence between the author and Linda France, 7 July 2023, first published in *The Stephenson Trail* booklet, produced by the City of Sunderland. Date unknown.
10 Jonathan Davidson, 'Bringing back the common-land', in *New Defences of Poetry* (Newcastle upon Tyne: Newcastle Centre for the Literary Arts, 2021), http://nclacommunity.org/newdefences/2021/07/16/bringing-back-the-common-land/ (accessed 7 July 2023).
11 The ampersand isn't a typo: I'm nodding to the Liverpudlian variation, which I enjoy so much.
12 William Martin, 'Malkuth', section 27, in *Hinny Beata* (Stamford: Taxus Press, 1987).

13 William Martin, 'Abuba Bide', in *Lammas Alanna* (Newcastle upon Tyne: Bloodaxe Books, 2000), p. 107.

Chapter 10. Light moved on

1 Andrew Waterhouse, 'Making the Book', in Neil Astley (ed.), *Land of Three Rivers: The Poetry of North-East England* (Hexham: Bloodaxe Books, 2017), pp. 165–167.
2 Peter Armstrong, 'Songs at Birtley', in *Risings* (Petersfield: Enitharmon, 1988), p. 10.
3 REfUSE, home page, https://refusedurham.org.uk (accessed 7 November 2024).
4 From personal email correspondence with Dr Carl Kears, November 2022. With thanks to Carl for drawing my attention to these words and their entries in the *Bosworth-Toller*. See Joseph Bosworth, 'lást' and 'mearc', in *An Anglo-Saxon Dictionary Online*, edited by Thomas Northcote Toller, Christ Sean and Ondrej Tichy (Prague: Faculty of Arts, Charles University, 2014), https://bosworthtoller.com/21193 and /55183 (accessed 7 November 2024).
5 North Pennines AONB Partnership, 'Froserley Marble', https://northpennines.org.uk/wp-content/uploads/2020/01/Frosterley-Marble.pdf (accessed 7 January 2025).
6 Katrina Porteous, *Two Countries* (Hexham: Bloodaxe Books, 2014), p. 150.
7 Elizabeth Oldfield, *Fully Alive* (London: Hodder & Stoughton, 2024), p. 163.
8 Visit Northumberland, 'North East England: Passionate People, Passionate Places', YouTube channel, https://www.youtube.com/watch?v=wO2vIYulhB8 (accessed 30 May 2024).
9 Peter Armstrong, 'Songs at Birtley', in *Risings* (Petersfield: Enitharmon, 1988), p. 10.
10 These references, citing scholarship by David Rollason, are from Sam Turner, Sarah Semple and Alex Turner, *Wearmouth & Jarrow: Northumbrian Monasteries in an Historic Landscape* (Hatfield: University of Hertfordshire Press, 2013), p. 199.
11 Ibid.

Chapter 11. The big meeting

1 Alex Glasgow, 'And I Shall Cry Again', from *Songs of Alex Glasgow Volume Three: Tyneside Songs Old and New*, released on MWM Records (1997).
2 Angelic Upstarts, 'Heath's Lament', on *2,000,000 Voices*, released by EMI Records, 1981.
3 Walt Whitman, 'Pioneers! O Pioneers!', in *Leaves of Grass* (1855), quoted here as seen on Chopwell Lodge banner.

Notes

4 In 2011. See Jonathan Glancey, 'The votes are in: your favourite British building', *Guardian*, 16 September 2011, https://www.theguardian.com/artanddesign/2011/sep/16/britains-best-building-readers-vote-results (accessed 7 November 2024).

5 Émile Durkheim, *The Elementary Forms of Religious Life*, trans. Carol Cosman (Oxford: Oxford University Press, 2001).

Davy

1 Jake Morris-Campbell, *Corrigenda for Costafine Town* (Edinburgh: Blue Diode Press, 2021).

Index

Page numbers in **bold** refer to illustrations

'A Creative Call to Arms' open letter 117
A1 224, 240
A19 161, 163, 215–216, 217
Abdul 142–143
Acklington Park 89
Ad Gefrin, Wooler 54
Adventure Sunderland 181
Aged Merchant Seamen's Homes 196
Aged Minerworkers' Homes
   Boldon Colliery 163–164
   High Moorsley 223
   Silksworth 214
   South Shields 259
AI 117, 257
Aidan, Saint 7, 19–20, 38–39, 40, 53, 58
Albany 214
Aldhun, Bishop 217–218
Aldred the Scribe 239–240
Ale Gate, Alnwick 68
Alnmouth 80–81, 82
Alnwick 51, 67–68, 72, 89, 90–91, 95
Alwnick Castle 76
Alwnick Gardens 68, 76
Amble 72, 84–89, 91, 182
Amble Harbour 87
Amble Links First School 85
Angel Numbers 47
Angel of the North 184, 243
Angelic Upstarts 254
The Animals 9
Arbroath, Hospitalfield 19
Armstrong, Peter 17, 210, 221, 235
arts funding 107–108, 116
arts practice, socially engaged 219
Ash Path, the 169–171
Ashbrooke 213
Ashington Group, the *see* Pitmen Painters, the
Ashington 72, 98, 103–110
   The Blacka 109
   Central Billiard Saloon 104
   colliery site 105
   Colliery Trail 105
   colliery workers' terraces 104–105
   The Hirst 107–108
   The Old Ash Dene 105
   Portland Park development 106
Ashington Cricket Club 104
Ashington Miners Amateur Boxing Club 103, 114

Index

avian flu 122
Aykley Heads 234

Baden-Württemburg 116
Bailiffgate Museum, Alnwick 89
Bamburgh 20, 51, 52, 57, 91, 129
Bamburgh Bones project 52, 54
Bamburgh Castle 38, 52, 55, 56
Barley Mow 243
Barter Books 68
Bartram, Sam 255
Bartram's Shipyard 194, 201
Batchelor, Paul 74, 105
Bath House, the 77
Beadnell 54, 59–65, 65, 76
Beadnell Bay 55
Beamish Museum 162, 234, 259
bearing witness 270–271
Bede, the Venerable 14–15, 40, 42, 55, 151, 167, 172, 175, 186–187
   achievements 20
   birth 153, 160
   on Caedmon 82–83
   Eccesiastical History of the English People 154
   grave 15
   Life of Cuthbert 79
   mission 158, 179–180
   Mouth of the Tyne miracle account 133
   on founding of St Peter's 182–183
   parable of King Edwin's conversion 147
   reputation 153–154
   things named after 184–185
   tomb 156
   travels 155–156

Bede Gallery 158
Bede Monastery Museum 152
Bede's Bakehouse 184
Bede's Cross, Roker Battery 177–180
Bede's Way 23, 156–158, 169
Bede's Well 47
Bede's World 152–153, 159
Belmont 224
belonging 17–18
Benedict Biscop 20, 155, 175, 182–183, 186
Bensham 102–103
Benwell 86, 142
Berwick-upon-Tweed 62
Bewick, Ernie 193–194
The Big Meeting (film) 223
Billy Shiel's Boat Trips 57
Bishop's Wearmouth 192
Blackman-Woods, Roberta 92
Blackstone 117
Blair, Tony 75
Bloodaxe 122
The Blue House, Hendon **188**, 202
Blyth 72, 121–122
Blyth, Chay 181
Blyth, River 111
Blyth South Beach 121, 122
Bogg, Edmund 24–25
Bolbec Hall, Newcastle upon Tyne 117
Boldon Book 167
Boldon Colliery 161–164
Boldon Community Association 247–249
Boldon Comprehensive School 167
border reivers 66
Boulmer 51–52, 78–79

Index

Bowey, Keith 159, 160, 161
brass bands 248, 251
Brenchley, Chaz 182
Brexit 72, 127
Britain's oldest house 77
British Library 9, 92
Britishvolt site 116–117
Brockley Whins 254
Brockley Whins Metro station 164
Broomhill colliery 86
Brown, Gordon D. 212
Brown, Michelle 154
Bunting, Basil 33, 124
Burne-Jones, Edward 180
Burton, Andrew 87
Butcher's Bridge Road 158
Byker 122, 155

Caedmon 82–83
'Caedmon's Hymn' 82–83
Cambois 98, 111–113, 116–118, 159, 200
Cambois Miners' Welfare Hall 110, 113–116
Cameron, David 127
Camino Inglés 23
Campbell, Alan 126
Campbell, John 142–143
Campbell, Joseph Redmayne 142–143
Camperdown, Battle of 198–199
Cappleman, Wilkinson 138
Carter, Raich **188**, 202
Catherine Cookson Country 23–24
Centre for Writing, Bolbec Hall 117
Ceolfrith, Abbot 20, 157, 186
Challis, John 121–130, 131

Charlton, John 111
Charlton brothers 108
Cherry Knowle psychiatric hospital 195
Chester-le-Street 7–8, 13, 40, 217, 231–245, 265
   Church Chare 238, 242
   Cuthbert's after-image 236–237
   Front Street 236, 237, 240, 243
   High Chare 238
   history 231–232, 237
   importance to Cuthbert hagiography 244
   Macari's Lindisfarne Gospels-inspired mural 233–234
   McCarrick Homes 235
   Riverside cricket ground 239
   St Cutbert's Walk Shopping Centre 236
   St Cuthbert's Hospice 236
   St Mary's & St Cuthbert's **230**, 232, 238–242
Cheviots, the 123, 171
Christian commodification 236
Christianity 6, 20, 21, 38–39, 147
Churches Conservation Trust 197
civic branding 24
Clanny, William Reid 46
class 72–73
Cleadon 167, 171, 173
Cleadon Hills 171–171, 177
Cleadon Water Tower **168**, 171, 214
Clement, Joanne 262
Cleveland Hills 171

Index

coal and coal mining 84, 98–102, 219–220
coalfield culture 253–254
Coalfield Way 222
Coast to Coast cycle route 181
Codex Amiatinus 157, 186
Coleman, Russ 37–38, 43
collective effervescence 261
collective memory 24
colliery workers' terraces 104–105
Collingwood, Cuthbert 134
Colls, Robert 24–25, 25–26
Collywell Bay 124–125
Colpitts poetry readings 262
community, sense of 26
Cookson, Catherine 23–24
Cooper, Julian 234
Copt Hill Inn **208**, 220–221
Coquet, River 82, 84, 85
Coquet Island 84, 91–92
Cornthwaite Park 175
cost-of-living crisis 214
Cotton, Robert 92
Covid-19 pandemic 115, 129–130, 150, 254
Cox Green 265
Craddock, Nicola 262–263
Cramlington 97
Cramp, Rosemary 149, 151
Craster 56, 66, 67, 71, 73–74, 75–76, 78, 175
Craster kippers 67
Crawford, Jack 198–199
Creswell 91, 95
Crown Works film studios 201–202
Cuddy's beads 44–45
Cuddy's Isle 81
Cullercoats 128–129

Cullercoats Bay 128–129
Cullernose Point 76–77
The Cumberland Arms, Byker 155
Cummings, Dominic 225
Cuomo, Mario 244
Cuthbert, Saint 7, 20, 21, 37–38, 44, 44–45
  after-image 236–237
  arrival at Durham 13
  cult of 8
  death 39, 55–56
  dun cow legend 16–17, 217–218
  final journey 7–8, 34, 39, 47–48, 89
  first burial site 37–38, 39
  fondness for birds 64
  incorrupt body 39–40
  interest in 227
  last stopping place before Durham 217–218
  love of avian and marine life 122
  memorial sculpture 42–43
  miracles 32, 79, 132–133
  move to Lindisfarne 39
  pectoral cross 43
  shrine 14, 226–227, 228
Cuthbert's Way 21

Dan (film director) 223, 225
Danelaw, the 8
Dark Ages 7–8
Darling, Grace 57, 91
Darling, William 91
Davidson, Jonathan 220
Davies, Winnie, Queen of the East End Carnival 201
Davy, Humphrey 46, 149

Index

Davy (Morris-Campbell) 266–267
debt 150
Definitions of Distance (Morris-Campbell) 204
deindustrialisation 97
Delaval, Sir Francis Blake 123
Delaval family 123
Department for Environment Food and Rural Affairs (Defra) 79
The Detectorists 153
disconnection 62
distressed and trapped dog 166–167
Dixon, Sally 234
Dixon, Sarah 81
Don, River 150, 151, 153, 157, 160, 164, 164–166, 167
Donnelly, Jim 87–89
Donnelly, Kate 87–89, 89
Donnison, Elizabeth 196
Donnison School, Sunderland 196
Double Maxim 68
Douglas, Charlie 60–61, 63
Doxford Park 215–216
Dragonville industrial estate 224
Draper, Daniel 37
Druridge Bay 94–95
Druridge Bay Country Park 94
Duff, Aaron 130–139
Duff, Tim 134
Dunholme 13, 217–218
Dunstanburgh Castle 65, 66–67
Durham 20–21, 40, 245
  arrival at 224–226
  County Hall 234
  County Hotel 251, 262
  Framwellgate Bridge 262, 264
  Lord Londonderry statue 250
  Market Square 249
  Prebends Bridge 25, 227
  The Swan and Three Cygnets 251
  The Victoria Inn 16–18, 225
Durham, Pilgrims (Zinkeisen) 16–17
Durham Aged Mineworkers' Homes Association 163, 214, 223, 235, 259
Durham Cathedral 8, 13, 17, 21, 23, 25, 26–27, 41, 93, 227, 270
  Bede's grave 15
  Chapel of Nine Altars 228
  Cuthbert's shrine 14, 226–227, 228
  Durham Miners' Gala service 259–261
  first glimpse of 224
  Galilee chapel 14–15, 227
  miners' memorial **12**, 14, 15, 15–16, 18, 261
  nave 227, 228
  Rose Window 14, 224, 259
Durham Coalfield 250
Durham County Council 234
Durham Elvet Station 225
Durham Miners' Gala 27, 32–33, 213, 247–263, 263
  banners **246**, 250, 251, 255–258, 259
  brass bands 248, 251
  County Hotel 251
  departure 264–265
  Durham Cathedral service 259
  the march 250–253

Index

political speeches 259
start 249–250
Durham Mining Museum,
　Spennymoor 45
Durham Priory, cellarer's
　account books 61–62
Durham Students' Union 259
Durham Women's Group 257
Durkheim, Émile 261
Dusseldorf 116

Eadfrith, Bishop 6–7, 241
Eardwulf, Bishop 243
Earsdon Church Hall 125–126
Easington Colliery disaster 209
East Boldon 189
East Coast Mainline 81,
　223–224
East Durham 219
East Rainton 222
Easthope 209–211, 223
*Eccesiastical History of the
　English People* (Bede) 154
Ecgfrith, King of Northumbria
　39
eco poetry 62
Elliot, Alistair 133
Elliot, William 197–198
Elliott, Bill 255
Embleton 65
Emma (friend) 25
Empty Shop concept 262
England Coast Path 94
Englishness 174
Escomb Church 23
Essen 116
Eucharist, the 171
European Union 127
*Everybody's Gone to the
　Rapture* (video game) 59

extinction events 62
Eyre, Charles 89

The Fall 88
Farne Islands 36, 39, 57, 58, 85
Feather Star Mantle (Coleman)
　37–38, 43
Feaver, William, *Pitmen
　Painters* 107
Felling Colliery disaster
　148–149, 270
Fender, Sam 136
Ferguson family 54
Finchale Abbey 23, 265
fire beacons 84–85
First World War 121
fishing 79
fishing community 60–63
Florence, Medicea Laurenziana
　Library 186
Floyd, Jimmy, *The Miner – Last
　Smoke Before Descent*
　101–102
folkloric ancestry 154
Ford, Harrison 136
Forfarshire, SS 57
fossils 44–45, 62, 238–239
Foxton Beach 80
France, Linda 19, 218–219
'Future Walls' initiative 191

Gannet, Hector 57, 130–131
gannets 122
Garfitt, Roger 21
gasometer, Hendon 202
Gateshead 102, 110, 243
　the Sage 130, 184
Gazza the Gull **70**, 87
general election, 2024 72
Geordie lamps 46

Gibbon, Elizabeth 171
Gilesgate Moor Hotel 224
Gilley Law 215
Ginsberg, Allen 124
Godric, St 265
Going Home (Hedley) 41
Gormley, Antony 184
Gospel books 6–7, 9
Grangetown 195
Great North Forest project 166
Great North Road 240
Great Northern Coalfield 21
Green, Robson 73
Gresford colliery disaster 112–113
Grey, Charles, Earl 77
Griffiths, Bill 63
Groundwork charity 152
Gut, The 85

Hadrian's Wall 142
Hairy Bikers, the 87, 136
Hall, Lee 100, 107
Hampel, the Reverend Canon Michael 259
Hardy, Stevie 198
Harris, Rodney 94
Harry Potter films 68
Hartlepool 171
Hartley pit disaster 125–126
Harton, South Shields 4–5
Harton Cemetery 220, **268**, 269–271
Harton Coal Company 3
Harton Collieries group 163
Hauxley 93–94
Hauxley Point 91
Hebburn Riverside Park 185
Hector Gannet, loss of 131
Hector Gannet project 131

Hedley, Ralph 41–42
Hemmer, Fred 148–151
Hendon **188**, 199–203, 214, 265
Hendon Beach 200–201
Henry VI (Shakespeare) 83
Heron, Eleanor 89
Hetton Bogs 222
Hetton colliery railway 215
Hetton Lyons Sheds 218–219
Hetton-le-Hole 219
Heworth 255
High Moorsley 222
High Newton 64
High Pittington, St Laurence's Church 223
Hilda, Abbess 82
Hine, Dougald 110, 216
Hipsburn 81
Hodgson, John, Reverend 148–149
Hodgson, Louisa 134
Hollis, Matthew 31, 33
Holman, James 159
Holman Hunt, William 41, 242
Holy Island *see* Lindisfarne
Holy Trinity Church, Sunderland 196, 197–198
Holywell Dene 123
Hopper, Joseph 163
Hospitalfield, Arbroath 19
Howick 76, 77, 77–78
Howick Hall 77
Huss, Esther 98, 113–116, 117
Hylton 265

identity 24
immigration 52–53
Ina Mactavish grounding 87

Index

inclusion 53
invasive species 48–49

Jackson, Dan 53
Jackson, Eleanor 6
Jamie, Kathleen 211
Jarra Slack 147
Jarrow 150, 151–152, 255
    St Paul's 14, 20, 23,
        147–151, 157, 270
Jarrow Hall 151
Jarrow March, 1936 150
Jarrow School 157–158
Jekyll, Gertrude 32
Jennings, Douglas 108
Jewish communities 102
Jobling, William, gibbeting of 158
John of Gaunt 66
Johnson, Kris 121–130, 131
The Jolly Fisherman, Craster 67
Jones, the Reverend Lesley 148–151, 161, 261

Kears, Carl 232–245
Kerr, Bobby 221
Kev (carrier of the Durham Miners' Gala banner) 253–254
Kilbourn, Oliver
    Half-time at the Rec (Welfare) 100–101, 106
    Rainy Day, Ashington Co-Op 110
King Edward's 131
King George's playing fields 159–160
King's College London 232
King's College Morris Men 154
Kirkup, James 26, 132, 139

Lacey, Andrew 46
Laidler, Frank, *Fish and Chips* 101
Laing Gallery, Newcastle upon Tyne 92, 107, 240
Lancaster, Thomas, Earl of 66
land, the, connections to 86
Lawson, Fenwick 151
Leam Lane 160
Leameside Line 223–224
Life of Cuthbert (Bede) 79
lighthouses 35
    Guile Point Lighthouse 36
    Heugh Hill Lighthouse 36
    St Mary's Lighthouse 124, 125
    Souter Lighthouse 175, 272
limekilns 58, 59
Lindisfarne 19–20, 21, 26, 31–44, 36, 79, 91, 252
    attraction 48–49
    causeway 47–48
    Emmanuel Head daymark 30, 32, 35–37, 55
    fossils 44–45
    genius loci 34
    Gertrude Jekyll's garden 32
    monastic community established 38
    pirri-pirri 48–49
    tranquillity 34
    village centre 37
Lindisfarne Castle 31
Lindisfarne Gospels 6–8, 9, 13, 39, 40, 239–241, 244
    repatriation campaign 92–93
Lindisfarne Priory 37–38
    Cuthbert memorial sculpture 42–43
    statue of Saint Aidan 40–42

Index

Literary & Philosophical Society, Newcastle upon Tyne 149
living culture, facilitating 216
Local Government Act of 1972 22
Londonderry, Lord 250
Long Nanny, bird sanctuary 64
Longhoughton Beach 78
Longsands 131
Lonsdale, Ray 135
Lovejoy, Lizzie 258
Low Buston 89–90
Low Hauxley colliery 90
Low Newton-by-the-Sea 65
Low Stead Links 78
Lumley, George Lord 238–239
Lumley, John Lord 238–239
Lumley Castle 239
Lumley family 238–239
Lunn, Stephen 86
Lynemouth 98, 111, 113
Lyon, Robert 99, 107, 108

Macari, Ant 233–234
McCabe, Rowan 258
McColl, Ewan 131
McDonald, Chris 225
McGuinness, Kim 53, 92
mackem, meaning 211
Mahler, Gustav 44
male identity 257
Malyan, Nick 222–223, 224, 226, 260, 262, 263, 264
Marden Rocks 80
Mark (volunteer) 262–263
marra 14
Marsden 265
Marsden Bay 16, 271–273
Marsden Rock 177

Marsden White Horse 172–173
Martin, Andy 190–196, 199–206
Martin, Bill 17, 18, 21, 209–210, 211–213, 213, 214, 216–217, 218, 222, 224, 226–227, 252
Martin, Bob 15
Martin, Graham 209–210, 215, 223, 224, 226, 258, 259
Martin, William 56
masculinity 257
material legacy 234
Matt (friend) 51, 56, 62, 66, 71, 76, 95
Mauretania, RMS 86
Mayhew, Gavin 221
Medicea Laurenziana Library, Florence 186
Menforth, Thomas 254
Mesolithic House, Howick 77
Michaels, Anne 166
Micky 248–249
Mike (friend) 25
Mike and Emma (Wrexham couple) 211, 225, 226
Milburn, Jackie 108
Miles-Watson, Jonathan 25
Miliband, David 75, 220
Mill Dam race riots, 1930 142
miners 17–18
miners' lamps 3–4, 5–6, 8–9, 10, 16, 34–35, 43–46, 89, 102, 148–149, 227, 249
miners' strike, 1984–1985 219–220, 224, 257
Mines and Collieries Act, 1842 250

Index

Mollett, Baz 46
Monkton 160
Monkwearmouth, St Peter's 14, 20, 23, 153, 182–183, 184–185
Moore, Nicholas
  grave **268**, 269–271
  miners' lamp 3–4, 5–6, 34–35, 43–44, 45, 46–47
  New Year's Day tradition 4–6
  tally number 47
Morden Tower 124
Morpeth 106
Morris, William 180–181
Morris-Campbell, Elma Dilys 3, 54, 125, 174
Morris-Campbell, Gruffydd 3, 5
Morris-Campbell, Jake **207**
  annual pilgrimage 15–16
  birth of daughter 54
  connection to Bede 156
  Durham Miners' Gala service 259–261
  education 176–177, 219–220
  inspiration 16–18
  itinerary 9–10, 19–21, 24, 26–27
  New Year's Day tradition 4–6
  personal and professional identities 26
  poetry 5–6
  psychosomatic symptoms 32, 33
  receives miners' lamp 3–4
  reflection 271–273
  role 19
  South Shields mug 21–22

Morris-Campbell, Kate 3, 58, 59, 122, 124, 125, 126, 130, 271, 273
Muslim population 102

Napoleonic Wars 72
National Coal Board 45
National Glass Centre 182–183
National Lottery 183
National Trust 58, 123
New Labour 220, 241
Newcastle Brown Ale 137
Newcastle Central Station 231
Newcastle Evening Chronicle 152
Newcastle Journal 33
Newcastle Kingsmen, the 154–155
Newcastle upon Tyne 252
  Bolbec Hall 117
  Laing Gallery 92, 107, 240
  Literary & Philosophical Society 149
  Live Theatre 107
  Roman altars 141–142
  Swing Bridge 141
  Theatre Royal 107
  Trinity House 35
Newton Garth Farm 167
Newton Point 65
Newton Steads 65
Nissan 116
north, the 176
North Blyth 111, 200
North East, the 17–18
North East and Yorkshire Film Archive 131
North East Combined Authority 53
North Sea Link, the 113

Index

North Shields 26, 135, 135–136
  Brewhouse Bank 137
  The Engine Room 137
  Fiddler's Green sculpture 135
  The Gut 135–136
  Herring Girl sculpture 135
  King Street Social 137–138
  lighthouses 35
  The Low Lights Tavern 136–137
  North Shields Master Mariners Asylum 139
  Northumberland Square 138
  Stag Line building 138–139
North Shields Fish Quay 136
North Shields Master Mariners Asylum 139
North Sunderland 58
North Tyneside 125
Northern Saints Trails 25
Northern Sinfonia 184
Northumberland 72–73
Northumberland, Duke of 71
Northumberland Coast Area of Outstanding Natural Beauty 58
Northumberland Coast Path 23, 26, 94
Northumberland County Council 106
Northumberland Gazette 72
Northumberland Park, pet cemetery 138
Northumberland's Colourful Coast project 85
Northumbria, Kingdom of 15, 52
  Golden Age 53, 234

Northumbrian hagiography 157
Northumbrian vernacular 62–63

Oates, Alex 98, 113–116, 117
Old Durham Gardens 224–225
Old Hartley 125
Oldfield, Elizabeth 241
Osred II, King of Northumbria 132
Oswald, King of Northumbria 20, 38, 52–53
Oswald, Saint 7
Oswiu of Bernicia, King 131
overman's lamps 249
oystercatchers 134

Pallion 201–202
Pann's Bank 189–190
Parbury, Kathleen 40
Passionate People, Passionate Places slogan 241–242
pebble-carrying tradition 36–37, 175, 185, 210, 227, 260, 270–271
Pelaw 200
Pelaw Wood 225
Pele Tower
  Creswell 95
  Seaton Sluice 124
Penshaw 265
Percy, Hugh, second Duke of Northumberland 72
Percy, Ralph, 12th Duke of Northumberland 74
Percy Tenantry Column 71–72
Perry, Grayson 257
Peter (walker) 223, 225
Peterlee 46
Petts, David 234

Index

photography 203, 204–206, **207**
Pickard, Tom and Connie 124
pilgrimage 47–48
pilgrimage wisdom 272
pillboxes 73
Pitmen Painters, the 99–102, 103–110
Pitmen Painters (play) 100, 107
Pittington 223
Pity Me 233
Poetic Licence gin company 221
poetry 33–34, 62, 63–64
pollution 129
popular consciousness 241
Porteous, Katrina 60–65, 219, 239, 259
Pound, Ezra 33
Prac Crit (journal) 60
Price, Narbi 98, 103–110
Pride of the Tyne 141, 143
Puffing Billy 218–219
punk bands 254–255
Pyrex 204

Queen Elizabeth Country Park 98
Quin, Joyce 92

RAF Boulmer 73, 78
railways 164–165, 215, 218–219, 223–224, 225
Rea, Vince 158–159
Readhead, Robert 270
Ready To Go Forum 194
The Red King 52
Redhills 223, 262–263
relic logic 34–35
Renton, Katherine 71, 72, 73–74, 76, 77, 81–82, 83, 84–90, 91

Ripon 40
Rising Sun 9
The Robin Hood pub, Monkton 160
Roker 179–181, 200, 265
Roker Battery 177–180
Roker Cliff Park 176
Roker Lighthouse 181
Roker Park 181
Roman occupation 10, 141–142, 237
Royal Quays 139
rural/urban divide 115
Ryhope 195
Ryhope Colliery 215

Sage, the, Gateshead 130, 184
St Aidan's Catholic Academy 213
St Aidan's Church, Bamburgh 52, 54, 57
St Andrew's Church, Roker 180–181
Saint Bede's Well 184
St Cuthbert's Way 23
St Ebba, Church of, Beadnell 59
St George's Church, Cullercoats 129
St George's Presbyterian Church, Sunderland 192
St Laurence's Church, High Pittington 223
St Lawrence's Church, Warkworth 82
St Mary's & St Cuthbert's, Chester-le-Street **230**, 232, 238–242
St Mary's Lighthouse 124, 125
St Oswald's Way 23, 26, 94

Index

St Paul's, Jarrow 14, 20, 23, 147–151, 157, 270
St Peter's, Monkwearmouth 14, 20, 23, 153, 182–183, 184–185
salt pans 87–88, 173
salt path, the 172–173
Salters' Trod 269
#Save the National Glass Centre 183
Schmitdke, Daniel 74–75
sea, the, paradox of 36
sea coal 74, 90
sea fret 98
Seaburn 175, 200, 252
Seaham 250
Seahouses 52, 57, 58–59, 63, 175
Seaton Burn 123
Seaton Delaval Hall 123–124
Seaton Point 79–80
Seaton Sluice 122–124
Second World War 78, 142
Seven Sisters, the 222
Shakespeare, William 83
shapers, poets as 212
shared rituals 261
Sherburn 224
Shield, Bill 247, 248
Shilbottle 67
shipyards and shipbuilding 84, 186, 190, 194
Shotley Bridge 60
Silksworth 214–215
Silksworth sports complex 215
Simon, Ed 35
Simonside Hills 214
Smith, David 72–73
Smith, Liam 213
Smith, Mark E. 88

social media 64
Society for the Prevention of Accidents in Coal Mines 148–149
Souter Lighthouse 175, 272
South Shields 19, 21–22, 139, 141, 164–165, 169, 173, 255, 259, 265
South Shields and Sunderland Water Company 171
South Tyneside 22, 175
South Tyneside Hospital 22
Southwick 194
Spanish City, Whitley Bay 127
Spennymoor, Durham Mining Museum 45
Spine Road, the 97–98, 109, 111
Springwell Park 158
Stadium of Light 191
Stanhope & Tyne Railway 164–165
Starlight Castle 123
Starmer, Keir 126
Stephenson, George 46, 218–219
Stephenson Trail 218–219
Stevenson, Anne 147
Stockton and Darlington Line 218–219
Stone, Degna 33–34
Storm Arwen 37
storytelling 244
'Stringing Bedes: A Poetry and Print Pilgrimage' project 159, 160
Stubbs, Frankie 214
Styles, Frank 194
Sugar Sands 77
Summers, Paul 183

Index

Sunak, Rishi 115
Sunday Sun 93
Sunderland 173, 206, 214, 216, 252, 265
   Aged Merchant Seamen's Homes 196
   Bangladeshi community 202–203
   Bull Lane 193–194
   The Clarendon 193–194
   Crowtree Leisure Centre 194–195
   Donnison School 196
   Eagle Building 192
   East End 199
   future 201–202
   'Future Walls' initiative 191
   High Street East 192
   Holy Trinity Church 196, 197–198
   shipyards and shipbuilding 194
   Villiers Street 190–192
   The Welcome Tavern 195
Sunderland, City of 175
Sunderland, University of 159, 182, 183
Sunderland Bangladesh International Centre 202
Sunderland Black and Minority Ethnic Network 192
Sunderland Boys' Orphanage 199
Sunderland City Council 191
Sunderland Marina 181–182
Sunderland Orphanage Asylum 198
Sunderland Road 169
Sunnilaws 170
Sunniside 192

Surf Café, Tynemouth 130–131
Symeon of Durham 243–244
Symonds, John Addington 256–257
Synod of Whitby 20, 39, 82

Tadorne 76, 78
Tebbit, Norman 258
Temple, Simon 152–153
thin places 48–49
This Is Wrexham 112–113
Tideroad, the 56
Tirtha 143
totemic items 27
tourism 65, 66, 132
Town Moor Railway Station 196
toxic masculinity 257
tradition, loss of 62
traditions, composting 216
Trafalgar, Battle of 134
Trevelyan Anne-Marie 72, 79
Trinity House 35
Tully, John 81
Tully, Sarah 89
Tunstall Hills 210, 213, 223
Turnbull, Anthony, Bishop of Durham 93
Turner, Frank 54–55
Tyne, River 35
Tyne and Wear 22
Tyne and Wear Development Corporation 151–152, 183, 189–190
Tyne and Wear Fire and Rescue, animal department 166–167
Tyne Bridge 141
Tyne Improvement Commission 135

Index

Tyne Tunnel 51, 95, 97, 156, 172
Tynemouth 128, 130–139
Tynemouth Priory 131–132, 134
Tyneside 184, 185

Uchtred, Earl of Northumbria 218
unemployment 151–152
Unfolding Theatre 115
Universal Basic Income (UBI) 150
Ushaw College 16

Vane, Lady Frances Anne 250
Vera 73
Victoria Viaduct 265
Viglianisi, Carlo 262, 264
Vikings 7, 20, 39, 56
Vindolanda 10
Visit County Durham Northern Saints Trails initiative 181

wages 74
Wallsend 132
Walney to Wear cycleway 181
Wansbeck, River 109
Warden Law 220–221
Warkworth 81, 82–83, 87
Warkworth Castle 83
Warkworth Harbour 84
Wars of the Roses 66
Washington 116, 214, 232, 265
watching on 237–238
Waterhouse, Andrew 232
Wear, River 25, 186, 225, 227, 235, 264–265
Wear Valley 172
Wearmouth, Richard 117

Wearmouth Bridge 186, 189
Wesley, John 81
Westoe 269
Whitburn 95, 173, 174–175, 176–177
Whitburn Bents 175
Whitburn Colliery 173
Whitburn Steel 175
Whiteleas allotments 169
Whitley Bay 125–128, 129–130
Whitman, Walt 256
Wilbourn, Colin 182
Wilkinson, Ellen 150
Williamson, Sir Hedworth 172–173
Woodhorn Colliery Museum 98, 98–102, 106–107
   Ashington Group Gallery 99–102
   miners' memorial **95**, 102, 108
Wooler, Ad Gefrin 54
Workers' Educational Association 99
Writers' Guild of America strike 257
writer's vocation, the 186–187

Yates Thompson manuscript 56
Yeats, W. B. 33
Yeavering 54
Youldon, Keviin 255
Young, Arthur Rousselange 82, 86
Young, Eleanor Mary 86
Young, John 86

Zinkeisen, Doris Clare, *Durham, Pilgrims* 16–17